CAPTIVE

Captive

A SURVIVAL STORY

Donalda J. Reid

Copyright © 2007 Donalda J. Reid
Off the Mountain Publishing
2nd printing 2008

143 West 26th Ave.
Vancouver, BC
Canada, v5y 2j6
offthemountain@shaw.ca

LIBRARY AND ARCHIVES CANADA CATALOGUING IN PUBLICATION

Reid, Donalda, 1943–

Captive : a survival story / Donalda Reid.

Includes bibliographical references.

ISBN 978-0-9784724-0-5

1. Reid, Donalda, 1943– —Captivity, 1998. 2. People in Arms for the
Liberation of Rwanda. 3. Rwanda—Militia. 4. Hostages--Congo (Democratic
Republic)—Biography. 5. Hostages—Rwanda—Biography. 6. Hostages—
Canada—Biography. 7. Reid, Donalda, 1943– —Health. 8. Post-traumatic
stress disorder—Patients—Biography. 1. Title.

DT658.26.R43 2007   967.5103'4092   C2007-905957-0

Cover art "Rwandan Women" by Donalda Reid
Photo of author by Dan Sheehan
Design and layout by the Vancouver Desktop Publishing Centre
Printed in Canada by Ray Hignell Services Inc.

To Dan with love
To Ian with gratitude and affection
In Memory of Doug, Ann-Charlotte and Jens

ACKNOWLEDGEMENTS

First and always, thanks to my husband Danny for getting me home and taking care of me. Thanks to Ian Macnaughton for helping me get it all sorted out and for encouraging me to keep working. To all the people in my writing groups who forced me to find my voice, especially Luanne Armstrong and Jane Broweleit, thanks for pushing me.

To the women of Rwanda—I haven't forgotten the promise I made on the mountain. In support of you and all the African grandmothers who are struggling to raise their AIDS orphaned grandchildren, the profits from the sale of this book will be donated to the Stephen Lewis Foundation.

BACKGROUND INFORMATION

"For I only am escaped alone to tell thee."

—*Book of Job*

uMuntu ne Suntu u zo na Bantu no' Ubuntu
(A human with soul is one with all humanity)

—*Traditional Zulu saying*

"Our deepest fear is not that we are inadequate. Our deepest fear is that we are powerful beyond measure. It is our light not our darkness that most frightens us. We ask ourselves, who am I to be so brilliant, gorgeous, talented, fabulous? Actually, who are you NOT to be? You are a child of God. Your playing small does not save the World. There's nothing enlightening about shrinking so that other people won't feel unsure around you. We were born to make manifest the glory of God that is within us. It is not just in some of us; it is in everyone. As we let our own Light shine, we unconsciously give other people permission to do the same. As we are liberated from our own fear, our presence automatically liberates others."

—*Marianne Williamson, "A Return to Love."*
Quoted by Nelson Mandela in his 1994 inaugural speech

ONE

It was late on Sunday afternoon, August 9th, 1998, at the market in Kabale, Uganda. The sun hung above the jagged tips of the distant mountains, still hot enough that we were comfortable in our short sleeved shirts and walking shorts. The market wasn't crowded. Most of the Ugandans had long since finished shopping and returned home. Only *wazungu*, Europeans like us, shopped so late in the afternoon. The unsold fruit and vegetables, displayed in piles of three or four on wooden planks in the rickety booths or on colorful lengths of cloth on the ground, had been well picked over.

My husband Dan and I were the odd couple walking through the open-air market loaded down with turquoise plastic tote bags overflowing with bread, fruit and vegetables. We stood out not only because we were white, but also because we were double the age of the Australian, American and British twenty-something-year-olds that made up the majority of our safari group. Dan and I were the gofers who had volunteered to carry shopping bags while Patrick, our Kenyan cook, shopped for the last days of our safari. The other sixteen people in our group were wandering, randomly checking the small kiosks in the market for souvenirs and drinking warm Fanta or Coke while keeping one eye on Patrick so they would know when it was time to head back to the safari truck.

As we meandered out of the dusty market square, Charles, the Kenyan safari leader and main driver, came hurrying up. He stopped in front of us, slid his sunglasses up to the top of his head pushing his shoulder length dreadlocks into a Medusa look-alike. "Do you still want to see the gorillas?" he asked, sweeping his eyes across the group.

"Ha, ha. Good joke, Charles," someone said.

"No, I mean it."

"Get real. If you're trying to get even with us for bugging you about the gorillas for the last three weeks, you're not succeeding."

The first thing Charles had ever said to us, before the safari began in Nairobi, Kenya, was, "Forget seeing the gorillas. It isn't going to happen." He wasn't telling us anything new. A month before Dan and I left home we'd received a letter from our tour company saying we wouldn't be able to see the gorillas. No gorilla viewing permits were being issued and groups wanting to go on a gorilla trek were not being given day visas to cross the border from Uganda into the Democratic Republic of Congo where the treks took place. The letter explained there were administrative problems at the Djomba Gorilla Park with booking and payment procedures which had resulted in the Park being closed. As a tour company representative, Charles had spent three months in Kisoro, the closest Ugandan town to the border, trying to find out when the dispute might be settled. He had been unsuccessful in getting any information and the border remained closed.

Long before we met, when my husband, Dan, was in his twenties, he'd done a six-month 'Across Africa' overland trip from Nairobi to London, travelling under extremely primitive conditions through a dozen African countries. In the early 1980s, under the aegis of World University Service of Canada (WUSC), he'd taught for three years in Zimbabwe shortly after its independence.

It was Dan who introduced me to Africa. On our first trip, in 1992, we'd gone on safaris in Botswana, Namibia and Zimbabwe, stopping to visit the schools where he'd worked. That trip had whetted my appetite for Africa. Watching animals I'd only seen in the National Geographic was magic. I wanted more.

For our second trip in 1998, Dan and I built a wide variety of places and animals into our thirty-seven day safari. When the letter about the border closure arrived we were disappointed. Seeing the gorillas was to have been the trip highlight. The company offered us a choice—cancel, reschedule, or accept a substitute visit to see chimpanzees in the Ugandan Budongo Forest. There was no way we'd cancel. Rescheduling wasn't an option, either. Both Dan and I were working in the public school system; Dan was a Secondary School teacher and I was the Principal of a Kindergarten to Grade Seven Elementary school. Since summer break was the only chance we had to go on a long African safari, we chose chimpanzees.

In Kenya, Tanzania and Uganda we'd visited ten game reserves and national parks; we'd seen all the big animals—elephant, lion, black and white rhinoceros, buffalo, leopard, hippopotamus, giraffe, cheetah and hundreds of zebra. My bird and animal log filled two pages. Although there are over twenty-nine varieties of antelope, I'd stopped recording at fifteen, content to watch them browse, tails flicking, ears twitching, alert for danger.

Elephants were my favorite animal. When Charles located a herd in one of the parks, he would turn off the truck engine and we'd wait. Because elephants need to eat huge amounts of vegetation, they browse for up to eighteen hours a day and are always on the move. In spite of their weight, they move almost noiselessly through the brush, often coming within five feet of the open side of the truck. As they strolled past, they seemed oblivious to the truck and all of us sticking out everywhere going click-click-click.

Elephants are amazingly ingenious and dexterous. While browsing, their trunk snakes out, wraps around a branch, effortlessly breaks or tears it loose, then twists it up into their mouth. In one park we watched an elephant shake an acacia tree, pushing it with his forehead until the seedpods dropped off. He used the two opposing prehensile parts on the tip of his trunk like fingers to pick up the individual pods and flip them into his mouth.

Every large group of elephants is a close-knit matriarchal clan under the leadership of the oldest female. The females are extremely protective of their young. When our truck inadvertently separated a baby elephant from the rest of the herd, the matriarch lifted her trunk high in the air, bellowed, and charged the truck. The average adult female elephant measures twelve feet forehead to tail, nine feet at the shoulder, and weighs up to 3500 kg. Above the huge body is a proportionally large head with flapping four-foot long ears and a trunk that needs to be curled so the end doesn't drag. As the elephant ages, her curved tusks increase in length. When I saw that huge elephant with long pointed tusks bearing down on my side of the vehicle, I ducked and screamed for Charles to get going, fast. Fortunately it was a mock charge and she stopped short of the truck. As the baby ran back to the herd, the matriarch, still bellowing, rejoined the other females who circled the baby protectively.

As large as she is, a female elephant looks small beside a mature male who can be over nineteen feet long and thirteen feet at the shoulder. When they are about twelve years old and reach sexual maturity, males are expelled from the female herd. If you see a lone elephant, it's certain to be a bull, a mature male. Bulls only join the female herd to mate a female in oestrous.

In Amboseli National Park, Kenya, we watched a bull elephant in musth lumber across the open plain toward a herd of females. Bellowing and dribbling urine from his engorged penis, he chased down and mounted a young, fertile female. With his front legs on her back and his body pushed against her, his bulk dwarfed the female. It seemed impossible that her legs could support them both, but fortunately the encounter was brief. Trumpeting loudly, the bull slipped back onto his feet and wandered away.

Near sunset in Samburu National Park, Kenya, we watched a herd of around thirty elephants splashing in the shallow, muddy brown river water of the Ewaso Nyiro River. Because elephants' skin is sensitive to sunburn and insect bites they were spraying water over their bodies with their trunks, rolling in the shallow water and scratching their backs and sides against the red clay mud banks. At a signal from the matriarch, the herd of adults and young, making sounds ranging from a bellow and trumpet to rumbling and whistling, splashed across the river, lumbered up the bank in front of us, circled past the truck and faded silently away into the brush. I knew, from my first trip, that it was impossible to capture an elephant on film. But that didn't stop me from trying.

As we neared the end of our safari, I was content. Even without seeing gorillas, it had been great. The only thing that hadn't been perfect was my health. A number of people on the trip had passed around a flu-y cold. I'd missed the fever, but, even after the antibiotics I'd taken as a precaution, I had less energy than usual.

Back when we were planning the safari, I told Dan I was concerned about making a fool of myself as I struggled up the mountains to see the gorillas. At the best of times I'm one step above a couch potato. The idea of hiking up hills and mountains ranks as low for me as having a root canal, to be done only when unavoidable. I have been known to use my physical problems—asthma, seasonal allergies and calf muscles so tight I go up even a moderate slope on my toes feeling like Frankenstein's monster—as excuses for not getting too active.

Dan, however, is my opposite. His idea of a good time is a ten-mile run up steep hills or a fast game of hockey. "Don't worry," he'd tell me. "If you have to go slow, we'll go slow. You can make it. You're not that bad." Dan always had more faith in me than I had in myself. I wasn't convinced. I was likely the only person in our safari group who had been more relieved than disappointed by the cancellation of the gorilla trek.

Even knowing there was no possibility of seeing gorillas, several unfailingly optimistic people in the group had extracted a promise from Charles that he would keep in close contact with the company's main office in Nairobi and, if the border opened during our safari, he'd try to arrange it so we could see the gorillas. Every day someone would ask, "Any word about the gorillas?" or "Have you heard about the border?" It had become an on-going joke, particularly with the Australians. Charles just smiled and ignored them.

That day in the Kabale market, the last thing on my mind was gorillas. As wonderful as the safari had been, travelling for a month through a dry, dusty country in an open truck and sleeping on the ground in tents could never be called a restful, relaxing holiday. I was a 'veteran' Principal. I knew that a week after we got back from Africa I'd be up to my eyeballs getting the school I had been reassigned to organized and ready for opening day. I was ready to kick back and relax for a couple of days. I was thinking about the lake Charles was taking us to, Lake Bunyonyi.

Although many people think all of Africa is oppressively hot, the climate varies, depending on the altitude and nearness to bodies of water or the Equator. Kabale and Lake Bunyonyi were close to the Equator but high in the mountains where it was sunny and pleasantly warm. As well, Lake Bunyonyi, unlike many bodies of fresh water in Africa, was free from bilharzias, a debilitating disease caused by a nasty, water-borne, flatworm that digests through the skin and takes up permanent residence in anyone who wades, bathes or even showers in infested water. Because the lake was bilharzias free, we'd not only be able to sun tan but swim.

As my arms filled with blue carry bags, my anticipation grew. Three days at the pristine lake would be the perfect end to our safari. I could see myself beside the lake—eyes closed, half read book lying across my chest, coolish beer by my side and memories of a million wild animals running through my mind.

Back at the truck, however, all conversation focused on the gorillas.

"You're sure you want to see them?" Charles asked us. Under his dark sunglasses, his face gave nothing away. I still retained some hope he was joking.

"Sure."

"Yes!"

"Any time," the rest said.

Charles broke into a wide grin, his teeth white against his dark skin. "Let's go then. The border is open. We're heading for it tonight." Without giving us any more information, he turned and hopped into the truck cab beside Justin, the Australian co-driver. With a whoop and cheer everyone tucked their packs up into the overhead bin and settled along the bench seats down the sides of the truck as Charles drove off for—someplace.

There was a lot of speculation in the back about exactly what would happen next. Charles hadn't told us how he knew that the border was open. Was it a rumor, information passed by word of mouth, or perhaps something he'd heard from local tourist guides? Conversation and supposition bounced back and forth.

"He might have called the Nairobi office."

"How would Nairobi know about it before people here?"

"Where are we going?"

"Where's the border? Who's got the map?"

"It's already five o'clock. It'll start getting dark in an hour."

"We can't cross after dark. The border closes. We must be staying in Uganda someplace."

"Where are we on this map?"

"Kabale."

"Where's that? Here, you find it."

"Charles is driving so fast."

"Maybe we're close to the border and he's trying to get there before dark to get us across."

"I don't think so. The closest border town on the map is here. Kisoro. Look at how this road twists all over when it hits the mountains."

"Bang on the cab and ask Charles where we're going."

His voice whipped back, "Kisoro."

Kisoro was seventy kilometers away over one of the roughest, steepest, most winding roads I have ever travelled. The dusty road climbed up and up, twisting around steep mountain slopes that were cultivated to the very tips, dotted with small houses tucked along the road or out in the terraced fields, lighted by the warm yellow rays of the setting sun and softened by a haze of wood smoke. It was like a drawing of the fabled Shangri-La. Along the edge of the steep gravel road, lines of people trudged with large bundles balanced on their heads: jerry cans of water, loads of bamboo, sacks of sorghum and other crops. Groups of children with huge green or yellow plastic water containers on their heads wound along the narrow tracks that dropped down from the road and stood patiently waiting their turn at trickling water pipes. Men leaned forward, the sinews on their thin, muscular legs standing out as they strained to push overloaded bicycles up the steep road grade, balancing brilliant green banana stalks, sisal sacks bursting with ears of corn, woven baskets of squawking chickens. One carried a wooden bed frame. Blanketed by dust as the truck roared past, they looked up only briefly.

Dusk lasts about twenty minutes at the Equator. We were still driving when the last light in the sky faded, plunging us into a pitch-black world. I peered out past the front of the truck. A small section of road momentarily lit by the headlights and spotlight was all that was visible. As we rounded sharp corners, the road would disappear. It looked as though we were driving into nothingness. People walking on the road edge would light up, then instantly disappear again. There was little other traffic. We travelled isolated in a bubble of light.

The back of the truck was drafty and the temperature dropped quickly. I pulled my Whistler sweatshirt down from the overhead rack and cuddled into Dan for warmth. "Are you excited?" I asked him.

"It will be great if we get to see the gorillas after all. I don't know how Charles is going to pull it off, though. We don't have much time. According to the guidebook, there's a maximum of six people allowed in a group. If we don't start to get in right away, not everyone will make it." Although I didn't tell Dan, I'd decided to stay behind if there were any problems with getting enough places. In spite of his assurances that he'd help and I could make it, I wasn't so confident.

Two hours after leaving Kabale, tired, hungry and covered by a light layer of desiccating dust blown up from the road, we pulled up in front of a building.

"Where are we?"

"The sign says the Virunga Hotel."

"But what town are we in?"

"We're in a town?"

"Who knows?"

There are few electric lights in African towns—no street lights, no lighted storefronts, no lighted house porches or windows. Stores and kiosks are lit by a single kerosene lamp and houses by a candle or lamp that forms a rich, deep, orange-yellow ball of light only in its immediate area. We had travelled down the main road in Kisoro unaware of either the town or the buildings.

The Virunga Hotel was on a short side street a few hundred yards from the main road. The truck had stopped in front of an eight-foot bamboo fence with closed gates. All we could see was a small patio with five tables and chairs at the front of the building.

"Where are we going to stay?"

"Are we going to camp or is Charles going to book us into the hotel?"

Twice before when we'd driven after dark and hadn't been able to put up our tents, we had stayed in a $5-a-room hotel with questionable facilities. The Virunga Hotel looked similar. It was a square, single story building constructed around a central courtyard. Although there were five small bedrooms down each side with two shared showers, two flushing toilets and a wash basin at the rear, we would be camping.

A moment later the gates swung open and our truck drove forward. Inside the fence were three other large safari trucks with cook fires burning near them and twenty-five tents pitched willy-nilly. The only artificial light was from one bare light bulb on the side of the hotel above a walkway into the courtyard and a light inside the drop toilet at the back. I wobbled down from our truck and, as quickly as our tents and thermarest mattresses were tossed down from the top storage bins, Dan and I found an open space and pitched our tent.

While I got the tent organized, Dan gave our friend, Doug, a hand putting his tent up next to ours. We had come to know Doug quite well over the five weeks that we had travelled together. Like Dan and me, he was considerably older than the rest of the group. He ran a small gardening company in New Zealand to supplement his retirement pension and travelled during his business's winter off-season. He and his wife, Mary, had previously travelled in southern Africa. This time he was alone because Mary had injured herself just before they were to leave. Several times when he and I were putting up tents together or scrubbing dirty clothes under the tap, Doug had commented, "I miss Mary. She's the one who did all the planning and kept everything organized."

"It must be hard travelling alone. But, you look like you're doing fine, Doug. If you ever need a hand with anything…"

"It's not that I mind being alone. I've been a hiker all my life and hiked alone for days in the mountains at home," Doug said with a sigh. "I miss Mary."

As soon as our tents were up, Charles called us together. "Tomorrow we'll all go to the border. I'll talk to the officials. I know them. I'll do everything I can to get you in to see the gorillas."

"What about all the other groups camped here?" someone said. "I was talking to one fellow who said they haven't been able to get permits."

"Their leaders are European, not African like me. The guys at the border and me, we talk the same language." He rubbed his hand across his forehead, turned and sauntered into the hotel bar.

Later that night our group sat around the fire talking with campers from other groups who had been waiting for up to a week to see the gorillas. One obnoxious, loud, drunk fellow with a particularly offensive manner hi-jacked the conversation at our fire. Disgusted by his obscenities, the majority of our group, including Doug, Dan and me, left. We didn't hear him mention a sign that had been posted earlier that week in the gorilla-viewing area. The sign warned that, if rebel demands weren't met, hostages would be taken.

Anyone who has read the small print in brochures advertising African trips is aware that Africa can be a dangerous place to visit. It means accepting a degree of risk that might be unacceptable in other places. Around the campfire one night near the beginning of this trip, I listened to our guide tell horror stories about trips gone wrong, where travelers were injured or killed. A baboon jumped into a safari truck at Nakuru and bit a woman on the neck. A tourist sleeping with his head outside the tent flap on a hot night was grabbed by a hyena and dragged by the head into the brush. A woman who got between a hippo calf and its mother was crushed so badly she was still in the hospital a year later. A man reacted badly to Larium, an antimalaria medicine, and tried to kill himself at Samburu by throwing himself off a cliff. Fortunately the guide and Masaai trackers found him before the lions. I'm sure some of the stories were the African equivalent of urban legends, but they did remind me that this was a wild country where anything might happen at any time. Often all that separated us from the wild animals was the thin fabric of a tent and Masaai guards with spears.

Wild animals were not the only problems. Several times I read in local English-language newspapers about Europeans being killed—a woman found dead in Nanyuki, a man shot in a Nairobi bar. Even our home newspapers occasionally reported snippets about tragedies in African countries. Before the trip I had checked the Travel Advisory issued by Canada's Department of Foreign Affairs which warned about various rebel groups operating in the north and eastern border areas of Uganda. Our safari route wasn't travelling in those dangerous areas, so I was puzzled when I noticed that Charles sometimes took a round-about route.

"This is the long way, Charles. Why not take this road?" I said pointing to the map when we stopped for lunch.

"That way is not good. There is unrest near there."

Without giving us any idea of how recently it had happened, Charles told us he was bypassing one area between Murchison Falls and Queen Elizabeth Park where thirty-three people had been killed by Ugandan guerillas. None of us asked for details, content to leave our safety in Charles' hands.

Like many of the group, I felt distanced from the history of violence in the countries through which we were travelling. Even startling events seemed unremarkable. While Dan and I were taking down our tent in preparation for leaving our camp beside the White Nile at Jinja, Uganda, one of the women in our group came hurrying up from the river. "There's a corpse in the water! It went bobbing past in the current."

"Where?"

"What did you do?"

"In the river, right down there. There was nothing we could do."

A minute later the rest of the group who had been by the river climbed up the bank. "God, there was a dead guy in the river. I wonder who he was and how he got in the water."

Charles called, "We're leaving in ten minutes. Get the rest of your things packed up."

"Charles, there was a dead guy down there in the water. What do we do?"

Charles shook his head and shrugged. "Get packed."

Silently, the group finished packing. Dan shook his head. "If we were back home and someone saw a corpse—how different our reaction would be."

On August 7, when bombs went off at the US Embassies in Nairobi, Kenya and Dar es Salaam, Tanzania, killing two hundred and fifty people, we were driving into Kampala, Uganda. Fortunately, the bomb in the US Embassy in Kampala had been found before it exploded, too. The two Americans in our safari group pored over the local newspaper and read articles about the bombs aloud. But, the only sign of conflict we had actually seen was a rusted derelict tank by the side of the road, a remnant of the Idi Amin regime. When the only news of the outside world comes from one paper every couple of days, it's easy to forget that a world apart from the truck even exists. Travelling in the Bedford truck was like being in a cocoon.

We drove for hours between one game park and the next with nothing to do but watch the countryside and people as we passed. To fill the time, several people began reading travel guides from the truck library. "Just listen to this," one of the young Australians said. He read us excerpts from the history of Uganda under Idi Amin when an estimated 300 000 Ugandans had been killed, many of them tortured to death. Later in the day when he got to Rwanda and the genocide, he began to read aloud again. Although the history of violence in the countries through which we were travelling may have been new for a few of the younger people on the trip, most of us had become aware of Rwanda in 1994 when scenes of mass murder and genocide exploded on our TV screens. We had seen the image of thousands of bloated bodies floating down rivers or lying in rag-doll positions along the roadside. Endless lines of people fled, their heads burdened with their few essential possessions. In the refugee camps, blue tarps floated in a sea of smoky cook fire haze. More bodies— the young, the old and the weak—everywhere.

"Don't read that to us," one of the women said. "Didn't you see enough of it on the news? Anyway, we're not going to Rwanda."

Although the Rwandan genocide had ended four years earlier, the underlying conflict between Hutu and Tutsi continued. In 1996, two years before our safari, Paul Kagame, the Tutsi head of the Rwandan army, had forcibly closed the Hutu refugee camps that sprang up after the genocide to end the Hutu militia's control in the camps and stop the still ongoing murders of neutral Hutu and Tutsi Rwandans. Many of the ousted militant Hutus and their families, rather than returning to their homes in Rwanda, had fled into the forested volcanic mountain areas in the northwest or moved deeper into Zaire. There they waited for the opportunity to once again take control of Rwanda. That tied the on-going Rwandan Hutu/Tutsi hostility to the neighboring country, Zaire.

In 1996 Zaire's corrupt government was headed by Mobutu Sese Seko. He was ultimately overthrown by Laurent Kabila with the support and backing of Tutsis in the Rwandan government and Zaire's Tutsi community, the Banyamulenge. Kabila declared himself President of Zaire in 1997 and renamed the country the Democratic Republic of Congo.

In spite of the key role Rwandan Tutsis had played in bringing him to power, Kabila was unable or unwilling to do anything to stop the Hutu hiding in Congo from continuing to attack the Tutsis in Rwanda. The mutual disenchantment between Kabila and Tutsis escalated. In 1998, just days before we arrived in Kisoro, Kabila fired his top military aid, a Rwandan Tutsi, and ordered all Rwandan soldiers to withdraw from Congo. The mainly Tutsi Congolese army troops stationed near Bukavu in eastern Congo on the Rwandan border, immediately rebelled against Kabila. The open hostilities shattered the fragile peace that had been maintained since the end of the genocide.

As I climbed into my tent at the Virunga Hotel, the only thing on my mind was whether I'd make it up the mountain to see the gorillas. There was no way I could have known that eleven kilometers from where I was sleeping in Kisoro, an uneasy political situation had exploded and would mushroom into a major war in central Africa involving rebel armies and military forces from nine African countries.

TWO

We were up shortly after daybreak the next day. At a signal from Charles, we left Patrick, the cook, with the breakfast dishes, piled into the back of the truck and bounced for eleven kilometers over rough gravel roads to the border, arriving just before its 9:00 a.m. opening. Charles and Justin, the co-driver, went into the Ugandan border office to talk with the officials while we waited in the truck watching a sea of people pass.

Unlike tourists, the Africans who lived on either side of the border crossed freely between Uganda and Congo. Young boys pushed wooden scooters loaded with water containers or sacks of produce up the hill into Congo. Others rode empty scooters down the hill away from the border into Uganda. A steady stream of women, most with babies on their backs, walked back and forth over the border balancing huge loads on their heads. Dressed in kangas—lengths of brightly coloured, patterned fabric wrapped and secured around their bodies, with a cloth around their heads serving as both a headcovering and a cushion for their heavy loads—the barefoot women turned to look at us as they passed. Children, dressed in a mishmash of outsized, dirty, mostly tattered western clothing, were every-where. Some were dressed in school uniforms with bright pink shirts for both boys and girls. We watched people pass; they, in turn, watched us.

Throughout the trip, anytime our truck stopped, people had appeared from nowhere, down the road or out of the countryside, to watch us. Per-haps *wazungu,* white people, were entertainment for them. The children looked on us as a possible source of gifts. As we drove past they chanted.

"Give me money."

"Give me pen."

"Give me sweets."

At this border town, like the others through which I'd passed, the vendors were almost as numerous as the children. They talked at me through the windows and held up goods to sell—bracelets, necklaces, carvings and fruit—hoping I might be enticed and buy something. "Buy this from me. I give you a good price. A bargain, just for you." The prices always started high; bargaining was expected.

As the time Charles and Justin were spending in the border office stretched on, I got tired of sitting on display so high in the truck. From the height of six to eight feet, I looked down on everything. Like watching a play from the theater balcony, it reinforced my feeling of separation, of being a spectator.

With several of the others, Dan and I climbed down the ladder at the back to talk with the crowd of giggling children encircling the truck. One woman in our group got mobbed when she gave away candy and a few pens. Another fitted a small barefoot girl with a pair of her running shoes, carefully double-knotting the laces. I wondered if the girl would get to keep the shoes or if they would be taken away and traded or sold.

Doug was talking with a group of teenagers. One young man said, "I have a good walking stick for you at my home. It will help when you go into the mountains. It is for you. Just the right size."

"I could use a walking stick," Doug told the boy.

"I go to get it now," the boy said and started to leave.

Doug stopped him, unsure of how much longer we would be at the border or how far the boy had to go. "We have to come back here in the morning. I'll buy it from you then."

It was an hour before Charles and Justin returned to the truck. "Get in," Charles said as he started the truck, ignoring the questions about whether he'd been successful. My anticipation and anxiety grew with each kilometer back to Kisoro. Would I see the gorillas or could I go back and suntan by the lake?

At the hotel, we gathered in a tight group around Charles. "The border is open for visitors. The officials who decide how many tourists are allowed in each day told me there's a good chance you'll all get to see the gorillas within a couple of days." He smiled as the group cheered. "We'll camp here at the hotel and go to the border every morning till you've all gone in. There's enough time before you have to be in Entebbe for your flights home.

"We have to go back this afternoon to get your visas stamped and pay all the fees. You'll need to pay everything in US dollars. If you need to cash any traveler's checks, I can do that for you." Charles was in charge of the safari kitty we had contributed to at the beginning of the trip. The kitty money paid for food, incidental Park fees, motel and camping costs. He obviously still had enough US dollars to exchange for the traveler's checks.

I calculated it would take a minimum of two days for us all to see the gorillas—six people in a group, two groups a day. In addition to the $150 US the tour company paid for our permits, each of us had to pay an additional $60 US for a visa and $5 US to have our vaccination records checked. These weren't official government fees, but monies that would go to the men at the border. The Park had been closed because of a dispute over who should get this additional money. Some travel books suggested that when the three contiguous parks—Uganda's Mgahinga Gorilla National Park, Rwanda's Parc des Volcans and Congo's Parc des Virungas—were set up to protect the gorillas and the last remaining forested area at the peaks of the Virunga Mountains in which they live, the local people had been promised a payment for the expropriated lands. It was unclear to me from what our travel company had said whether this money had ever been paid to the local people and who got the collected fees, the government or the border officials. The only money we were sure of was the $2 US tip we were told to take for the Rangers who would lead us on the walk.

The few remaining wild mountain gorilla family groups in the Virunga Mountains usually avoided people and remained hidden when humans were close. As part of the governments' efforts to protect the gorillas through a combination of ecotourism, education and anti-poaching, two of the families in the Virunga Mountain area had been gradually habituated or made less wary of humans. They were the groups we would be visiting.

After lunch we all went back to the border while Charles got the visas and other paper work done. I recognized a group of young boys from that morning; they were Border Rats, kids who hung around there all the time. I climbed down again from the truck. Since French is the second official language of the area, I tried talking with two of them in my high school French. It was quickly obvious they had no idea what I was saying. With a smile I drifted back to the truck.

Doug and I were standing at the side of the truck in the shade talking about the heavy loads the women were carrying when a voice called from behind us. "Mister! I have your stick." It was the young man from the morning with the walking stick for Doug. I left Doug to do his bargaining.

When he came back beside the truck, Doug showed me the stick. "Look. This wood is green. The stick's just been made. He must have gone right home this morning and made it."

"It looks good, Doug," I said, not knowing anything about walking sticks.

"Unfortunately, it's too long, too big in diameter and too heavy. I paid him most of what he asked. I didn't bargain much, but that isn't important. This is one way the people here can earn a little money. It's better than begging. I get upset when some of the people with us bargain too hard."

Several of the group used to tease Doug about his generosity. One day early in the trip while we were waiting for the last people to return from shopping, someone sitting at the front of the truck gave a young boy a cheap pen for school. The boy came around to the back of the truck and sold it to Doug for twenty Kenyan shillings or about 50¢ Canadian, far more than the pen was worth. Doug just shrugged. He didn't give anyone money, but he'd buy anything.

While we waited, I finally told Dan what I'd been thinking since Charles first said we might get to see the gorillas. "If there's a problem with getting enough places, I'm staying back at camp."

Dan shook his head. "They'll put us in the same group. Don't worry. I'll be there." Charles came out of the office with a fist full of passports. All of them had been stamped with one-day visas for Congo. Since we each had a visa, we were all going, including me, whether I thought I could do it or not.

When we drove back to the hotel, three European women returning from a day of gorilla viewing caught a lift with us. One, who was 56 years old like me, raved about her experience. Without much prompting, she described her day. After the vehicle dropped them off on the mountainside, the Rangers had divided the people in two groups, putting her and the other two older women on the short walk trip. The beginning was a fairly demanding, hour-long climb up a long steep hill to the jungle. Once they reached the top, she said it got easier. The previous day the Rangers had marked the area where they'd seen the small gorilla family: a silverback male, a pregnant female and their three-year-old young. Starting from the marked place, the Rangers bushwhacked through thick undergrowth following the spoor, feces and broken foliage. Although gorillas wander freely wherever food grows, browsing on bamboo and over fifty other plants, they are fairly sedentary, rarely moving farther than a kilometer a day. They located the gorillas quickly and the women spent about an hour with the animals. From what she described, I figured I could manage the short walk. As long as I didn't have to go too fast, I'd make it.

That night Charles told us more about the two families of gorillas. Although groups going to see both families started from the same place and spent the same amount of time with the animals, the distance they hiked was different. The 'short walk group' would see a gorilla family close to the drop off point and be gone a total of three hours. The hike for the 'long walk group' was physically demanding and lasted seven hours or more. From the drop off point they would hike for three hours before their long climb into the forest where the gorillas were located. The long-walk-group would see more gorillas, one silverback, his females and their young; about thirteen in all. Charles stressed that both groups got the same time, an hour, with the gorillas.

"Who's going on the short walk?" he asked. I was the only one who put up my hand.

Dan stood there with his hands in his pockets shaking his head. "Just look at who wants the long walk," Dan said. "Who do they think they're kidding? I'm in better shape than most of them and I'm going on the short walk." The one problem with a safari holiday for anyone as physical as Dan was the enforced inactivity. I could hear the frustration in his voice. I knew he needed a good workout after five sedentary weeks. I didn't want him to get stuck in the wimpy group holding my hand.

"Look, Dan, you should go on the long walk. I know you said you'd stay with me, but I'll be fine. Go in the other group." But he didn't want to leave me by myself.

"Maybe we won't have a choice," I said, "but if we do, I want you to go on the long walk. It's not like I'll be alone. It sounds like the Rangers will put five other people in the short walk group whether they want to be there or not." He finally accepted that I'd be fine without him.

The next morning I was up by 5:30 a.m. I wasn't sure how many of us would be seeing the gorillas that day, though Charles had told us all to be prepared. I wore my hiking boots, a pair of light cotton trousers, a short sleeved t-shirt and a white cotton sun hat. In case it rained, a near daily occurrence in the high mountains, I zipped my Nikon camera in a plastic bag and carried it with a light rain jacket in my canvas totebag. I added a bottle of water and my lunch: a passion fruit, a banana, a jam and peanut butter sandwich and some cookies. Tucked in my pocket was enough money for the tip and to buy a pop when we got back.

Shortly after we arrived at the border, a Land Rover pulled up and two young couples we'd seen camped around the hotel got out. Their driver, a heavy man with shoulder length wavy hair joined Charles and Justin and the three of them disappeared into the Ugandan customs office with all our passports.

I was subdued as I waited in the truck. Most of the others were bubbling about the gorillas, but my excitement had been overwhelmed by a growing anxiety about the climb. "I should be using this time to get caught up on my journal," I said to Dan without making any effort to get the book out of my locker.

"You'll have so much to write about tonight that you'll be writing for hours," he said. After half an hour in the truck I felt I'd explode.

"I've got to move," I said, climbing out of the truck with my canvas bag over my shoulder. I was itching to take pictures of the passing people, but left the camera in my bag. Borders are not good places to take photos. I had been told the guards get quite aggressive if they see a camera. Several others from our group also got out and we stood shifting from foot to foot, watching and waiting. Two of the Border Rats came over and asked us, in English, if we were going to see the gorillas. Their English was good. No wonder they hadn't understood my French the day before. They likely didn't even speak French. Unlike the vendors, they had nothing to sell, but were curious, asking questions about where we were from and what we had seen in Africa.

After an hour, the three guides reappeared. "You're all going at the same time," Charles said striding over to our truck. "Today. Follow me." With a whoop of excitement, our entire group and the four from the Land Rover walked across 'no man's land' into Congo. On the other side we waited while the Congolese authorities checked our passports and vaccination certificates. Charles and Justin collected our visa fees and the other monies we had to pay.

"Look at all the cash," one of our group said. "Someone's getting rich today."

The local people walking back and forth across the border stared at us as we eagerly handed over our $65 US. "Imagine what they're thinking," I said quietly to Dan. "We're paying more money to see a gorilla for an hour than they'll earn in months of hard work. Gorillas may bring a lot of money into the country, but the people don't seem to benefit. They must think we're millionaires."

"We are, compared to them."

We were herded toward a twelve-seat van and a pickup truck hired to drive us to the drop-off area. A crowd was milling around the vehicles: drivers, Rangers in yellow jackets, guards with guns slung over their shoulders, teenage porters. Dan pulled me toward the van. "You don't want to ride in the back of the pickup," he said. Dan and I squeezed into the van with fourteen others, a mix of gorilla trekkers and Africans. Everyone else rode in the back of the truck.

The farther from the border we travelled, the more the road deteriorated, narrowing to two twisting, jarring tire tracks. Along the road tucked in the fields of corn, sorghum and beans were small, widely spaced, mud plastered huts with dozens of children playing in the dirt yards around them. The children waved and ran after us. Women with babies on their backs stood silently watching as we passed.

The drop-off point was about eight kilometers from the border. We emptied out of the van and waited for the truck. After what seemed like an inordinate length of time, the pickup finally arrived.

"What happened to you guys?" someone called as the truck pulled up.

"A rock blew our tire. There was no spare. We had to wait for someone to come from the village with another tire."

There was a flurry of activity as the back of the pickup emptied. The young men who had come from the border jockeyed for jobs as porters. "Hello, my name is Ben. I will carry your things. Please remember me when you need something."

The head Ranger announced, "Those who have travelled in the van will go on the short walk. Those in the truck will go on the long walk." Pandemonium broke out as the people in the van who had wanted the long walk began to protest.

"No way," I told Dan, pushing him toward the group by the truck. "You're going on the long walk. No matter what, just go with the rest of our group. I'll be fine."

The head Ranger pointed to Doug. "You will join the short walk group." I gave Dan another push.

Everyone continued to mill around—hikers trying to position themselves near the long walk group, porters vying for jobs, Rangers trying to make two groups. Suddenly the head Ranger threw up his hands. Pointing to Doug and me and the four who had joined us at the border, he said, "You go on the short walk. Everyone else, the long walk." Immediately he set off across the hill followed by a phalanx of tourists and Africans, with Dan near the back. I waved good bye and set off at the back of my group, up the hill to see the gorillas.

The hill was long and steep. The rest hiked up as though it were flat. I soon abandoned any attempt to keep pace with them. One of the Rangers stayed with me as I struggled up the hill stopping to catch my breath every dozen steps or so. I knew I wasn't in great physical shape, but the altitude, approaching 7000 feet, added to my breathing problems. By the time I got to the top of the hill, the others were resting outside an abandoned and vandalized building that had once been used as a lodge. Although there was nothing left in any of the rooms, from the size of the outbuildings and the extensive overgrown gardens around the main building, it must have been a wonderful place to stay. From the front verandah, you could see the hills and fields below stretching and fading toward the distant horizon. All our head Ranger could tell us was that it had been empty a long time. I thought, perhaps since the Rwandan refugee exodus.

Before we headed into the jungle, the head Ranger talked about the gorillas. I had read Dian Fossey's *Gorillas in the Mist* and seen videos of her and the gorillas around her research station. There are just over 300 mountain gorillas remaining in the Virunga Mountains area. Although the family we were seeing had been habituated, contact with humans was kept to a minimum. Only one group of people was allowed to visit a day, for no more than an hour. We were cautioned not to talk, not to touch the animals, and to stand motionless if the silverback came near us.

After a short rest, we moved on and I headed up a narrow path behind the lodge into the jungle forest. Although I could see nothing along the path to differentiate one spot from another, the Rangers suddenly stopped and left the path, pushing through the thick brush, slashing a trail through the nettles and thorn bushes with their machetes. With my eyes peeled for anything unusual, I climbed over logs and ducked through foliage, careful to avoid the sharp, jagged ends of jutting branches. Now that the climb was over, my excitement was building.

When the Ranger placed his finger to his lips to signal silence, I looked around in bewilderment. I didn't see anything. With his machete, the Ranger carefully pushed some leaves aside. There, about twelve feet away, like a giant midnight-black mountain of shiny fur, sat the silverback. He was looking directly at me, motionless. His deep brown eyes, shaded by heavy brows, seemed to be taking stock of me. *My god*, I thought, my mouth open and my breathing suddenly shallow. *He's huge. He's magnificent.* I tugged my totebag around and felt inside it for my camera. My eyes never left his.

The Ranger signalled us to move closer. All six of us were fumbling with our cameras, tripping over the underbrush and each other in an attempt to get a photo of this magnificent animal before he disappeared, but he sat there as if we didn't exist. Keeping a respectful distance, we took turns, in pairs, photographing him. The only sound apart from our heavy breathing and the clicking shutters came from the Ranger. He made a deep sound in the back of his throat, a combination of vibration, hum and growl. The Ranger motioned for me to go and stand right behind the gorilla so Doug could take my picture. *Whoa,* I thought as butterflies fluttered in my stomach. I raised my eyebrows in question and pointed to the gorilla and then to me. The Ranger nodded. I thought, *OK, you're the boss.* Trying to be as light and invisible as possible I tiptoed across the small clearing, stepped gingerly around and behind the gorilla, growling deep in my throat the way the Ranger had done. It was only then that I realized how big the silverback actually was. Seated, his head was chest level on me, over four and a half feet high. The thick short shiny fur on his back was silver in contrast to the deep black everywhere else. His powerful heavy hands rested on the ground in front of him.

While Doug snapped several photos of me, the gorilla stared straight ahead as if he were posing. Then, as though he realized each of us had had a turn taking pictures, the silverback very slowly tipped forward and stood up, his front paws still on the ground. He put his left hand just in front of my foot. I took a long, slow breath in and held it. My shoulders lifted and my body seemed to lengthen. I was nearly levitating. His right hand swung forward coming even with my legs. "Grummph," I crooned, my hands dangling by my thighs.

"Don't move," the Ranger whispered between the soothing sounds he was making. With casual languor the gorilla sauntered past, so close his shoulder brushed against my leg. Only my eyes moved, following his slow movement. As though it had a life of its own, my little finger stretched out toward his shoulder. A centimeter separated my finger and his fur; I could almost touch him. As the round slope of his back disappeared behind me, my shoulders dropped and I let a long exhalation escape. The Ranger smiled and continued his soothing growl.

The silverback wandered a few feet, cracking off lengths of bamboo, which he held between his fingers and his palm, peeling away the hard outside with his teeth and eating the soft white inner flesh. He tipped his head back and whoofed a few times. From somewhere deep in the surrounding brush, a smaller gorilla, about half his size, popped her head through the leaves and looked at me. It was the female. Right behind her was their three-year-old young, smaller still. The silverback gave a loud, screeching bellow and charged straight through the bushes knocking the female flying. I ducked and took a couple of fast pictures, thankful he hadn't charged at me. The gorillas wandered and browsed within a dozen feet of me as I continued to take pictures until I ran out of film. With my camera back in the plastic bag, I stood watching, a wide smile on my face. The Ranger lifted his hand. It was time to go.

We pushed back through the brush until we were well away from the gorillas and then stopped for lunch. When it was safe to talk, Doug and I burst out, "Did you see…?" "I thought when he…" "Wasn't that fantastic when…" Our words tumbled over each other.

"I'm not sure I got your camera in focus when you were standing behind the silverback," Doug said.

"Don't worry about it. Even if it's blurry it will be great. I was shaking so hard I'm not sure anything I took will be in focus. I took three rolls of 24! I hope the other group gets as close as we did. I thought we'd have to stay a lot farther away, but I guess the Ranger knows what's right."

The other two couples who were from Sweden were talking as excitedly as Doug and I. Seated on a log, with a thick green canopy overhead, I pulled out my lunch. The peanut butter and jam sandwich hadn't survived the climb. I knew I'd be able to get something more appetizing back in Kisoro, so I offered it to the boy who'd carried my bag. He wolfed it down while I ate the banana and passion fruit.

With lunch over, we found a path and headed out of the forest. Clear of the thick bushes and on the sunny mountainside, our pace and the temperature picked up considerably. Even though we were going downhill, I was hot, sticky, and puffing with the effort of keeping up with the others. Going down the mountain, braced against the slope with my toes pushed into the front of my boots, was as hard as climbing up into the forest. All the muscles in my legs were quivering from my unaccustomed exertion. I wanted to get back to the truck and sit down. The only person behind me was a guard, his gun slung casually across his body.

About half way down to the waiting vehicles, the head Ranger stopped. Darting glances down the mountainside, he and the guards huddled in a hurried conference. They seemed uneasy and quickly set off down the slope again at an even faster pace.

Suddenly the man in front stopped. "The trucks are on fire!" he said, pointing down the mountain. "There are bandits! We must go another way." The head Ranger immediately set off across the slope through knee-deep grass.

What's he talking about? I thought. Hustling now to keep up with the others, I strained to look down the mountain to see what had upset the Ranger. *Burning? Where's the smoke? I don't see any smoke. Where are we going? If those vehicles are burned, can't we wait for others to be brought up? Surely whoever vandalized them won't still be there. The police would get them.*

"Quickly!" the guard with me said.

Because the mountains are so steep, soil is terraced across the slope in mounds eighteen inches to two feet high and two to two and a half feet wide to trap the rain and prevent soil erosion. The terraced area we were traversing was covered in a coarse, dry, knee-high grass that obscured the ground. There was no way to tell with each step exactly where my foot would land. I hurried. Up, down, along, grass catching in my boots—up, up, down. I was at the back. "Hurry, hurry. We must get away from here," the guard with me urged. I hurried as quickly as I could, knowing that if I tried to go any faster, I wouldn't be going anywhere at all. I hated myself at that point.

I didn't understand why the vehicles' being vandalized was causing such a panic among the Rangers and guards. *Where are we going?* I asked myself. *We're away from the paths and those trucks. Why are we still rushing? I can't do this. Why don't they slow down? God damn it, I knew I shouldn't have come on this damn trip.* All thoughts of the glorious hour with the gorillas were erased.

We angled across a wide swath of field and down through a dry creek bed. Walking on the rocks was easier and the streambed headed down the mountain. Irritated at the Ranger, in my ignorance of the seriousness of the situation, I thought we should head down the creek bed. I glanced down and had a flash that I should just leave the group and go down the rocks. Or I could sit down and huddle out of sight for a while. But I hurried onto the next section of field.

"Hurry! Hurry! There they are!" the guard exclaimed, looking back and pointing. "Bandits." I turned to look back. Far away, high on the grassy slope down which I had previously come, were eight tiny figures bounding effortlessly down the hill. *Wow,* I thought, *look at how fast they're coming.* There was no way I was going to outrun those men.

"Run!" As I twisted around to start back down the hill, the bandits began shooting. Simultaneous with the gunshots, time slowed down. I saw and heard everything in real time, but there seemed to be an infinite amount of time to think. The shots made two sounds: a crack as the gun was fired, and then a following sound, a thunk. I didn't know if they were aiming at us or over our heads. I did know that if they wanted to shoot me, there was nothing I could do. I couldn't get away. I could neither run fast enough to escape nor fight them successfully. Strangely, I wasn't afraid. A voice in my head began talking, giving me directions, telling me what I should do next. A continuous stream of talking flowed through my head as though I was listening to someone else. *If it's time for you to die, then you'll die.* The group in front of me began running—fast, faster; yellow Ranger jackets flying through the grass, two young Swedes growing smaller, porters throwing away packs and bags in their rush down the mountainside. Crack. Thunk.

Try running. I tried running a few steps, but the unevenness of the terrain and the thickness of the grass made it futile to even try. *Put your hands up so they know you're not trying to resist.* I raised my hands high over my head and continued walking down the hill. Crack. Thunk. The bullets whined overhead and out of the corner of my eye I saw the other Swedish couple drop to the ground. Crack thunk. Crack thunk. They continued their crawling scramble down the slope. And there I was, out in the open, walking upright with my hands in the air. *With your hands up you're a bigger target. Crawl.* I tried crawling through the shoulder high, matted mesh of dried grass and quickly realized that if running and walking were difficult, crawling was impossible. The grass that caught and pulled on my clothing masked the unevenness of the ground. One of my hands plunged deep into a hollow tipping me forward so I almost smashed my nose, while my other hand jammed into the rising slope of the next hillock. I stood up. Crackthunk. Crackthunk. The shots were a lot closer; the interval between the bullets' crack and thunk was very short. Crackthunkcrackthunk.

To my left a large patch of bramble bushes was growing along the edge of the dry creek bed. I headed toward the brambles in a crouch, thinking they might provide a hiding place. Doug and the Swedes appeared in front of me. I couldn't see the group who had run ahead of us any more, but passed the bags and packs the porters discarded in the grass.

Brambles are brambles no matter what country they're in. As I crawled into the first sparsely leafed vines, the thorns scratched and speared my bare arms. The Swedish couple was much farther ahead of me in the brambles. I was amazed at how they were able to just push through. I couldn't see Doug. *This is stupid,* I thought to myself. *There is no way these will hide us. The colours of our clothes will give us away no matter how deep we go.* I stopped and pulled off my white hat in what I knew was a futile attempt to be less obvious. Then, I waited.

THREE

S creaming men jabbed me with guns, forcing me out of the brambles. I didn't understand their words, but I knew they were telling me to get out and stand up. Once I untangled myself from the thorns, they pushed me into a group with Doug and the two Swedes and began herding us back up the mountain.

Oh god. Not up. We didn't go back the way we had come, but angled to the left, through the grass, over the mounds and up the steep slope straight toward the forest. The men shoved me across the back with their rifles and jerked on my arm, screaming in my face, "Faster, faster! Vite, vite!" Up, down, over, along! Up! Those damn mounds of dirt! That fucking grass! The harder I tried to keep up, the more I stumbled and fell. *Damn, damn. I can't do it. Please let me stop!*

I gasped for breath unable to suck enough oxygen. My heart nearly burst out of my chest. The men yelled and prodded me with their guns.

Move faster. Faster!

I can't.

In every language I thought they might understand I pleaded for a rest, to go more slowly. "I can't go faster! Pole pole! Lentement!" Stopping wasn't an option. If I couldn't keep up I was sure I'd die.

Doug kept shouting at the men to leave me alone, that I was sick, that I had a bad heart. He was wonderful; he was lying to help me. I don't know whether or not they understood him, but I did. Deep inside, I smiled.

In spite of my exertions, I was slowing the whole group down. Like an engine revved beyond its upper limit, my body was ready to explode. I grew huge and heavy.

Suddenly, all the strength left my muscles and I collapsed. One of the men reached down, hauled me upright and looped my arm around his neck. He began hauling me up the hill. With my eyes shut I had no idea how far we still had to go. I hung limply, eyes closed, boots dragging through the thick matted grass. I had no control of my body. I was dead-weight. Soon there were two men carrying me, one on each side. As they jostled and sweated me up the mountain slope, their bony shoulders pounded my underarms like sandpaper-covered clubs.

Suddenly the men dropped me. I lay on my side in powdery earth as soft and welcoming as a feather bed. Every muscle vibrated and then, slowly relaxed. Completely limp, eyes closed, I lay panting. My breathing began to steady and my pounding heart slowed. *Don't move. Stay there. Don't let them know you're recovering.* I lay motionless, a panting heap on the ground.

The air around me was filled with an angry buzz as our captors conferred in short unintelligible bursts. I heard Doug say, "There's nothing you can do, mate. You have to leave her." The Swedish man must have done something, I thought. I lay there, body motionless, mind racing.

I felt my feet being tugged and jostled. The pressure of the bootlaces on the front of my feet lessened, and with a twist, my boots were pulled off my feet. They're taking my boots, I thought. What are they going to do to me? *They might kill you now. Don't move. Lay still.* Every cell in my body was tingling. I listened for the swish of a machete. Would they chop my head or my neck? Would I die immediately or would they slash me again and again? I lay there and waited. I breathed.

Mixed with the murmuring voices I heard the sounds of people moving away. They were leaving. As the sounds faded, two male voices, one on each side of me began to whisper. *Maybe they'll kill you now that the others are gone. Stay still. Keep panting.* Except for the whispering voices, everything was quiet. *Maybe they'll leave, too.* I didn't change my position but continued to pant and moan softly.

I felt something brush my waist and twist my fanny pack around until the clasp was at the front. I heard a click and, as the fanny pack was pulled off, felt a tug when the clasp snagged my t-shirt fabric. A hard finger hooked the top of my socks and pulled them off. The chain on my reading glasses slipped over my head catching in the hair at the nap of my neck. I lay motionless as a sharp tug freed both the chain and several tangled hairs. The whispering continued. *That's all you have. There's nothing else to steal. They haven't killed you yet. Maybe they will leave.*

But they didn't. Hands grabbed me and rolled me onto my back. Fingers slipped under my elastic waistband and my slacks began to slide down my legs. The possibility of being murdered was replaced by the near certainty that I would be raped. I knew the probability that they had AIDS or

HIV was high. Over 12% of the population in that area was infected. It didn't make any sense to get free if I ended up infected by HIV. My mind raced as I thought of every possible option and quickly discarded most of them—scream, fight, scratch, run, lay still. I was unwilling to alter my apparently comatose state in the hope that they would still go and leave me behind, but recognized I had to do whatever I could to stop them raping me.

Everything I remembered from a lecture on rape prevention raced through my head. *Make yourself as unattractive as possible; have a bowel movement in your pants.* I did that. *Tell them you have a venereal disease or herpes.* I began moaning over and over, "No, I have syphilis. I have gonorrhea. I have my period now. Don't hurt me." I thought I'd heard some French words when the men were shouting at us earlier, so I tried to say the same thing in my broken French. I thought I heard one man tell the other that he had been immunized against syphilis. *I didn't know that there were preventative shots for syphilis,* my voice commented curiously. I lay there with my slacks and underpants around my calves and waited. What would they do? Other than their whispers and my breathing, there were no sounds.

Without warning a heavy male body dropped on top of me. Coarse fabric rubbed against my skin as a knee was forced between my legs bound together at the ankle by my clothes. Unable to escape, I shifted my body, twisting my legs and angling my pelvis to obstruct his access to my body as much as possible. With a chorus of accompanying grunts, a semi-hard penis was pounded against my groin. There was no penetration. He became increasingly soft and with a few sharp words, rolled off my body. *Yes!*

Suddenly my pants and underpants were ripped off. My body jerked along the ground and my t-shirt bunched up under my shoulder blades in the back. Strong hands grabbed my ankles and pulled my legs straight and apart. He knelt between my thighs and began poking and prodding the soft folds between my legs with sharp nailed fingers. I was at the end of my menstrual period and was wearing a tampon. He didn't seem to notice it. Knuckles dug into my inner thighs as he thrust himself forward, holding his penis straight and trying to push inside me. *This guy's serious. Keep your body turned. Move your knee in.* I moaned and wiggled to angle my body. He was persistent, though no firmer than the first man. Fingers spread my labia, but between my body angle and the tampon, he got no farther. He pounded his body against me, jolting me up the path. Then, with a sharp exclamation, his weight lifted from my body. I waited, my nerves as taut as a strung violin. All the while the two whispered feverishly and I repeated my mantra—I have syphilis. I have gonorrhea. I have my period. Don't hurt me.

The thought that they might resort to anal sex popped into my head. I buried it somewhere deep. Then, one of the men cursed angrily and a boot was slammed against my ribs four times. Just as I braced myself for another sideways kick, the boot stomped down on my stomach forcing all the air out of my body. As I lay there winded, the tone of their voices suddenly changed. *Something's happening.* Hands held my ankles and I felt cloth being worked over my feet. *Someone's coming.* Awkwardly and hastily my slacks were tugged and twisted up my body. *They wouldn't put your clothes back on if they were going to kill you.* There were a few more whispers and then silence. Where were they? *Gone!*

I lay without moving, a slack muscleless body, my cheek cushioned on the soft earth. The voice in my head cheered—*You escaped. They're gone. Congratulations. You stopped them. Well done.* Something made them run away, I thought. What did they hear? Was someone coming? More bandits?

I lay motionless. My breath was slow, calm and deep. My heart, back in my chest, beat as it should. But, my mind raced. What should I do next? My first thought was to get up and run. S*tay where you are. Don't move in case they came back or more bandits come up the path.* My collapse, though involuntary, had been a successful strategy. I was reluctant to abandon it. *Lay there. Don't move. Wait.* How long should I wait? I tried counting to keep track of how much time had passed, but I kept forgetting what number came next. I lay motionless and hyper-alert for what seemed like an hour, but likely wasn't more than a few minutes.

I opened my eyes hesitantly. The thick, green brush growing along the edge of the taupe dirt path was interlaced with a matted underlayer of grass, weeds and vines. Rolling my head slightly, I looked up at a high canopy of vibrant greens, a tunnel formed by the branches of tall trees stretching across the narrow path. I was in the jungle. Should I crawl into the brush and hide in case anyone was coming? I looked back at the thick bushes beside me. *Get out of the jungle.*

I rolled onto my hands and knees, pushed myself up onto my haunches, and looked down the path in both directions. All I saw was a narrow brown path curving into the green jungle. Using my hands to steady myself, I slowly stood up. My legs didn't feel strong enough to hold me and my knees threatened to buckle and drop me to the ground without warning. Like a reed in the wind I swayed back and forth in small circles.

But my mind was racing. All I could think was that I had gotten away from the men. I celebrated my freedom; I rejoiced at my deliverance; I delighted in my victory. I had to get out of the forest, back down the path toward the village the Rangers had been trying to reach. My eyes had been closed before we even entered the forest and I had no way of knowing, for sure, which direction to go in. I reasoned that, when I was dropped onto the ground, I likely fell forward. I turned to face down the path. There, in the dirt in front of me, were my soiled underpants. I stepped over them and began walking.

Slowly and deliberately I placed my bare right foot in the soft, thick dirt, paused, and then lifted my left foot, placing it in front. I thought each step. *Move your foot. Right. Left. Slowly. Down the path*. I kept trying to lick my cracked lips but my tongue was dry and moistureless. Somewhere close, just out of eyesight, a loud, steady, pounding drum kept rhythm with my steps. Step, boom, boom, step, boom, boom. Suddenly I recognized the drum. It was my heart.

I moved with intense concentration, one foot in front of the other. Dirt puffed between my toes. There were no rocks. It was like walking on velvet. *You did it. You got away. You stopped them from raping you. You're going home. Good. Keep walking*. I knew that all I had to do was keep going down the path, out of the jungle, to the houses below the grass. I'd be able to go home. Free.

Ahead of me I heard a movement on the path. Branches rustled as if someone had ducked into the bushes and disappeared. I peered into the brush as I passed, looking for some sign of a person in the thick undergrowth. "Help me, please. Au secours," I called softly. There was no answer. My heartbeat echoed in my ears, with a steady thump, thump, thump. Suddenly, without any warning or sound, a man dressed in dusty, ragged black clothes appeared on the path in front of me. A black cap with earflaps covered his head and a long, black raincoat hung unbuttoned over his black shirt and pants. Ragged black shoes, the soles partly unsewn, covered his feet. Everything about him was the dusty gray-black of continual use and many washings. For several long seconds we stood motionless staring at each other. "Help me, please. Au secours," I whispered again, but like a wraith he stepped soundlessly past, even his footsteps making no sound behind me on the path. Breathing slowly, steadily and deeply I continued down the path, one foot in front of the other.

At the end of the shady path, like a beacon, I could see a shimmering ball of golden light. The end of the jungle. Another dozen steps and I emerged from the cool shade of the verdant tunnel into intense sunlight. I closed my eyes and lifted my head. Behind my eyelids the sun shone red and the heat radiating from the sear land beat against my body. For a moment I stood there, relief washing over me at having made it out of the jungle. Then the voice in my head began again. *Start walking. Get to the houses.*

I opened my eyes squinting in the brightness. In front of me the path split. To my left it headed steeply down, back toward the grass area where we had been captured. To the right, just visible above the thick, steeply sloping grass field were the roofs of two houses. A few steps ahead of me the soft dirt path changed into a narrow line of trampled broken grasses. I glanced down at my bare feet remembering how the grass caught and pulled on my boots. With a quick plea cast toward the heavens that my bare feet would be tough enough to survive the rough, dry grass path, I straightened my shoulders and took two steps toward the houses.

I heard something behind me. I spun around. The ragged dusty man stepped out of the forest. With him was a young man who appeared to be in his early twenties. He was wearing a white, stiff collared dress shirt under a pullover sweater in a deep wine, navy and gray geometric knit. His gray trousers hung unwrinkled over well-polished oxfords. His hair was closely cropped and when he smiled, his teeth gleamed white and even. The ragged man hadn't ignored me, I thought. He went to get help.

The young man spoke to me in gentle tones and words I didn't understand. His whole manner suggested the need to be hidden within the safety of the forest. Were there bandits in the houses below? Hands outstretched toward me, the young man slowly stepped backward, urging me with his body to come back to the forest. The young man looked so clean and safe I allowed myself to be inched back to the forest. I didn't yell or fight, I just went. The voice in my head was shouting. *Don't go. Don't listen. The forest is bad. Dangerous. Keep out.* This man will help me, I argued. As though agreeing, my feet moved me back up the path into the forest. When we passed my underpants, already torn and shredded by some animal, I moaned aloud. I knew with certainty then that I was not going to escape.

Since thwarting the rape, I had been congratulating myself on how well I had done. I was sure I had managed to escape through my ingenuity and intelligence. I outwitted them. Not escaping showed me I was wrong.

As we followed the path deeper into the forest and higher up the mountain, I kept my eyes focused on my feet. My slow pace was a mix of fatigue, dehydration and shock, with an overlying determination that, if I were going to have to go up that goddamn mountain again, I'd do it at my speed. I walked slowly but I thought quickly. I had already come up against my physical limitations. I knew if I was going to survive I had to take care of myself. No one else could control my thoughts or how I reacted to and interacted with others. Controlling even small things helped me keep my fears in check. I talked to myself. *OK, Donalda, you're not going to escape. This is your life. You'd better make the best of it. No regrets. If the next few moments are all you have left, live them with as much dignity as possible.*

Twice the young man shoved me on the back and said something I didn't understand in a sharp tone that I did. I glared and shrugged him away. I didn't rush or allow myself to be hurried. I just watched my feet and took one more step, and then one more step.

A pair of black gum boots with red toes appeared beside my feet. I looked up in surprise at a new man walking beside me. Soon there were six young men around me walking slowly, staring at me and talking. I was desperately thirsty. I mimed lifting a cup to my mouth, but no one had any water.

A woman walked by. She's a woman, too. She'll help me. Our eyes met and I waited for her to say something to the men. It was naïve of me to think she would say or do anything. A traditional Rwandan expression is "The hen does not crow in the presence of a cock." African women don't have much of a role in decision making, nor do they openly question what the men do. She passed without giving any sign that seeing a barefoot white woman trudging up a path deep in the mountain jungle was unusual.

We eventually came to a small clearing where we were joined by a group of older men with guns and grenades in their belts. One of them, a handsome man about thirty years old, spoke to me in French. I didn't understand everything he said; I hadn't yet begun thinking in French. "Courage, madam, courage! N'as pas peur. Je m'appelle Frère *Something*." When I heard the word *Frère*, I thought he was a priest or religious person who would help me. Relief washed over me. Although he repeated his name several times, it wouldn't stay in my mind. What I understood was, "I am Brother *Something*. Don't be afraid. We are not going to hurt you." He told me he was a Christian and reassured me that I wouldn't be hurt. I believed him; he didn't want to hurt me.

I showed him the tiny guardian angel pin inside my fanny pack. In my rusty high school French I told him I, too, was Christian. I knew the majority of people in that part of Africa belong at least nominally to the Catholic Church. I didn't realize how many times I would give thanks to God, acknowledge my Catholic background, and share my guardian angel. When my friend, Daphne, gave it to me, I had no idea I would show it to my African captors as the angel who looks after me.

Because my husband, Dan, had lived in Zimbabwe for several years, I was aware of the importance *face* plays in all interactions in Africa. I lacked the French vocabulary to say anything complex, but speaking with deference and extreme politeness, I explained I had to go back to my husband in Kisoro, Uganda. Brother *Something* laughed rather pleasantly. "Ce n'est pas possible. That is not possible," he said. "I am taking you to my home… chez moi."

"Where is your home?" I said. "Is it in Uganda?"

"No," he said, "Rwanda."

"Rwanda?" I said astonished. "Where is Rwanda?" He looked behind me over my shoulder and pointed.

"C'est là. That way," he said.

When I turned to look where he was pointing all I could see were huge, cone shaped mountain peaks soaring mauve above the green trees. They looked incredibly high, steep and vast. My heart dropped and my legs turned to jelly. If they tried to make me go over those mountains I would die. I turned to Brother *Something*. "Ce n'est pas possible! No way! There is no way I can ever get over those mountains! Ils sont trop grand! Shoot me! You might as well shoot me now, because I can't do it." I wasn't sure what he would do, but I knew what I couldn't do. There was no way I would make it over those mountains.

He looked puzzled when I said, "Shoot me!" but I didn't know how to say it in French. I put my index finger to my temple, said, "Bang!" and let my legs collapse me toward the ground. He just laughed, held out his hand to help me up, and told me that they would help me. "It is only a little way up and then the rest of the way is down." Whether I wanted to or not, I was going to Rwanda.

Geographically, Rwanda's a small, mountainous, landlocked African country in the Great Lakes Region of Eastern Africa. It's bordered by Burundi, Tanzania, Uganda and Democratic Republic of Congo, where we had seen the gorillas. Even after 800 000 people died during the genocide and one million more people fled the country, the 1996 population of Rwanda was estimated at seven million, over 900 people per arable square kilometer. Almost half the population is under fourteen, a joint legacy of the high birth rate and the genocide. As in many other African countries, infant mortality is very high and life expectancy is only around 40 years. The majority of Rwandans is poor and earns less than $250 US per year.

Although Rwanda is a predominately agricultural country with over 90% of the labour force working in agriculture, only 30% of its land is suitable for growing crops. The dense population exerts intense pressure on the land. Marginal land and areas previously part of the forest or other woodlands are increasingly being used for cultivation, causing widespread deforestation from uncontrolled cutting of trees for fuel, soil exhaustion and soil erosion. Except for the very tips of the mountains, such as the land set apart for the gorillas, every piece of land, no matter how steep, is cultivated.

Continued ongoing fighting and the uncertainty of safety have undermined the ability of ordinary Rwandans to carry on with their day-to-day lives. Businesses have been devastated, farming interrupted and economic activity brought to a standstill. The severe economic hardship gripping the country had left no money for basic necessities such as food, medicine or schooling. Although I would never have chosen to visit Rwanda, I had no choice.

Still shoeless, I started down the path again surrounded by a growing crowd of nameless, faceless men, most dressed in shabby, mismatched dirty clothing. One fellow came up beside me and pulled a pair of white running shoes with a pink flash down the side out of a turquoise plastic bag and held them out to me. I looked at the shoes intently. They were too small. Dan teases me about my tender feet and I knew that if I tried to walk in shoes that didn't fit well I would be in worse shape than being barefoot. As long as the earth stayed soft, the soles of my feet, toughened to some extent from wearing my sandals for the last month, would be fine. I rationalized that if the African women could go barefoot, so could I. I shook my head and smiled. "C'est bon. Non, merci." At my response a flurry of excited comment exploded around me.

Then I spotted a green plastic water bottle dangling from another man's belt. "Please!" I begged him, "just one sip. Une morçeau d'eau." He untied the sisal twine and passed the water bottle to me. Gripping the bottle in both hands I poured the water into my mouth gulping frantically. Before I could drain it a hand reached out and took the bottle from me. I almost cried.

The path we were on had been gradually rising, but with the slow pace, I was managing well. Suddenly, the path changed direction—straight up. I lifted my head; in front of me was an endless cliff of soft, dusty dirt rising vertically higher than I could see. The men around me began climbing quickly, drawing me up with them. After a few dozen steps, my legs turned to rubber; my feet weighed a thousand pounds. I scrambled in the soft dirt, grabbing at dust and trying to pull myself up with my arms. When I stopped to breathe, a long line of women with huge packs balanced on their heads climbed quickly and steadily past me, sparing me less than a second's glance. I didn't think I would ever reach the top. First one young man, and then a second, was sent to help me. As they strained to hoist my body up the cliff sweat ran down their faces in rivulets and dripped from their shirts. I cried in pain from the pressure of their shoulders digging into my underarms and groaned with the effort of trying to move my leaden legs. With no steps cut into the cliff-face, it was a scramble, up and up and up, even more difficult than trying to walk through the long grass. Four or five times as they pulled me sweating and panting up the never-ending cliff I glanced up. All I could see rising above me was the dusty crumbling earth. I knew, even if I collapsed again, there was no way my captors would leave me. I would never be able to escape.

Finally, I was push-pulled over the upper edge of the cliff and collapsed on the ground. There, surrounded by men with guns, were Doug and the Swedish couple.

FOUR

I dropped like a rock as soon as the men unhooked my arms from their necks and lay my head on one of the packs. The Swedish woman, a young, long haired blonde in her late twenties, handed me a plastic bottle containing about a cup of water. "It's fine to drink. It has been purified," she said in slightly accented English. It smelled faintly of iodine but tasted delicious. I drank it all then lay down again.

Although we had all camped at the Kisoro Hotel campground, it was pure happenstance that the Swedish couple and I were in the same gorilla-viewing group. On the hike up the mountain to see the gorillas, they stayed at the front of the line with Doug, while I brought up the rear. We were strangers travelling together for a few hours; there had been no interaction between us. During the hour we spent with the gorillas and while we ate our lunch, we had been in three separate groups: the Africans, the Swedes, and Doug and me. Now, it was four of us together.

One by one, rather hesitantly, the men began passing back my belongings. I was relieved to get my boots back since I knew I wouldn't be able to walk forever in bare feet. When they pulled my jacket out of the Granville Island Market cotton bag I had been carrying, the contrast between my memories of calm order that the bag evoked and where we were was stark. From behind one of the men near me, a hand appeared holding my socks. I shifted so I could see the man who was holding them. He kept his head down and his eyes averted. He was no different than any of the other dozen men around us. Slowly I reached out and took my socks, then sat methodically pulling embedded grass and seed heads from the wool, stalling for time. A hand pushed my shoulder and waved at my socks and boots. Nodding, I pulled the socks over my filthy feet and laced up my boots. It was time to go.

We continued in a long slow line through the forest. Fortunately the terrain rose only slightly. As Brother *Something* had promised, it was much easier. As we reached a large clearing that appeared to be a main resting place at the top of a mountain pass, the afternoon sun dropped behind the surrounding trees. The four of us were directed to sit on a long, low, bamboo bench along one edge of the clearing. From our bench seat we looked around cautiously, saying little. Throughout the clearing, near bundles piled on the ground among the litter of cornhusks, corncobs and ashes, small groups of men, women and children stood silently watching us. Most of the men who had come with us gathered talking around a fire. None of them paid any attention to us.

A man brought a jerry can over and filled the others' water containers. I was still very thirsty and tipped water from Doug's bottle into my parched mouth. "Stop!" the Swedish man cautioned. "It hasn't been purified yet." Reluctantly I spat the water on the ground.

I stared at the water in the bottle and then at the Swede. "I don't care. I have to have some water." The man with the jerry can said something we didn't understand and showed us a small plastic tube of white powder, likely 'magic powder', the same chemical Dan had been using to purify our water on the safari.

The Swedish man reached into the top section of his backpack and took out a blister pack of small tablets. He put a tablet into each of our containers. "We don't need their powder. I have water purification tablets, enough for seventy-five liters." The ten minutes waiting for the tablet to work seemed more like an hour. I wondered if the man with the jerry can had been trying to tell us he had already purified the water.

One of the men by the fire brought us an ear of corn. It looked like the corn on the cob we eat in Canada, but some of the kernels were blackened from being roasted over the open fire. He broke the ear in half, handed half to Doug, half to the Swedish man, indicating with a gesture that they were to share the halves, a quarter ear each. Doug handed the corn to me. "You go ahead." I bit off four kernels and began to chew. The kernels were mature, dry and starchy. I passed the cob back to Doug and chewed. I seemed to have no saliva and the corn became a mass of thick, grainy paste, impossible to swallow. When, finally, the ten minutes to purify the water had passed, I swished a tiny sip around my mouth dislodging the corn pulp and finally swallowed. Doug passed the corn back. After two more inedible bites I gave up. Doug managed to eat the rest. "Have you ever tasted anything like it?" he asked. His look said everything.

We were also given two avocados to share and four fried pita-sized bread. Anticipating creamy, smooth, rich avocado I took a big bite. To my dismay, like the corn, it became a layer of slime coating the inside of my mouth. Eating was futile. I stared at the avocado and the golden brown bread. Who knew when we might get more food? Prudently I put the bread in my pocket and sat holding the avocado.

In a few minutes my stomach began gurgling and churning. I had to go to the bathroom. I looked behind me at the thick brush that began about eight feet behind the bench. None of the men gathered around the fire were paying any attention. I took a deep breath, slipped the avocado carefully into my pocket, cut side against the bread, and stood up. No one called as I walked into the bushes or came over to check where I had gone.

I'd had a part roll of toilet paper in my missing fanny pack. That was gone, too. Looking around for some fat leaves, I saw a crumpled torn sheet of lined paper caught in the base of a bush near where I was squatted. I pulled it loose. It was a page of school exercises in French. I used half and tucked the other half in my pocket. When I pulled my slacks up I noticed the label was at the front. To turn them right way round, my boots needed to come off. I left them backward.

Nearing the bench, I was suddenly too exhausted to take another step. Certain the men didn't care if I sat on the bench or not, I slid down and curled in a fetal position on the ground behind the bench. A minute later Doug came and lay down beside me. "Doug, would you hold me?" I said. He pulled me back against him like nesting spoons and put his arm over me. With the avocado in my hand so it wouldn't become mush in my pocket, I tried to go to sleep. A few minutes later the Swedish couple joined us and we lay together as the sky darkened to indigo.

"Good Morning! Good Morning," one of the men called. "Time to get up."

Up? I thought in bewilderment. We had just lain down! When I saw Brother *Something,* I protested. "I'm tired. Fatigué."

"Not much farther," he replied.

I held back the urge to stamp my feet and have a temper tantrum. "I can't go up any more." He had promised I wouldn't be hurt; walking uphill hurt. I was pissed off and increasingly frustrated with my inability to communicate. "How do you say 'climb up' in French? C'est impossible aller en haut. Pas d'en haut!"

Brother *Something* reassured me again, "It will be easier. It is down."

We walked single file into the forest, the four of us sandwiched between the men, me staying as close as I could to the Swedish man ahead of me.

The slimy avocado still coated my mouth. I scraped my tongue against my teeth to clear the slime and pushed the residue onto my lips. No matter how hard I spat, it stayed glued there. Finally, in desperation, I cleaned my lips with the side of my hand and rubbed my hand on my leg. It wasn't as though my pants could get much dirtier.

Within half an hour it was so dark that I could no longer see where I was stepping. A few of the men turned on the flashlights they had tied to their belts. Someone handed one to me. I continued walking, the flashlight in my right hand, the avocado in my left, carefully shining a narrow beam onto the path in front of the Swedish man ahead of me. The two-foot wide path became alternately rutted, rocky, rough and steep; it was crossed by tree roots and cut deeply in the center as people walking in soft soil over the years had worn a rut as much as eight inches wide and twelve inches deep. Concentrating intently, I managed to watch my feet so that I didn't step into the rut, keep the light shining far enough ahead so the Swedish man could see and hold the avocado.

As I stepped precariously over and between a series of intertwined roots, a young man beside me held out a walking stick. I looked at the flashlight and avocado. I need a third hand, I thought. Unwilling to put the avocado in my pocket again or try to eat it, I held it out to the young man. He squeezed the avocado, sucked the soft flesh into his mouth and discarded the peel with a toss. With a firm grip on the walking stick, I moved more confidently as we wound slowly down through the darkness.

We came to a large muddy area which we skirted, stepping carefully on higher mounds where the sticky, slippery mud had partly dried. When we came to a second, even larger boggy area, the man behind me gripped my upper arm and guided me left around the far side of the mud. He began talking in a soft voice. Not understanding what he was saying, I paid no attention. I concentrated on walking without slipping; my flashlight playing over the area in front of me as I looked for the drier, least shiny places. We'd covered about ten feet when he said something that made my stomach spasm. "… couchez…" When I was young I had giggled over a French slang expression for having sex; *Voulez vous couchez avec moi?* I jerked to a stop and looked around. He and I were alone. On the far right side of the bog a string of bobbing lights was heading away from me. Everyone else was going the other way. I jerked my arm away from him. "Je suis mariée. I'm married! Ne couchez pas! No going to bed!" I strode through the middle of the mud hole, sliding in the ankle-deep gumbo until I reached the others, not checking over my shoulder to see whether he was following. As I slipped back into my position behind the Swedish man, I told him about the 'couchez' comment and suggested he stay close to the woman with him at all times. He understood.

We travelled single file through the darkness for about an hour and a half, our world restricted to the narrow band of light provided by the flashlights. The Africans in front of me suddenly stopped and turned off their flashlights. Instead of the expected blackness, warm, russet light from the dying flames of a small fire illuminated the milling group. We were in another clearing. Determined to rest whenever I could, I sat down. In a second my body wilted. As I leaned over to lie down, my hand touched a very warm rock. Before I could move farther, one of the men put his hand on my shoulder and said something. He pointed at the ground beside my hand where the dying embers of a fire glowed red under thick ashes. The rock was on the edge of a fire circle.

A minute later someone reached down and pulled me to my feet. Time to go. We didn't follow a path, but pushed into the brush surrounding the clearing. There was no light, just the sound and feel of people ahead, the pressure of branches and tickle of leaves on bare skin. I kept my hands up in front of my face to prevent being scratched or accidentally whipped as the branches, released by the people in front, flew back toward me.

I broke through the bush and, momentarily disoriented, stumbled against something large, warm and hairy. I heard a low moo and something wet brushed my hand. In the faint, orange-red light that came from someplace, I could just make out the highlighted backs of a number of lowing cows that were jostling each other and me. The people in front of me pushed through the cows toward the light. I followed with my arms raised above my head to avoid the cows' long, curved, pointed horns. On the other side of the cows there was a small fire and another group of men. With men milling everywhere, the four of us were herded to a six-foot square shelter of bent, split bamboo on one side of the fire. We huddled together at the back of the shelter and waited. It was soon obvious from the men's relaxed actions around the fire that this was where we were going to stay for the night.

Exhausted, I inched forward and eased back onto the floor, laying with my feet out the opening. The others pushed their packs along the back wall to use as pillows; we curled into each other and lay without talking.

It was impossible to sleep. All my senses were focused on the men. Without looking at them directly, I watched their flickering shadows on the shelter walls and their fire-lit bodies as they moved into and away from the fire. My ears strained to listen to their voices, a low murmur punctuated with sharp laughter, though I couldn't understand anything they said. I lay motionless; I wanted to be invisible so they'd leave me alone. I hoped they might somehow disappear if I ignored them. When a man sat on the edge of the platform beside my feet, my discomfort skyrocketed.

I became aware of a long, very uncomfortable ridge in the platform floor that ran the length of my body and dug into my ribs and hip. Though I tried to remain motionless, I was finally unable to ignore it. Careful not to disturb either of the people lying beside me, I ascertained that I could move it. Slowly I worked it out from under me. It was my walking stick.

At some point, the men stopped moving and began to lie down. The fire burned down and died. Someone came over and threw an unzipped sleeping bag over us. Although we were lying close to one another and wearing all our clothes including jackets and hats, it had been getting steadily cooler. When we camped at Kisoro we needed sweaters and coats at night, even around the campfire. The temperature at this higher altitude was much lower.

The sleeping bag cover, though welcome, was not entirely successful. Lying in the middle, I began sweating from the combination of sleeping bag, body heat and my clothes. Doug and the Swedish man, lying on the outside, were only partly covered. Every time any of us turned, the bag pulled off their bodies. As much as possible, I tried not to wiggle. I don't know if any of us slept. I had listened to Doug snore in the neighboring tent for four weeks, but that night he didn't snore at all.

FIVE

As the sky lightened, a man collected the sleeping bag. Without it, the air had a definite nip. Still trying not to draw attention to myself, I watched from the corner of my eye as a man started the fire. He pushed small slivers of bamboo into the ash-covered coals from the previous night's fire and, as the wood began to smolder, blew them softly into flame. Then he balanced a pot filled with a watery, reddish beige mixture on three stones placed in a triangle around the flames. The mixture boiled gently, stirred periodically by passing men. When it was cooked it was poured into three jugs, like plastic gallon vinegar bottles. Bits of torn turquoise plastic bag were tied with string over the openings.

There was a flurry of motion as the men gathered their guns and other belongings, signalling that it was time for us to stand up. Off we went in a single file. It was the start of our second day as captives.

After leaving the night camp, we continued for about an hour and a half walking at a leisurely pace down a narrow mountain path, the four of us interspersed among the men. All I could see were the backs of the people in front of me, the dirt path under my feet, and a solid curtain of tall, slender bamboo stalks covered with clumps of thin graceful leaves rising high above my head on both sides. At a spot that looked no different than any other spot we had passed, the men led us off the path where we beat our way up a short hill through thick bamboo undergrowth. We broke out into a small, rectangular, grassy clearing about fifteen feet by twenty-five feet. Thick bamboo, shaded by scattered high trees, encircled the clearing, forming a visual and physical barrier. "Welcome to my home," said Brother *Something* in French.

I looked around the small clearing in bewilderment. There was nothing there, only grass and bamboo. "Ici chez vous? *This* is your *home*?" I asked. He just laughed and repeated that this was his home. Speaking rapidly in

French, he told me something else—none of which I understood—and disappeared through the bamboo brush and trees in a different direction than the one from which we had come. Four men armed with guns, grenades and machetes stayed with us. I sat down along one edge of the clearing and waited. As the sun rose higher and got increasingly warm, I shifted to another place where I could stay in the heat without facing directly into the sun. Though the sun wasn't overly hot, the combination of high altitude and no sunscreen made me cautious.

I was silent, lost in a mental fog, still dealing with the shock and fatigue of the previous day. From time to time I lay down but was too anxious to sleep.

After noon, a man brought over one of the jugs of the soupy mix they had cooked that morning and handed it to me. I wasn't sure what I was supposed to do with it. "Pardonez moi," I said as I held up the jug. "Qu'est-ce que c'est? What is this?"

"Sorgo," one of the men guarding us called back confirming my guess that it was cooked sorghum.

The men were passing another of the jugs around, taking turns drinking it; in imitation, I pulled the plastic off the spout and took a cautious sip. The slightly sweet, textured soup tasted unusual, but not unpleasant. As grateful for the liquid as for the food content, we drank about half of what we were given before passing the jug back to the men. I wondered when I'd get another peanut butter sandwich.

At about 4:00 p.m. the Swedish man suggested we build a bamboo shelter. Though I hadn't understood anything Brother *Something* said before he left, the Swedish man had recognized *lit*, the word for bed, and *nourriture*, food. He thought Brother *Something* had gone to get food and we were responsible for building ourselves a place to sleep. A superabundance of living bamboo with long leafed lacy foliage formed a thick mat around the clearing, across the area below us and around the towering volcanoes visible in the distance. Twenty foot tall, dark gray stalks of dead bamboo, the skeleton of leaves ringing the trunk at three foot intervals like matted birds' nests, pushed through the green growing vegetation. Bamboo became our building material.

With his Swiss army knife, the Swedish man cut down some bamboo. Doug pulled out his own knife and the two of them quickly cut two front posts and a couple of sections for roof supports. Lifting the roof supports about four feet off the ground, they pushed one end into the thick growth at the edge of the clearing. The challenge became how to fasten or tie the other end to the front posts. A vine and braided dry grass didn't work.

The men sat watching us from the other end of the clearing. As our various attempts to secure the posts failed, one of the men slowly got to his feet, picked up his machete and sauntered over, the machete dangling beside his leg. I took several steps back. With quick swipes of his machete he chopped down a small tree with a forked top, lopped off the extra branches, and braced one of the roof poles in the V top. With another swift chop he split one end of a green bamboo pole and wedged the second roof support into the split. Working together, the Swedish man, Doug, the machete man and I soon had a slant-roofed lean-to framed into the brush, large enough inside for the four of us to lie down. Two open sides and the top were closed in and covered with branches and bunches of bamboo leaves. Leaf debris was spread on the ground inside. When the shelter was complete, the machete man turned and went back to the other side of the clearing. Though it wasn't waterproof, the lean-to afforded a small amount of privacy and some shelter from the wind and sun. The four of us sat in front of the shelter in the sunlight and waited.

As the sun began to drop below the horizon, a number of men carrying pots and bags arrived, pushing through the bamboo curtain. One man, wearing a cap with *Commander in Chief* printed across the brow, carried a large cloth bundle. He untied his bundle, removed a large blue tarp, and brought it to us. Printed across the middle were the words, United Nations High Commission on Refugees. The English words were one of the few things I had seen since I was captured that I understood. I read the words again and again. I didn't make the obvious connection between the tarp and the Rwandan refugees. The tarp was obviously one of thousands left from the huge Rwandan-filled camps that sprang up in Congo after the 1994 genocide. The Commander in Chief indicated the tarp should be placed inside our shelter. Working with him and the machete man, Doug and the Swedish man got the tarp up under the roof, lining the top, the back and part of the ground.

The rest of the men were busy opening bags that contained potatoes and other foodstuffs. One young man with a bright red crocheted tam sat steadily peeling potatoes with a huge knife and dropping them into one of the pots. Another young man climbed into the clearing shouldering a big, well-used green jerry can spotted with numerous gray repair patches, dented around the base and sealed with a piece of blue plastic bag tied with vine. The man in the red tam opened the jerry can and poured a stream of water into the pot of peeled potatoes.

Water!

Because my water bottle had disappeared with my Granville Island bag,

Doug had been sharing his water with me. We had been strictly rationing ourselves and still had half the 750ml we'd been given the first night. When I saw the abundance of water pouring into the potato pot, I knew water wasn't so scarce that they would refuse to give me some. I went over to the Commander in Chief, who seemed to be the man in charge, and asked for water. "Pardonez-moi. J'ai besoin d'eau. Voudrez-vous nous donner la?"

He nodded and motioned to the man with the jerry can.

"He'll fill our water bottle. Doug, we should take a good drink first." We quickly drank most of the water remaining from the day before. The Swedish couple pulled three partly filled one-liter bottles out of their pack and refilled them, too. I was surprised when I saw three bottles. I had never seen them drink anything. The Swedish man dropped water purification tablets into all four bottles.

The Rwandan men began a fire using dry, dead bamboo chopped from around the clearing and dragged back by the armful. Four-foot lengths of bamboo, pushed under the pot and fed continuously into the center, burned furiously, providing a hot, but short-lived flame and a residue of fine ash with few coals. When there were stones available, as there had been where we slept the night before, they were used to support the pot. But there were no stones in this clearing, just grassy dirt. The cooking pots were suspended on a tripod of green bamboo that didn't burn, or were balanced on green bamboo supports with the fire in the center. Soon supper was ready: beans, rice and potatoes.

We looked in bewilderment as two square billycans—one heaped with boiled potatoes and the other rice topped with beans—and two spoons were set on the ground in front of us. There are no rules of etiquette or hygiene to advise how four people should eat with only two spoons. It took a while to puzzle it out. Self-consciously we scooped a mouthful from the heap before passing the billycan and spoon on, unsure whether to wipe the spoon before or after we used it. Since we had drunk the sorghum only a short time before, none of us was particularly hungry. I was still too tired and tense to have much of an appetite. After we had each eaten few mouthfuls I passed the uneaten food back to the men. "Asante sana. Thank you. Nous sommes fini. Ça suffit. We're finished. That's enough." They quickly ate their food and the remains of ours.

By this time it was completely dark. Two men brought a small pile of dry bamboo over and lit a fire in front of our shelter. Throughout the evening they kept an eye on it, keeping it well stoked. As we sat staring into the flames, a second group of young men emerged from the bushes in front of our shelter. Laughing and bantering among themselves, they called greetings to the men with us. One newcomer with a broad smile, who appeared to be around twenty years old, came over and began to speak to us — in English. Although his English was easy to understand, the rhythm and his accent sounded exotically foreign.

"Good evening my friends. I am Pascal. I am to buy food for you. But, I am sorry to tell you that we are poor, very poor. I must ask you for some money so I can go to get the food at the market." I had started the climb with only enough Ugandan shillings (USh) in my fanny pack to buy a cold drink at the end of the hike and $6 US that I had given to the Rangers as a tip.

I looked at Doug. "I don't have any money. Dan has it all. I didn't think I'd need any money up in the mountains."

"Don't worry. I'll put some in for you," Doug said.

"Thanks, Doug. Dan will pay you back as soon as we see him." Both Doug and the Swedish man assured me they would cover me and we'd settle the money when we were released. After a convoluted discussion with Pascal, they handed him $25 US.

Relieved to able to talk to someone who understood English, I explained to Pascal that I had been carrying medicine in my fanny pack and would like to have it back if possible. On the truck I'd been carrying a film canister with Tylenol 3 and aspirin as well as my Ventolin puffer for my asthma and an Epipen in case of an anaphylactic reaction with me so I didn't have to dig them out of my under-the-seat locker. I wasn't particularly optimistic about getting the fanny pack back, but thought it was worth asking about the medicine. Pascal didn't respond. He and the group who came with him left with the food money, through the bushes and down the hill.

That night the men put up a night shelter. They macheted sharply pointed bamboo poles and pounded them into the soft soil by hand until the poles were embedded deeply enough to stand securely upright. One large tarp like we'd been given was suspended from the poles about three feet off the ground and a second tarp placed under it on the ground. The Commander in Chief pulled two sleeping bags out of a large green plastic bag. He brought one to us and kept the second for himself. The rest of the men unwrapped lengths of colorful cotton cloth that they wore tied around their waists or wrapped around their shoulders during the day and used them as covers.

About 8:30, our fire was reduced to embers. We slipped back into the shelter, curled up together and tried to get some sleep. We lay on our sides like a series of spoons, the other woman and I in the middle with Doug and the Swedish man on the outsides. We each had a space about a foot and a half wide; my front was pressed tight against the other woman's back, my bottom arm curled up around my waist, my top arm resting lightly on her shoulder. Doug lay behind me, holding me the same way. The closeness was somehow comforting; I was surrounded and protected by the others. The fact that we were strangers seemed unimportant. Because the shelter's back wall jogged in on Doug's end, the top of his head was level with my neck. He and I lay close for warmth. Since he was concerned that he'd be cold at the back of the group, I tried to keep the sleeping bag from being pulled off him.

Unlike the night before when I had used part of someone's backpack as a pillow, I had nothing under my head. I hoped one of the others would offer to share again, but they said nothing. I already felt like I was sponging by taking their money for food, so I didn't say anything either. I scrabbled a small pile of leaves together, but those soon compressed to nothingness.

It didn't take long on the hard ground before my body began to ache. I was very conscious of the woman and Doug pressed against me. I knew they felt every twitch I made. Not wanting to disturb them, I tried to ease the aches by tightening and relaxing my muscles, making minute shifts in the position of one leg on the other, adjusting my angle to the ground and flexing my feet—though with boots on, this wasn't easy. Lying on my back would have been better but in that position I would have used more space under the sleeping bag and Doug would have been uncovered.

I stayed in one position as long as I could. When I finally had to turn to my other side, Doug turned as well and I curled against his back. It seemed I was awake most of the night fighting with my aches and the discomfort of not being able to move freely. Given how twitchy I felt, I was amazed that the Swedish woman never seemed to move. Sometimes I knew Doug was sleeping because I heard him snore. That made me feel better, because he was so careful to keep me warm and covered. Although I was convinced I was constantly awake, I knew I'd been sleeping when I remembered a dream.

At first light, a voice called to us. "Réveillez! Wake up!" The men were busy folding their night shelter tarps. After rolling his sleeping bag, the Commander in Chief stashed it and ours in a green garbage bag out of sight in the brush.

"Ça va?" he asked.

"Ça va bien," I replied. That signalled the beginning of our third day. On the other side of the clearing, the young cook lit a fire and heated our breakfast, rice left over from the night before. Although the food we were given each day we were captives was monotonously similar, the way it was given to us varied. One morning everything was heaped in a metal bowl; another morning it was in the two billycans. The number and type of utensils depended on how many men were eating at the same time: one spoon that we took turns using, a spoon and fork for pairs to share and once, four spoons. After fumbling awkwardly passing spoons around through two meals, I decided it was easier to pick food like potatoes up with my fingers or spoon a heap of rice onto my palm and eat out of my hand. Somehow sharing spoons seemed more intimate and less hygienic than eating with dirty hands. We rarely finished all the food we were given; I passed what we couldn't eat back to the guards.

For the first three days all of us were completely self-absorbed. The Swedish couple usually sat together inside the shelter, while I sat out front with Doug ignoring our captors as if they weren't there or only glancing at them out of the corner of my eye. During the day, individuals and small groups of men were constantly coming and going. They were anonymous except for a few who seemed to be there all the time or wore some piece of distinctive clothing—the cook in a red tam and the Commander in Chief in his baseball cap. Each day fewer men were left to guard us; by the third day, there were only two. By then the shock was wearing off. I became less absorbed in my own thoughts, calmer, curious about our captors and a bit bored.

Whenever the Commander in Chief left the clearing he told me, in French, that he was going to go talk with his commander and that he would return. I had no idea where he was going or how far away it was. Because he was gone for several hours every time, I surmised he either travelled a long distance or had a lot to talk about.

SIX

On the third day the Commander in Chief had gone to talk with his commander and we were sitting in the sun in front of the shelter staring blankly out across the vast mountainside of green bamboo. The morning rice had been heavily salted. "Doug," I said, "may I have a drink of water?"

"Oh, your name is Doug," the Swedish man said turning to look at Doug and me. "I think we could be here for a while. We should introduce ourselves. My name is *Yens*." Unfamiliar with the name and pronunciation, I asked him to spell it for us. "J-E-N-S." The Swedish pronunciation of the woman's name, Ann-Charlotte, was hard for Doug and I to duplicate, so we used default anglicized pronunciation, where the *ch* sounded like *sh*.

It seemed that introducing ourselves opened the door to conversation. The four of us sat in front of the shelter and talked quietly about what had happened, why we might have been captured and how long we might be kept. Although we didn't think anyone in the group understood English, we were very circumspect.

A little later, using a combination of sign language and single words, Doug found out the Christian names of the two young men guarding us: Richard and Oscar. Richard, the cook, was a teenager with a quiet, but happy, disposition. When he smiled, which was often, his front tooth, broken in half on the diagonal, along with his crocheted red tam were his main identifying features. A hard worker, he cheerfully chopped bamboo, tended the fire, or peeled a twenty-pound sack of potatoes for a meal. Oscar, the guard, had his gun with him at all times. Pascal, the young fellow who had gone off with the food money, hadn't returned yet and we were certain we'd never see him or the money again.

When the Commander in Chief returned that day, he explained that some people were coming to talk with us. When they were finished, we would be allowed to go home. HOME! They were going to let us go.

"How far do you think they took us?"

"We walked for more than eight hours. It was mostly up hill. It could be as far as twenty kilometers."

"Most of the way back will be fairly level or downhill. It could take six or seven hours to get out."

I knew I would be the slowest and didn't like the thought of being separated from the others. "I'd like to be somewhere in the middle if possible and not at the end. It's hard for me to go up hill but I'm able to keep up a reasonable speed downhill." We decided we would walk in the same order that we slept: Jens, Ann-Charlotte, me, and Doug.

What was nearly as exciting as hearing that we were going to be released was the Commander in Chief handing me my fanny pack and my empty water bottle. Missing from the fanny pack were my calculator, two pens, the Ugandan money and my Epipen. I wondered why they had taken the Epipen. It looked unimportant in its plastic tube. However, the instructions inside were in both English and French. Although I had been fairly certain I wouldn't be stung by a yellow jacket while I was in Africa, I'd brought it as a precaution. For anyone with potentially fatal allergies, it would be valuable. Still in the fanny pack were the part roll of toilet paper, a comb, my canister of painkillers and my Ventolin puffer. Tucked in the back was a single sheet of paper, the British Air flight information for our trip. More than anything else, I was comforted to see it. It was the only thing I had with my name on it, my only piece of identification. If I died and my body was eventually found, that paper could help identify my remains. Dan would know what had happened to me.

If anyone had asked me, I would have reassured him that I was dealing very well with everything that was happening. But, several times during those first few days, my body would begin to tremble and shake. The shaking never lasted long and I worried at first that I might have malaria. But, apart from the shaking, I had none of the other symptoms like fever, chills, headache, muscle aches and tiredness.

One morning after our breakfast rice, my stomach began knotting and dipping. I tried to swallow it back in place and deep breathe it level before I gave up and went into the bushes to heave and gag. Doug came to check on me.

"Are you OK?"

"Yah," I said. "I'm OK, just having a nerve attack." He put his arm around me and walked me back to the shelter. I lay my head on his shoulder, grateful for his help and concern.

We waited impatiently for the men who were coming to talk with us to arrive. To fill the time, I took off my boots and set my innersoles and socks out to dry. It was the first time in three days my boots had been off. The bottoms of my thick, gray wool socks were a hard, crusty beige-brown. The dusty residue from my barefoot march up the mountain was caked black in my foot creases and between my toes. I searched the grass deep in the shade and under the bushes hoping to find some remaining dew. I gathered the dampest grass I could find and used handfuls to clean my feet and between my toes, restoring the usual pink to much of the skin. But my socks were filthy; sweat had cemented the dirt into the fabric.

While I was rubbing my feet with grass, the Commander in Chief, on the other side of the clearing, took out a basin, stripped to the waist and began washing his face and arms. He scooped water over his chest and arms, splashes flying everywhere. Working up a soapy foam on his hands, he rubbed his skin with the suds and then splashed the soap away. He dumped the basin over his head and shook himself dry like a dog that had just come out of the ocean. When he saw me trying to clean my feet, he told one of the men to bring me the basin filled with clean water and a bar of hard, dark green soap. I gave him a huge smile. "Merci. Merci beaucoup!" I got wash water without asking.

As dirty and sweaty as I was, I knew the others were just as dirty and in need of a wash. The basin of water had to be shared. I showed Jens and Ann Charlotte a technique I'd learned during my first two weeks in Africa for washing using minimal water called 'washing out of the basin'. Much as the Commander in Chief had done, we cupped our palms and scooped a scant handful of water out of the basin to wet our skin. Then, careful not to drip into the basin, we soaped, then rinsed off, letting the dirty water drip onto the ground. By using the basin as a water source rather than a sink we were all able to wash and rinse with clean water. When all of us had washed our faces and arms, I used the remaining water and gave my feet a thorough wash. As I air-dried my pink toes I decided not to wash my socks. We were going home that night. I could last one more day with dirty socks.

The sun moved slowly across the sky. We waited. And waited.

Just before sunset, Pascal, the young man who had taken the money for food, reappeared carrying a number of turquoise blue plastic sacks. As he walked past us he handed Jens five avocados and a plastic bag filled with two dozen fried bread rounds. The bread was very fresh, still gleaming with the sheen of the oil in which it had been fried. I could smell the yeasty smell of fresh bread and my mouth began to water. "No sense saving all of these. We're going out tonight and they'll just get stale." Jens handed one to each of us and stored the rest in the shelter. I pulled the bread that I had been given the first day out of my pocket. It was dry, but hadn't gone mouldy. I looked at it and the new bread in my other hand. The turquoise bag full of new bread was in the corner of the shelter. I tossed the old bread into the bush and bit through the crunchy, brown crust of the new bread. It tasted like the fried bread my grandmother used to make.

Over in the cooking area Richard and Pascal emptied the other bags—potatoes, small bags of rice and many types and colours of beans. They pulled a ragged edged piece of meat from the last bag. While travelling in Africa I had eaten giraffe, zebra, warthog, antelope and crocodile. I didn't think this was an exotic game meat, but more likely a chunk of goat, which was a common meat in the villages. At the markets and in the small bars in Kenya and Tanzania there were often signs advertising roast goat—nyama ya mbuzi choma. On ceremonial occasions a whole goat would be roasted or barbecued. I could feel a prickle of anticipation from the salivary glands at the back of my jaw and my mouth began to water. After sitting doing nothing for three days, my appetite was returning. The meat went into a pot and the pot onto the fire. Several other young men arrived and began chopping dead bamboo, piling it by the cook fire and our shelter. Soon there were three different pots cooking on their tripods.

The sun set and daylight disappeared. Any hope I had of going home faded with the daylight. There was no way I could walk a long distance in the dark. I would certainly be there for one more day. As our disappointment became palpable, Jens said, "We shouldn't be too optimistic about being released. We still don't know why we have been captured, or what they want us for." I didn't care who they were or why. I just wanted to go home.

Pascal came back to talk with us while the food was cooking. He was a cheerful, outgoing young man of eighteen or twenty. He reminded me of a wiggly puppy. He'd learned to speak very good English at school where he'd completed the Fifth Form. "What kind of pop do you like?" he said. It was such a bizarre question, given where we were, that none of us answered. He must have wondered if we understood him. "Which do you like, Coke, Fanta Orange or Fanta Citrus?"

We looked at each other, shrugged and answered with as much seriousness as if we had been asked which we liked better, the Tooth Fairy or Santa Claus. Our mouths dropped open when he produced six bottles of pop, two orange, one coke, one lemon and one ginger beer. He popped the tops off, levering one bottle open with another and handed us our choice. After days of having nothing besides water to drink and bland food to eat, the intense sweetness of the pop was jarring. I sipped slowly, swishing the warm liquid around my mouth before letting it trickle down my throat. None of us wanted the ginger beer so Pascal and Richard shared it.

In most African countries businesses will only sell you beer or pop if you drink it there and return the bottle immediately. When you buy take-away beer or pop, you must have bottles to exchange or pay a deposit on the bottle that is usually greater than the cost of the pop. Mindful of this, when we finished drinking our pop, I set the bottles by the wall of the shelter to be returned later. When Richard tossed the empty ginger beer bottle into the bush I laughed aloud. I guess they weren't into recycling!

The Commander in Chief returned. "Ça va?" he said as he passed.

As usual, I answered, "Ça va, bien." Whenever the men brought us something, helped us, or talked to us I thanked them in all the languages I knew. I had picked up one or two Swahili words from the Kenyan cook—'Please / Asante sana' and 'Thank you / karibu'. Whenever I said anything in Swahili, the men laughed and corrected my pronunciation. I wasn't sure if I was getting the words wrong or if the pronunciation was different in Rwanda. Much later I realized they were speaking Kinya-rwanda, which along with French, is the official language of Rwanda. The two Swahili phrases I'd used most frequently right after I was captured were 'pole / sorry' and 'pole pole / slowly'. However, you can't hold a conversation with three or four Swahili words. As the days passed, although I had to think carefully, I found it increasingly easy to talk with the men in French, using very basic vocabulary I remembered from high school French and evening conversation classes I'd taken when I lived in Ottawa. Understanding what the Africans were saying back was harder; they used words I didn't know and my ear wasn't attuned to their speech rhythms. I kept having to say, 'Encore une fois / One more time. Je ne comprend pas / I don't understand. Répétez s'il vous plaît / Please repeat it.'

Dinner that night was the usual heap of rice covered with beans, with potatoes on the side. We got none of the meat. We looked at the billycans, then at each other, shrugged, and ate. After the pop, my disappointment was easier to bear.

As I handed our unfinished food back to the men, someone we hadn't seen before appeared from below the clearing. He walked straight to us. "Hello," he said, speaking English with great enthusiasm, "I am Emmanuel. Do you know what my name means? God! Emmanuel means God." An especially appropriate line from an old Christmas hymn ran through my head, 'Come, oh come, E-mman-u-el and ransom captive Israel.' Emmanuel told us he was Catholic and assured us that we didn't have to worry about being hurt. Feeling much more religious than I had for years, I told him that I, too, was Catholic and showed him the guardian angel pin on my fanny pack. He asked what church the others attended. We all wanted to be cooperative. Doug said he was a Protestant and Jens and Ann-Charlotte said they were Christians.

Emmanuel asked our nationality. "Not American?" he exclaimed when we told him we were from Canada, New Zealand and Sweden. "The men who captured you thought you were Americans. The government of Congo is very friendly with the United States. No white people come here except Americans. They saw you with the gorillas and said you were from the US of A." We assured him that we were *not* Americans.

So that's why they grabbed us, I thought. If our capture was politically motivated and Americans are the bad guys, I want to make sure they know I'm Canadian. The book title 'The Ugly American' popped into my head. How fortunate neither of the Americans in our group had come on the short walk.

"Are the men treating you well? Do they give you enough food?" he said. When you are sitting on the ground, sleeping crammed together in a bamboo lean-to and passing a spoon around so you can eat off a common plate, it's hard to know how to answer questions like those. Since the Commander in Chief had said we would be released after we were questioned, co-operation was at the top of our agenda. I spoke for the group.

"We're fine. The men have treated us well. But," I said gesturing to Ann-Charlotte, "this lady cannot eat the beans." Emmanuel laughed and said he understood. That was the last time we were served beans. From then on we only got rice and potatoes.

"Why have you come to this area? There is much fighting and wars. It is not a good place to come," Emmanuel said. I explained our only reason for coming was to see the gorillas. We had understood there was no danger from rebels or warring factions in the part of Congo that we were visiting. We trusted our guides would have told us if there was any reason we shouldn't cross the border.

Emmanuel continued questioning us: How old are you? How long did you go to school? What jobs do you do? Jens and Ann-Charlotte said they were thirty and thirty-one. When Doug said he was sixty-seven and I said fifty-five, he exclaimed that his mother and father were those ages. When he heard I had two children, a son twenty-seven and a daughter twenty-five, he responded quite excitedly, "I am twenty-seven! You are my mother. You are my father. You are my brother and my sister!" From then on the men addressed me as 'Mama', a polite form of address reserved for older women. I explained that I ran a school for little children and had been in school for nineteen years. Doug said he was retired but was a gardener. Emmanuel was most interested in Ann-Charlotte, a veterinarian, and Jens, an engineer who worked with radio and television. Emmanuel had studied zoology at University. With obvious pride he showed Jens his radio, a multi-band, battery-run radio about five inches by ten inches with the antenna attached by wire. Jens looked at it for a moment and commented, without much interest, that it was very interesting.

Most of the men who were guarding us carried battery-powered radios. They turned them on several times a day slowly scanning all the bands. Most of what they listened to was in a local language or French. Though we couldn't understand much of what was broadcast, the names of towns stood out. News seemed to be primarily about the growing conflict in Congo and the fighting around Kinshasa. Once or twice we heard English, but the station was quickly changed. I wondered if anything was being broadcast about us.

Emmanuel told us that he had been a second year student at University in 1994 when war had broken out. He was forced to leave school and had been unable to return to town because he was a Hutu. If he tried he would be stopped and beaten or perhaps put in jail. He told us things in Rwanda were very bad for the Hutu and would need to improve before he could go back and finish school. As he got ready to leave, we asked when he would come again. "I will not come again. Tonight some men will come to talk to you. When that is done, you will go back to your home." He wished us well and left down the slope of the hill. Although we now knew why we had been captured, we still had no idea what they wanted from us.

We settled in around our evening fire, passing the time mindlessly watching our guards around their fire much as we would watch a TV show at home. Suddenly, a whole group of men holding automatic guns appeared out of the darkness and surrounded the shelter. We all jumped up and I held my breath. In the flickering firelight it was difficult see their faces clearly, but their manner was so palpably threatening that everything but them vanished. Would they start shooting? Then I remembered Emmanuel had said men would be coming tonight. Were these the men?

One of the two uniformed men spoke English. In a harsh, unpleasant tone he began firing questions similar to Emmanuel's at us. "Where did you come from in Uganda? Where did you enter the Democratic Republic of Congo?"

Why would they want to know that? Who knew what the towns were called, I thought, confused and in near panic. The towns were like the antelope; I'd stopped remembering their names. I just rode in the truck and went where I was taken. I turned to the others. "Does anyone know the names of where we came from? All I can remember is Kisoro."

Jens pulled a small map about the gorilla trek area out of his shirt pocket. In the dim light he and I strained to read the small names. After a few seconds I gave up. Without my reading glasses, I couldn't read anything in the dim light. "Here," Jens said pointing to the map. "It says the border is Bunagana and the name close to the mountain is Djomba."

"What are your nationalities? Why had you come to Congo?" At least I knew that answer. I'd just told Emmanuel all this, but repeated it patiently and sweetly. Whatever they wanted to know was fine, just as long as we got to go home.

"Didn't you know there was a war on?"

"We came to see the gorillas. We had no idea there were any problems in this area. We thought the travel companies knew what was going on and wouldn't take us any place that was unsafe."

The two men in charge seemed annoyed and angry about my answer. "You know nothing about our country. Don't you listen to the BBC to find out what is happening in Africa?"

That was complicated to answer. How could I get them to see that we came from a completely different kind of country? "The BBC programs you hear in Africa are short-wave broadcasts for countries that don't have their own English stations. In our countries we don't have BBC broadcasts. We only get local news on the radio. Our newspapers print very little about African countries." It sounded feeble, but being as honest as I could be seemed the best option.

Then came a question that almost stumped me. "What have your countries done to help Rwanda during their conflicts?" My brain was flying, digging for vaguely remembered facts buried in my general knowledge of African issues. If only I'd paid better attention to the news. What had I seen on TV? I wished I had Dan beside me. As a history and geography teacher, he knew everything and remembered it all.

"Canada provided a lot of help to people in the refugee camps after they had fled Rwanda. We gave a lot of financial aid to the UN and sent soldiers as UN Peacekeepers." Helping refugees is good. Money is good. Peace is good. Would they accept my answer? They didn't respond. Fuck!

Jens said, "Sweden has a seat on the UN Security Council. It gives us a voice in international affairs." Doug didn't say anything. I wondered if he had his hearing aid in. He'd been taking it out for most of the day to prolong the battery life.

I knew the United Nations War Crimes Tribunal, set up to bring those responsible for the 1994 Rwandan genocide to justice, was operating in Arusha, Tanzania. I wasn't sure who our captors would consider the bad guys, the Hutu or the Tutsi, so I didn't say anything about the Tribunal. I did comment that a Canadian general had been in charge of the UN forces in Rwanda during the genocide. "Roméo Dallaire," one of the men responded.

Lt.-Gen. Roméo Dallaire headed the United Nations Assistance Mission for Rwanda (UNIMAR) sent to oversee the implementation of provisions in the Arusha Peace Accords signed by President Juvenal Habyarimana and representatives of the Tutsi Rwandan Patriotic Front. In January 1994, Dallaire sent a fax to the United Nations warning of an imminent wholesale slaughter. The fax stated the Hutu government was compiling death lists of Tutsis and moderate Hutus and training militiamen to do the killing. The fax also warned that they had become aware there was a plan to kill Belgian Peacekeepers and cause a withdrawal of Belgium's UN troops from Rwanda. Dallaire said he intended to raid the Rwandan government's weapons caches to thwart the genocide plan. Between January 22 and March 13, 1994, Dallaire sent five additional memos warning the UN of the coming massacre. However Lt.-Gen. Dallaire was instructed not to act against the Hutus. He was ordered not to seize any arms or take aggressive action against the Hutu government, but rather to ask the government to stop arming citizens. Given these orders, Dallaire and his forces were powerless to stop the killing.

On April 4, 1994, Rwanda's leader, President Habyarimana, and Burundi's President Cyprian Ntayamira were killed when Habyarimana's plane was shot down as they were returning to Kigali. Concurrent with the plane crash, the genocide began. Among the first casualties tortured and killed by government troops were Agathe Uwilingiyimana, Rwanda's moderate Hutu Prime Minister, and the ten Belgian soldiers sent by Lt.-Gen. Dallaire to escort her to a radio station where she was to appeal to Rwandans for calm after the President's death. As predicted, with the deaths of the Belgian soldiers the Belgian Government withdrew their troops who were the largest part of the UN peacekeeping contingent and the genocide proceeded unchecked.

An exhaustive French parliamentary inquiry report released in December 1998, blamed the United Nations for failing to avert the Rwandan genocide and said that the United States government bore special responsibility for resisting demands to boost the UNIMAR force. The Americans had likely refused because they were still smarting from the 1993 debacle in Somalia where eighteen American soldiers, part of a UN force, were killed and images of the body of a dead American soldier being towed through the streets were shown on world television. The French inquiry neglected to include the fact that, before, during and after the Rwandan genocide, France continued to provide arms and military assistance to the Hutus.

How would our captors view Dallaire? "Yes, Roméo Dallaire was the Canadian." I said nothing more.

The two men questioning us wanted to check our packs. I thought they meant the bags we had with us. To my surprise, from somewhere in the darkness at the back of the group, all the bags that had been dropped on the mountainside the day we were captured were set in front of us. I identified the Granville Island canvas bag that now held only my camera in a ziplock bag. They took it. "Where is your money?" I repeated the story of not bringing any. I unzipped my fanny pack but they weren't interested in the contents.

Then they thoroughly searched each of the backpacks the other three had with them. The men took Doug, Jens and Ann-Charlotte's cameras, all their film, used and unused, and their watches. The men in charge looked closely at Jens' watch. "It is broken."

"It's not broken," Jens said and showed them how to display the time, activate the stopwatch, etc.

"Bloody hell," Doug whispered to me with a catch in his voice. "I hate to give my watch up. It has great sentimental value to me."

The men were busy with Jens and Ann-Charlotte. I whispered back. "I know, Doug. But the most important thing is getting free. We have to keep focused on that." It crossed my mind how fortunate it was that I had nothing of value with me. I remembered thinking before we left that I should leave my watch, my gold jewelry and a cross from my Mother that I always wore at home so they wouldn't be stolen or lost.

They checked Doug and Jen's wallets, but didn't take any of their money. The man questioning us said, "You will need your money to pay a tip to the men who guide you out tomorrow. For each the tip is $20 American money. You will give them this money at the end."

"But," I began.

"Don't worry about the money," Jens said to me. "We'll settle it all later."

I thought, at this point, that the men were going to turn and melt away into the darkness as quietly as they had appeared. We'd been questioned and our bags had been ransacked. There was nothing else we could give or tell them. But, I had a question. "When will we be released?"

"Tomorrow. At one o'clock." We sighed. Now they could go.

But they didn't leave.

The man in charge said, "Write down your names and the addresses where you live on a paper. Put it down two times, on two papers." His request was as bizarre and disconcerting as the questions he had asked earlier. Why would they want that information? They were letting us go the next day. Had we misunderstood him? We all stood there, not moving.

"Write your names," he demanded impatiently. All of us jerked into action.

"Does anyone have a pen or paper?" I asked. The only paper I had was my flight itinerary, and there was no way I was going to give that to anyone. Doug dug in his pack and pulled out a nice drafting pen and his journal. He tore out a sheet of paper and handed me the pen and paper.

"I'm no good at printing," he said. "Will you put my address down here, and you can add yours onto the bottom." He still sounded upset about his watch. Writing his address was the least I could do. I took the pen and paper from him. But, from the darkness beyond the firelight, a hand appeared holding a small notebook.

"Put your names in this book." It took me a while to get the information down as Doug had to spell parts of his address. When I had finished printing our information once, the man in charge said that was enough and took the notebook away. Jens wrote his and Ann-Charlotte's address on the back of his business card and handed it to the man in charge.

I was puzzled why they were collecting personal information. To ask our countries for ransom? Maybe if they knew Dan was at the Virunga Hotel, they'd contact him; we wouldn't have to wait for them to contact our countries, or something equally slow. "Is it possible for someone to take a message to my husband at the Virunga Hotel in Kisoro?" I asked the head man. Doug echoed my request; he was worried that his wife would have heard about him being captured. He hoped someone in Kisoro could get a message to her that he was fine.

"It is not possible to send any message." The tone of the response was final.

"What group do you belong to?" Jens asked. "Are you…" He mentioned several names and acronyms. His question hung in the air unanswered and ignored. A chill rippled through me. They would tell us only what they wanted us to know. I hoped Jens wouldn't ask any more questions.

No longer speaking English, the leader said something to one of the men who then handed Ann-Charlotte's watch back to her. He said something else to our regular guards by the fire, had his men gather our bags and belongings, and then faded into the blackness.

I stood for a minute staring into the dark. Had I given the right answers? I thought about Dan waiting for me and wished him good night.

We sat around our dying fire and talked about what had happened, almost giddy with the relief of having got through the questioning without provoking them unduly. We decided they might use our names to contact our tour groups or families to ask for money. But that didn't make sense to me. If it was money they wanted, they'd have taken Doug's and Jens's money. Other than their original mistaken belief that we were Americans, I still had no idea why we had been captured.

As we fed the last pieces of bamboo into the fire, we speculated about what the others in our tour groups were doing. "The group will stay as long as they can. Dan won't go home until I get there," I said with assurance. "Someone from the company will be in Kisoro by now. When we get out they'll be waiting at the border for us."

"We're on our own," Jens said. "We'll have to work everything out ourselves." He and Doug were certain everyone would have moved on. They discussed the problem of our lost passports and visas and what we might have to do to get back across the border to Kisoro.

Doug and Jens made an agreement, when we were released, that they would give the men who guided us out all the money they still had left, even though it would likely be more than $20. Jens was carrying quite a bit of cash in his wallet. He took about half and hid it between the two inner-soles in his boot. The remainder was more than enough to pay the tip for all of us.

Doug still had about $100 US and a bunch of Ugandan shillings. He looked down at his beat-up running shoes. "I'd like to hide some money, too, but I can't hide anything in these. If I give them all the money I have, I won't be able to get home. I need $10 US to pay the airport departure tax. And I need money to make a phone call when I get to the border."

I shook my head. It seemed incredible to me that they could believe four people could disappear and no one would be waiting and looking for them. I wasn't about to argue. We'd know who was right when we got to the border.

I didn't know who Doug would be phoning from the border, but I had a suggestion for his money. "Give the money to me, Doug. I'll hide it in my bra."

As we were talking, one of the guards called in French from their fire, "Mama, how much did the fancy watch cost in American dollars?"

When Jens called back, "$300 US," a burst of excited words erupted. "They don't want to sell it for too little," he commented. I thought they were curious and astonished at the price.

We sat staring into the dying flames. I thought about Dan and saw him sitting thinking about me. He'd be so pleased when I walked into town tomorrow. I could see him smile. Only a few more hours.

SEVEN

I woke up excited. I'm going home today! As soon as the Commander in Chief collected the sleeping bag, we began to dismantle the shelter. We took the inside tarp down, folded it and I handed it to him to bundle with the tarps from their sleeping area. He looked at me a little strangely, but took the tarp. With my limited French it was too hard to explain that we wanted to be ready to go the second someone said we could. Predictably, he said he was going to go talk with his commander and would be back soon. As he left, he added something about us leaving at seven o'clock that evening. My mouth fell open and I stared at his back as he disappeared through the bamboo. I turned to the others. "I think he just said something about us leaving at seven tonight. That can't be right."

"I heard seven o'clock, too," Jens said.

"But the man said one o'clock when I asked him last night."

"Remember, don't get too set on any particular time. We still don't know for sure what's going on or who these people are," Jens said. "Who knows when they'll let us go?" I wanted to roll my eyes. I didn't need him to remind us of that or to be negative. I preferred to believe what had been said the night before, that we would get out soon. There was no point in arguing, however. Like whether there was anyone waiting at the border or not, we'd have to wait and see.

Richard came over to borrow Doug's lighter. "You can keep it, mate," Doug said as he handed it to Richard. Doug turned to us. "We're going to be leaving soon. He might as well keep it." Richard went back to start the fire, smiling and flicking the lighter top off and on. After our breakfast we waited.

Sometime in the middle of the morning, Pascal arrived back in camp. "Hello, my friends. How are you this morning? Good, I hope. I need to get some money from you so I can buy more food."

I looked at the others in confusion. We were going to be leaving shortly. I was afraid to ask Pascal why he thought we would need more food, because I didn't want to hear what he might say. I couldn't imagine the tough, armed men last night going to Pascal and conferring about what they should do with us. I rationalized that he was one of the 'little frogs' and had no idea what was happening. Go with the flow, Donalda, I told myself. Don't start worrying without knowing what it is you're worrying about.

Jens explained that we needed our money to pay a tip when we were released and couldn't give him any more American money. Doug pulled out his Ugandan shillings, but he was low on those, too.

"There won't be anyone at the border waiting for us," Doug said to me. "Can you keep this 500 Ugandan shillings someplace safe for me? I'll use it to make a phone call when I get to the border." I tucked the money, which was worth about 50¢, into my fanny pack by my itinerary. Doug seemed calmer after giving me the money.

Pascal overheard Doug. "You do not need to worry at the border," he said. "I have already been to the border. I told them you would be coming out today. There will be someone there ready with transportation."

Suddenly everything was too crazy. Money. Food. Borders. Pascal was a kid, the grocery boy. He was obviously an opportunist, a minor player. He must be lying. Why did he need more food money? We were to be released. We weren't going to be there for any more meals. And there was no way we'd eaten $25 worth of rice and potatoes. He couldn't have been to the border that morning. It was too far away. It had taken us a whole day to get here. Where were they going to release us? Djomba? Kisoro? Some other border place? I ignored the rising thought that perhaps we wouldn't be released. I wanted to go home.

I sat alone in the sun and waited. The sun was warm. As the hours passed, the heat melted my anxieties. Let it go, Donalda. It doesn't matter. Nothing matters except getting home.

All the men except Pascal and Richard had gone. The two of them were sitting together by the men's fire chattering and knotting bits of blue plastic bag. Since the first day, Richard had borrowed Doug's lighter and his knife. He must have seen Doug lend me his pen the night before. Today he walked over and held out his hand. "Stylo," he said to Doug. After drawing some kind of game board on a scrap of paper he returned it. "Merci."

Curious, I wandered over to the men's fire and watched. They were taking turns putting their markers on the cross-corners of a series of intersecting lines, playing a variation of 'three in a row' with the plastic knots as game pieces. They played quickly and seemed well matched, though Richard won two games before Pascal left. Watching them play a game brought a weird sense of normalcy to everything that had happened since we were captured.

Back at our shelter we waited for some kind of signal that it was time for us to leave the clearing. In a cheerful mood, we sat talking. Doug and I described what we had done on the safari, the places we had been and the animals we had seen. Jens and Ann-Charlotte told us they'd come to Uganda for a week to see the gorillas and relax at Lake Bunyonyi before going on to Tanzania to climb Mt. Kilimanjaro. The day they arrived in Nairobi the bomb went off at the American Embassy. On their third day they were captured. Jens said they didn't know what they would do when they were released. I knew I'd be going home almost immediately. It was only a few days until our flight left Entebbe. I had no doubt I'd be on the plane, sitting beside Dan, going home.

Like all our conversations, this one petered out quickly. We really didn't have a lot to say to each other. We hadn't been and weren't going to be buddies. We were strangers. I knew that once we returned to our home countries, we'd never see each other again. We rarely discussed what was happening. Living as a captive was bad enough without talking about it, too. The overriding thought in my mind was always to get free and go home.

Time moved at glacial speed; there were still several hours until noon. Jens and Ann-Charlotte cleared the ashes away from our fire pit and played X and Os in the blackened dirt. Richard came over to watch and indicated he didn't know the game. By the time we'd played a couple of games he'd worked out how to win or draw each game. After days of sitting and waiting, even playing a simple game of X and Os was fun. Richard suddenly seemed more like a friend than our captor. We were playing games and soon I would be going home. I wanted more of that feeling.

I decided we needed a more complex game to play, Checkers. I borrowed Doug's pen though the paper in his journal was too small for a game board. The only large sheet of paper we had was my flight schedule. Each time I looked at it, I counted the days until our scheduled flight out of Entebbe. It's OK, I'd say to myself, our reservation at the Sheraton isn't until Saturday, or, the plane to London doesn't leave for two more days. That paper was my identity, the only proof that I existed outside of the small clearing. I painstakingly drew a checkers board on the back of the flight schedule, careful not to obliterate any of the printing.

Richard watched curiously as we knotted enough blue plastic pieces for one color of checkers and broke twigs for the other. Doug and I played the first game; he was sticks and I was knots. We were both concentrating on the game, strategizing so our pieces would be in the best tactical position. I moved a knot forward to a square that would force Doug to jump me and, in turn, I'd be able to jump two of his men and land in the Queen row. He didn't jump.

"No. You have to jump this man."

"No, I don't." he said. "I can leave it."

"The rules in checkers are that you must jump if you can," I said.

"We're not playing checkers," Doug said. "We're playing Draughts."

As we were laughing and arguing whether he was forced to jump or not, Emmanuel reappeared in camp. "Hello. Hello, Mamma. Hello, Papa. Hello, my brother and sister," he called as he broke through the bamboo. Ah, good, I thought. He's come to take us home.

"We have finally heard about you on the radio. The news said that four foreign tourists had disappeared on a gorilla-viewing trip, taken captive by an unknown group." He was quite excited. "Why has it taken so long, four days, to get it on the radio?"

Good question, I thought, then realized it wasn't rhetorical. I frowned at Emmanuel. How the hell would I know? I thought, but replied dryly, "We have no idea what's going on. We're in the forest with you."

"We are contacting the Head Commander," Emmanuel said. "He will be coming to talk with you." Who? Talk? When? We're leaving today.

"You will take some papers with you and information so the world will know the truth about what is happening in Rwanda. When you have spoken to the Head Commander, then you will be released." Then? When is then? Not today?

I stared at him. I knew I'd understood, but I didn't want to believe it. Fuck.

"What do you mean, Emmanuel? Where is your Head Commander? The men last night said we were going out today. At one o'clock."

His answers were vague and confusing. "The Head Commander is busy fighting… and he might not be able to come right away." We couldn't pin down exactly where the Commander was or how he was being contacted. Only one thing was clear—it was going to take a while. On my list of people whom I would never believe again, Emmanuel climbed over Pascal.

"Emmanuel, while you are contacting the Commander, could you send a message to Kisoro that we're all right?" I knew what he would say, but I wanted to make sure he was always aware that someone was down the mountain waiting for us. My husband was there.

"No," he said, "it isn't possible." No surprise. As he got ready to leave he said something about coming back soon with some information, or a communiqué of some type, to prove he was telling us the truth. I shook my head, rolled my eyes and snorted in disgust. Sure. What part is the truth?

The truth was, we weren't leaving. It was as though a heavy black cloud had covered the sun. I pulled my itinerary out from under the twigs and plastic bits, folded it, and put it carefully in my fanny pack. Dispirited, I walked back and sat at our shelter. I stabbed the ashes in the pit with a shard of bamboo, my thoughts as black as the burned earth.

"We have to be careful about putting a time frame on our leaving," Jens cautioned for the fourth time. I knew he was right, but he didn't need to keep saying it. I kept stabbing the dirt, caught in my own thoughts.

"I think if we'd finished that game," Doug said, "I'd likely have won. I was in better shape tactically."

A loud explosion somewhere down the hill below the clearing shattered my thoughts. Not breathing, I stared frozen in the direction from which the sound had come. Though the explosion had been loud, it didn't sound extremely close. I wished for x-ray vision, trying to bore through the bamboo. I couldn't see anything. In quick succession the clearing reverberated with the motley sounds of battle—the rapid rat-tat-tat of machine guns, the deep thump of explosions and the irregular tattoo of rifle volleys. What was happening? In my head the men from the night before, their mouths pulled back in grimaces, crashed through the bamboo, their bloodcurdling screams mixed with the deafening guns. I slipped back into the shelter, cowering with my hands pressed tightly over my ears. I scanned the bamboo brush. How close would the fighting get? Again I imagined men with blazing guns crashing through the bamboo, shooting. Was this fight because the Head Commander was coming? I hoped no one would shoot me. Did I look white? I took my white crocheted hat off so anyone coming into the clearing would recognize I wasn't Rwandan. I opened my fanny pack and checked that my flight itinerary was safely tucked at the back.

The sounds of battle didn't get any closer. After about fifteen minutes the barrage stopped. The silence echoed around me, as unnerving as the shooting had been. I sat and waited. Any semblance of civilization had been blown away with the mortar fire. One by one men, whose faces I recognized as one might recognize a rattlesnake curled up on a rock, filtered back into the clearing and sat around the other fire pit talking quietly. Who had they been shooting at? Had anyone been killed? The gunfight ended any expectation I had that I might be out with Dan that evening. I wasn't going to die, but it seemed obvious we weren't leaving.

Anger was boiling in my chest. I felt dirty, everywhere. When I'd washed my feet the day before, I'd rationalized putting my dirty socks back on because we were going to be released. If they weren't going to let me go, I was at least going to get my socks washed. Take care of your comfort. Be in control. I unlaced my boots, pulled off my socks and walked over to the group of men. With my socks dangling from one raised hand, I pointed to a basin and addressed the Commander in Chief, "Mon ami, J'ai besoin d'eau. Je veut laver mes vêtements." Telling him I needed water to wash my clothes was as close as I could come to 'I want to wash my socks.'

The Commander in Chief stood up and took the socks from my hand. Calling a young man to come over and help him, he pulled the plastic plug out of the water can. While the young man poured a slow stream of water out of the water can, the Commander in Chief bent over spread legged and squeezed and rubbed the socks in the trickling water. Once the socks were soaked, he took the bar of green soap and began rubbing the socks and soap together. He worked for quite a while to build up a good lather, then, with a quick rhythmic rubbing motion, he scrubbed the socks against each other, scouring them thoroughly. I stood mesmerized. His hands were incredibly strong and efficient. When he judged the socks were clean, he signaled the young man holding the jerry can to begin pouring and he rinsed them until all trace of the soap was gone. I raised my hand to take them from him, but he shook his head. He walked toward the shelter, wringing the socks until they no longer dripped. He stretched each one straight then threaded them upside down over the sticks that supported our roof so they would dry. My socks were clean.

"Asante sana. Thank you, my friend. Merci," I said. "C'est merveilleuse." My emotions were spinning. In less than ten minutes I'd gone through fear, anger, surprise and gratitude. I didn't know what to think about the Commander in Chief washing my socks. It was so incongruous. He was one of the group who had captured and tried to rape me—and he did my laundry. What kind of a man was he?

The Commander in Chief didn't go back to sit with the other men. He asked me if I'd seen the gorillas. He seemed interested that we liked animals enough to come so far to see them. I told him about the three we had seen: the silverback, his mate and one young. I used gestures as much as words. He filled in what I didn't know. He told us about the different gorilla groups that lived in the Rwandan forests. Although lone silverbacks were dangerous, they seemed less aggressive once they were in families.

The Commander in Chief asked us if we knew of Dian Fossey. "I worked for her," he said. Dian Fossey had been murdered thirteen years before, in 1985. I remembered pictures I'd seen of her and her helpers sitting in the jungle with the gorillas. That kind of man would wash socks. I looked at him closely. He had a few corkscrew gray hairs over his ears and appeared to be in his forties.

"Tell me, Mate," Doug said to the Commander in Chief, pointing at the high cone-shaped mountains to our south, "What are the names of those volcanoes?"

The Commander in Chief named the volcanoes, pointing at each in turn: Muhavura, Gahinga, Sabinyo and Muside. Then the Commander in Chief asked me if I had known about the war and disruptions in the Congo. I explained as best I could in French that we were ignorant of the situation. If we had known there was this much trouble, we would never have come into Congo. I tried to convey the irony of our situation with my tone of voice as well as my words. "Je ne suis pas stupide. Je suis seulement une touriste. I'm not stupid. I'm only a tourist."

After he went back with the other men, the four of us sat silently in the sunshine. Although we had been together for four days in the most intimate of circumstances, we knew almost nothing about each other. Jens and Ann-Charlotte had been spending most of their time sitting together in the shelter talking quietly. Ann-Charlotte rarely said anything to Doug or me and was eating almost nothing. I was concerned about her. I was sure that if I could get us all talking together, the distraction might help her. Doing anything that had an air of normalcy was better than obsessing on the bad things. Certainly for those few minutes when the Commander in Chief was washing my socks and we talked with him, I hadn't been as fixated on when and how we'd be released. I took a deep breath and turned toward her. "You're a veterinarian, Ann-Charlotte. What kind of animals do you work with?" I asked.

She explained that she didn't actually work with animals. She worked in personnel certification and office processes. She fell silent again. Since I knew nothing much about animals and little more about office practices, that almost ended the discussion. I vaguely remembered listening to one of my English cousins tell about his government job breeding and raising cattle. I dredged some half-remembered facts out of my memory, enough to keep us talking—about artificial insemination and the difference in the amount of milk produced by African cows and those raised in Europe. Not the kinds of topics I'd normally be involved with in my job as a principal, but for an hour or so, we talked about something besides our situation.

That evening, when all the men had returned to the clearing and were gathered around their fire, the Commander in Chief came over and stood in front of me with his hands behind his back. He obviously wanted something. "Ça va?" I said.

"Ça va," he answered, then asked me something. I wasn't sure what he was asking since I didn't recognize one of the words he used.

I looked at the others. "I don't remember what *lait* means."

"Milk." Jens said.

I looked up at the Commander in Chief. "Lait?" I asked. He nodded and repeated his question. "Do you drink milk?"

I wasn't sure how to answer since I don't usually drink milk. I began to dither, "Umm-m," then turned to the other three, "I don't drink milk, but do you?" Jens said he and Ann-Charlotte did.

"Oui, nous buvon du lait, merci," I said, relieved to be able to give a positive response.

The Commander in Chief handed me a small plastic jug of milk from behind his back. I thanked him and passed it to Jens who pulled the plastic off the top. I hoped Ann-Charlotte would drink some. She was hardly eating anything. As Jens tipped the bottle up I stupidly said, "I don't think it will be pasteurized. Do you think there might be a problem with tuberculosis?" As soon as the words were out of my mouth I knew I should have kept quiet. He looked at Ann-Charlotte, then put the plastic back on top and set it down. Damn. If I hadn't mentioned TB, they'd have drunk the milk, no problem. I looked up and the Commander in Chief was standing there looking from me to them.

Doug said, "Give it to me. I sure drink milk." He took the jug and tipped it up, drinking about half the milk. He wiped his mouth with the back of his hand and set the jug down. "You can tell him I've had enough," Doug said. I thanked the Commander in Chief and gave the jug back to him.

As he walked away Jens whispered, "I didn't think anyone spoke English here. But now I'm not sure. Someone must have listened to us talking about cows and milk this afternoon." We became even more circumspect about what we said after that. Several times Jens would engineer a discussion about what we could do when we were released that would support the Hutu cause in the Rwandan conflict—whom we could talk to or give information to.

Emmanuel returned that evening as we sat by the fire after our supper of boiled potatoes. "I am to tell you about Rwanda." Like a professor lecturing in a large hall, he stood straight in front of us holding sheets of notes. His lesson was on Rwanda's history and the current state of affairs. What Emmanuel told us was accurate, but incomplete.

He began, "In Rwanda there are three ethnic groups: the Tutsi, about 15% of the population; the Hutu, about 85%; and the Twa or Pygmies, who are less than 1%. For hundreds of years the Tutsi and Hutu have intermarried and lived in harmony. These two groups were both involved in government and education, both together."

Rwanda is unique among African nations where there are often hundreds of tribes in a country. It is inhabited by a single group, the Banyarwanda, made up of three subgroups, Hutu, Tutsi and Twa, who share a common language, culture and customs. Historically the Tutsi were cattle owners, the Hutu were farmers, and the Twa laborers or servants. In 1939, while Rwanda was a colony of Belgium, the Rwandan people had been divided bureaucratically by the Belgians into permanent unchangeable groups by how many cows they owned. Owning more than four cows made you a Tutsi—the 'have' group—while those who owned fewer than four cows were Hutu—the 'have nots'.

During the 1930s the Belgian colonial government ruled through the Tutsis, providing Tutsi children with a better education than Hutu children. However, in the 1950s, like groups in other African countries, the Tutsis began to demand independence and self-government for Rwanda. In response, Belgium switched their favour to the Hutu and began encouraging them to act against the Tutsis. In 1959 a peasant revolt erupted over access to land held by the Tutsis. Tens of thousands of Tutsis were murdered and an equal number fled into exile in the surrounding countries. This massacre solidified the division between Hutu and Tutsi. When Rwanda was given its independence from Belgium in 1962, the Hutu set up the government.

After the 1962 independence, there were periodic bloody conflicts between the Hutu and Tutsi that resulted in the deaths of thousands of Rwandans and the displacement of thousands more. Those Tutsis who had been forced into exile in neighboring countries continued to look upon Rwanda as their home and talked of returning one day to reclaim their place. This on-going conflict between Tutsi and Hutu set the stage for genocide, the murder of 800 000 Tutsis and moderate Hutu that began on 6 April 1994.

Emmanuel continued, "In 1994, there was a war where one group was pitted against the other and many, many people were killed. At the end of the war the Tutsis were given all the power—they formed the government, judiciary, military and security forces. No Hutu was given any position of authority. Many people were put into prison. Some of those put into jail were criminals, men who had killed many people, but many Hutu prisoners were put in jail simply because they were Hutu. They had not been involved in any killing. They were jailed anyway, along with many who were guilty of crimes."

What Emmanuel didn't say was that, unlike most countries where only the military is involved in wars, in Rwanda, tightly organized militias throughout the country deliberately involved as many civilians as possible in the atrocities. The slaughter was not spontaneous, but rather a planned and organized campaign of genocide. Everyone was involved in the carnage. Many Hutus had to choose between being a killer and being killed. In areas where too few Tutsi deaths were reported, experienced killers were brought in from other areas to complete the task.

The Rwandan genocide was accomplished almost entirely without firearms. As Elliott Leyton said in the book *Touched by Fire: Doctors Without Borders in a Third World Crisis*, '... it took many strong and eager arms to carry out the strenuous work of raping, burning and hacking to death a half million people (and mutilating many thousands more by slicing off their hands, their breasts, their genitals or their ears) with pangas (machetes), kitchen knives, farm hoes, pitchforks and hastily improvised spiked clubs.'

Emmanuel continued telling us what it was like being a Hutu in Rwanda. "Even though the war is over, the killing continues. In the refugee camps and in the towns, Tutsi soldiers and criminals who escaped with the refugees indiscriminately kill anyone who is strong and Hutu. Men are the first to be killed, but the women and children are also killed, their goods stolen and houses burned. The worst thing is the killing of Hutu women and children. None of these people are soldiers, just innocent civilians.

"The Hutu have no power. The Hutu want to have a part in the running of the country since our ethnic group forms the majority of the citizens. We also want purely political or ethnic prisoners set free. Hutu are persecuted because they are Hutu. Because all the judges are Tutsi, any Tutsi accused of a crime is set free; any Hutu accused of anything is sent to prison. Above all, the Hutu want to have freedom, democracy and security."

"Emmanuel," I said, "so you're a Hutu? Are the other men who captured us also Hutu?" He nodded. "From what you tell us, right now, all of you are being persecuted because you're Hutu." He nodded again. So, finally I knew. This was what it was all about. If he needed me to believe him, then I'd believe. "How can we help you?"

"You must tell the world for us. Tell them what is happening."

"We've been talking about that. Once we're free, we can take this information to our countries, to our governments. We will be able to help you when we're free." Just let me go!

Emmanuel smiled. "I will be getting more material, written material that you can take with you. The Head Commander will bring it. He wants you to see with your own eyes that what I'm telling you is true. When he comes you will go to see the destroyed villages and the killing—the truth." There it was again. That wonderful truth.

I was prepared to agree to almost anything. We all spoke enthusiastically about Emmanuel bringing us information. Although I listened and responded sympathetically, I was only interested in one thing, getting free.

After he left, I thought about what Emmanuel had said. I was clear on the facts in the history lesson, but confused about when and how we'd be released. Freedom was still up in the air. It seemed we'd have to travel quite a distance to get to this devastated war area. Somehow I got the feeling there was a vehicle involved, though I was unclear whether it would take us to the border or bring the Head Commander to us. As I tried to imagine what might happen, pictures similar to those I'd seen in movies flashed through my head. Driving up to a town while bombs exploded all around us. Being pushed out of a moving jeep amid gunfire and being left to make my own way across the border. Crawling or running, crouched against the concussion of explosions. All the Vietnam War movies I'd seen were replayed with black Africans as the combatants.

When the fires died down, the Commander in Chief brought back our sleeping bag and the tarp we'd taken down with such enthusiasm that morning. The last few nights the sky had been clear and the temperature had dropped. Doug and Jens were most affected by the cold. Even lying close to each other didn't generate enough heat to keep them warm since the sleeping bag didn't cover their backs. It didn't look like it was going to rain, so we decided to try putting the tarp on the ground and wrapping the sides up around Doug and Jens' bodies. The African men watched us with great interest as we spread the tarp on the ground with the edges pushed up the walls. Once we were lying down and covered with the sleeping bag, Doug and Jens pulled the edges of the tarp down over themselves. It helped. Doug snored.

EIGHT

O n Saturday morning, our fifth day, we waited while the Commander in Chief went to see his commander. The day stretched long in front of us. Suddenly Jens hopped up and pulled his Swiss Army Knife out of his pocket. "If we're going to play games," he said, "we'll need better game pieces." With his saw he cut a series of round, hollow pieces from a section of dead bamboo. He stared at the other plants growing around the perimeter and lopped a branch off a tree. From that he cut a series of solid round pieces the same diameter as the bamboo. He lined them up on the grass in front of the shelter. "There. Now we can play again."

After working out a compromise on the rules, Doug and I played a game of Checkers / Draughts. Before I made any moves I checked whether I could force him to jump or not. He was a keen player and sneaky. He caught me a couple of times when I let my attention slip. But I pushed my pieces to the back row and got a bunch of queens. "Ah ha! I got you!" I won.

Richard and Pascal watched closely as we played. I asked Richard if he would like a game, but he shook his head, no. Pascal said, "I know this game. I'll play with you." I won again.

The sun was shining warm and bright; we had our jackets and hats off. Black and white, African and Caucasian, we were playing together. We laughed, we talked, and we had fun. Having fun was fun. Every laugh wiped another gun shot from my mind. The men who had started out only as our guards were slipping into another parallel role as companions. I didn't want to think what they might become if something went wrong.

After our games, Doug, Jens and I sat in the sunshine talking about beer. Like bread, beer seemed to be universal. Every country I could think of had some kind of beer. I enjoy beer of any kind, cold, straight out of the bottle. At any time in our fridge at home we have eight or ten different brews to choose from. Jens was a beer drinker like me. He told me about the vast German beer gardens and I told him about the growth of microbreweries in Canada. I could almost taste the cool crispness of a Lager.

The familiar late afternoon dark clouds were building over the mountains. Every day when the thunder rumbled, I asked the men, "Is it going to rain?" It never had. But that day, the clouds looked especially ominous. They boiled high and black, building thick over the volcanoes and finally blocking the sun. With a shiver as the temperature dropped, we pulled the tarp over the lean-to roof and kept an eye on the clouds. Pascal, Richard and a couple of other men fished their tarps out of the bushes and began to tie one to the bamboo posts. It was the first time they'd put the tarp up during the day. Usually they waited until dark, after we finished eating.

As I watched them work, I heard women's voices. Several times in the preceding days I had heard children's voices and people singing. The voices always sounded close, but I was never able to see anyone through the thick vegetation. At night I had checked the area outside our clearing for light or fires, but I'd never seen anything that indicated there was a village nearby.

However, in the days since we were brought to the clearing, the area immediately around it had been slowly denuded of dead and living bamboo for the fire and pot tripods. Curious about where the women's voices were coming from, I wandering behind the shelter toward the bathroom area, peering through the bamboo. I caught a glimpse of something bright down the hill. Emmanuel was leading a long line of brightly clad women up the hill into our clearing. The flash of patterned reds, oranges, blues, greens and yellows in eyepopping combinations filled the clearing with a riot of color. After long days of staring at our monotonous, green surroundings, the women were like a flock of exotic Technicolor butterflies come to rest. They wore traditional kangas. One multicolored length of bright patterned cotton fabric wrapped around their legs served as a skirt. A second fabric with a different color and pattern was wrapped bust high over a blouse or t-shirt. A third, different again in color and pattern, was fashioned into a headcovering. Most of the women, who seemed to be between the ages of sixteen and thirty-five, carried babies in cloth slings on their backs. Two women had big golf umbrellas with alternating panels of yellow, red, green and blue.

Outside the shelter, standing under a sky growing increasingly ominous, we greeted them. Continuous rolls of thunder filled the air with the rumble of a bowling tournament. Fat, heavy raindrops splashed down in warning. One umbrella went up. As the raindrops swelled in size and frequency, I crouched low in the shelter opening motioning Emmanuel and the women standing right beside him to come in. The second umbrella went up. The women nearest to us hesitated, looked up, and then ducked for cover as the sky opened. Several women with babies huddled together under the umbrellas. The rest squatted with their babies under the men's tarp. Emmanuel, four of the women and the four of us squished back into the shelter. Emmanuel reached up and pulled the edge of the tarp down over the opening of the shelter, enclosing us in an intimate blue space. Outside, the rain poured down as though a faucet had been turned on.

Inside the shelter nine adults squatting on their haunches jammed together in the tiny space. I lasted less than two minutes before my calves cramped. I wiggled further back into the brush at the rear of the shelter until I could kneel down without pushing against the women in front of and beside me.

Emmanuel began speaking. "I am still waiting for the High Commander to respond to me. He is a long way and he is busy with the war. Yesterday, did you hear the guns?"

The rain pounded on the tarp, louder than the explosions. I shivered. "Yes, we heard them."

"Tutsi soldiers came up shooting and killing to the area where these women live. Nearly fif-a-ty—fif-a-ty—people! Dead! Women and children! All murdered by the soldiers yesterday." That certainly explained the sounds of a gun battle. But, women and children killed? I shivered and wondered if it had been soldiers looking for us.

One way Hutu rebels, the Interahamwe, provide themselves with protection is to surround themselves with uninvolved civilians, including women and children, like human shields. Since the Rwandan army, made up of Tutsis, didn't distinguish between civilians and rebels, many civilians were killed during open battles. This not only increased the instability and chaos of the region, but also further alienated the general public from the Rwanda government.

Emmanuel told us the women with him were widows. Their husbands, sons, or brothers had all been killed within the past few months. He spoke briefly to each of the women in the shelter, then pointed to them in turn and translated their words. "This one, her husband is killed, one month. This one, three months. This woman, her family, four men, brother, husband, father. All killed." The women sat silently listening to Emmanuel speak though they wouldn't have understood what he was saying.

Directly in front of me, less than six inches away, were the heads of two babies cradled in their mothers' arms. I looked down on them as Emmanuel talked. One, about two months old, was busy nursing. The other, a six-month old, stretched a tiny hand out as though he was going to pat the two-month old on the head. With an almost imperceptible gesture the nursing mother signaled the other. In one fluid motion she adjusted her kanga and the older baby began to nurse. His tiny fingers rested softly on his mother's chest. The front of the women's t-shirts and blouses had been cut away over the breast area. By lowering the top cloth wrap a few inches the babies were able to nurse easily. The babies' eyes followed us while we spoke.

"This woman, she is the oldest." Emmanuel translated as the senior woman sitting in front of me near the front of the shelter spoke in a soft, flat, emotionless voice. "Her family has all been killed." She wiped her eyes with the palm of her hand. "Her house has been burned. She has no place to stay. All her household goods are stolen. She has no place to sleep or pots to cook her food. She sleeps in the forest so she will be safe from the soldiers."

She lifted her head and looked directly in my eyes. Tears pooled on her lower lashes and threatened to overflow. She reached up and ran the heel of her palm across her eyes again. "She asks you to help her get peace and security so she can have a home again." Her voice was very soft. It was only her hand wiping her eyes that showed how she felt. I didn't know if Emmanuel was telling the truth or not, but I believed the woman's tears. Sitting there she was *Everywoman* who had ever been caught powerless in a war. She was me.

Then she began to speak with vehemence about their lack of security. I caught the name Kagame several times. She told us the Vice-President and Defense Minister of Rwanda, Paul Kagame, was a very bad man. He was responsible for having the soldiers come and kill their families. Emmanuel explained that Kagame, one of the ethnic group he held responsible for the current wave of genocide, was in charge of security and the military for Rwanda. Because he was a Tutsi, their enemy, the Hutu could not appeal to him for protection. Like the woman, Emmanuel spoke with great passion. He certainly seemed to believe what he was saying, but I had no way of judging its accuracy. I decided the best strategy was being open and accepting.

I responded with passion, addressing only what the woman had said. "Emmanuel, this is terrible. These women shouldn't have to live like that. I don't know what my country can do to help. But I will tell them. There must be some way to get help for the women now, to buy them new household goods." I had seen a line of stalls in every village market filled with brightly colored plastic dishes: bowls, basins, cups, plates. The goods were available, but how could we get them to the women?

"These women are Hutu. Hutus cannot go to town. They will be beaten or put into jail. It does not matter if they have done nothing wrong. They are Hutu, which is enough." I nodded. It's like us going to see the gorillas, I thought. We haven't done anything wrong, but we were there. That's enough.

"How can we, from the western countries, help? When we get home, we can send money so they can buy what they need. Perhaps through an Aid agency or a church. Aren't there churches around that can help?"

"The churches cannot help. Many churches have been burned and the priests killed." He shrugged and shook his head to indicate there was no way we could get help for the women.

I asked him to translate for me. "My heart is sad for you. I, too, wish for peace, safety and security. When I am gone from here, I will not forget you." Emotions washed over me as I imagined them being attacked, raped, shot at, taken away from the safety of their homes and loved ones, and forced to live in bamboo shelters in the jungle. I understood; it had happened to me. We all wanted the same things. Though we weren't soldiers or involved in the fighting, we were horribly affected by the conflict. I couldn't help them any more than I could help myself. The overpowering emotions of loss, pain and fear had to be pushed away and hidden; only in numbness was it possible to keep going. All I could do was promise that when I was released I would tell my world about the women of the Rwandan forest.

I was relieved when the rain finally stopped and we could clamber out of the shelter. My legs tingled with pins and needles when I stood up and gingerly stretched. The air felt cool and fresh after being confined and jammed together in such a small space. The women who had been standing outside under the umbrellas and squatting under the men's tarp gathered around us talking softly to each other. The ones who had been outside appeared to be the youngest; all of them carried babies and toddlers in bright patterned back slings. The solemn faced children watched us soundlessly. I doubt they'd ever seen other white people, but they were obviously too young to be afraid. I smiled and crooned in a singsong tone to one of the older babies. He grabbed onto my finger and smile back.

"Emmanuel, I love children," I said. His mother lifted the baby over her shoulder out of the sling. He was about eight months old, dressed in a tattered t-shirt, his bare bottom and chubby round legs dangling as she handed him to me. I slid my arm under his bottom, saying a quick prayer that he wouldn't pee on my jacket. As I continued to talk to him, he wiggled his sturdy little body and let me hug him close. I smiled at his mother, who looked to be about eighteen years old. "Asante sana," I said. I couldn't imagine being her, a young widow with a baby and no support, facing a harsh life in a harsh country. I promised the women and myself that, even if I couldn't do anything soon, I would not forget them.

"We must go, Mama," Emmanuel said. I handed the baby to his mother and watched as Emmanuel led the women back into the forest. Once again we were alone. The clearing seemed stripped of life. But the vibration of the women's plight echoed in my heart. I didn't understand the politics in Rwanda. I wasn't sure who was good and who was bad. Emmanuel certainly was making an effort to show us how the women of the Rwandan forest were suffering. How could a person not be touched?

"We need to be careful. The Stockholm syndrome, you know," Jens said, referring to the attachment prisoners often develop toward their captors. I just looked at him. There's a big difference between empathy and brainwashing. I could be touched by the women without grabbing a machete and chopping people to death.

When the Commander in Chief came to camp that night he was carrying a plastic jug with him. "Ça va, Mama?" he called. He came over, picked up one of the pop bottles still propped against the shelter wall, rinsed it, and filled it with liquid from the jug. When he handed it to me, I looked at him and the liquid quizzically. It was slightly cloudy and colourless. The smell wasn't distinct, so I took a tiny sip. It was banana juice. I had no idea you could make juice from a banana. "Delicieux!" I told him. "Merci, beaucoup! Asante sana! Thank you very much!" He corrected my Swahili pronunciation again. I gave the bottle to Ann-Charlotte first, explaining that it was banana juice. We shared the juice equally, savoring the smooth, sweet taste.

When Richard began cooking supper we saw him push a few small, orange-skinned potatoes into the coals to bake. "Look, sweet potatoes!" After the sweet of the juice, the thought of a moist, orange yam or yellow sweet potato was exciting. Unfortunately, when the supper tin came, there was just the usual rice and potatoes.

Emmanuel returned again after dark. He was obviously upset. "I have been told that someone has ravished you!" My heart jumped. Who told him? I began shaking my head and motioning, no, with my hands. I hadn't said anything about what the men had done beyond warning Jens about the 'couchez' remark. If the others found out now it would make things worse. I was concerned about Ann-Charlotte. I didn't want her to have more to worry about.

Ignoring me, Emmanuel continued, "You have been ravished. Your belongings have been taken away. People have stolen your money. I will find out who has done this wrong thing and they will be made to return your things." When I realized he meant robbed when he said ravished I was so relieved I almost laughed. My hands dropped and I settled back sitting on the ground.

I knew it was essential that we all stay calm until we were free. I didn't want any problems to erupt about the things the men had taken. Whatever happened, we'd end up the losers caught in the middle. The only thing that mattered was getting back to Dan. I said to Emmanuel in my most conciliatory voice, "Jens and Doug still have their money. We aren't worried about the small amount of money we paid to buy food and water. We know the Rwandans aren't rich people. However, some of our things were taken away and we would like to get them back." Acknowledging that much seemed safe. I didn't mention that the man who had come and taken the cameras and watches appeared to be his superior.

Jens casually said, "If we had a camera, we could take pictures of the things we are seeing, like the women that came to visit us today. We would have powerful images to take back to our countries." I wanted to kick him. I figured he had some kind of strategy, but we weren't in any position to bargain or demand anything.

Emmanuel didn't take the bait. "I have no camera for you," he said. "We must wait for the Head Commander. While we are waiting I will return tomorrow with more information for you to take to your countries." Tomorrow. At least one more day. After Emmanuel left, Jens and I agreed there was little chance that we would actually see any of our things again. They had likely already been sold. The Rwandans were poor people.

After the rain, the sky stayed clear and the temperature dropped. Since we weren't going home, we needed to make some decisions about the shelter. Jens decided it would be wiser to leave the tarp on top of the shelter though that meant it wouldn't be available as a cover. As we were getting ready for bed, Doug whispered how upset he was that Jens and Ann-Charlotte were using more of the sleeping bag than their share. He felt like he was being 'left out in the cold', though when I tried to see how much the other two had covering them, it didn't seem they had any more than we did. The bag was just too small for four.

That night I tried to keep a grip on the sleeping bag holding it in place so Doug wasn't uncovered when Jens or Ann-Charlotte moved. My hips ached; I was the restless one. I couldn't stop thinking, if things had gone as planned, Dan and I would have been in the Kampala Sheraton. I could almost see the big king-sized bed with a soft blanket folded back. Maybe it would have a mosquito net draped in billowing folds from the ceiling like the princess bedroom we had in the Arusha hotel. I dreamed about that bed.

The morning of our sixth day passed as usual; after collecting the sleeping bag at dawn, the Commander in Chief told me that he was going to go speak with his commander. We waited, watching the sun rise and the clouds over the volcanoes burn off. Richard tuned his radio to a Sunday church service. Although I didn't recognize the words, it sounded close to the Latin High Mass I had attended as a child. A single voice chanted, sang and spoke in sonorous tones, with a choir singing responses and hymns, and everyone praying in unison. I couldn't see Richard from where I was sitting, but I could hear him. He was obviously familiar with the litany and hymns from when he was a child, but his voice had changed. Unable to reach the high soprano notes, he still tried, singing in an unselfconscious mix of screech and falsetto. I kept my hands pressed over my mouth and didn't look at the others. I didn't want to laugh out loud.

Around noon Emmanuel returned, bringing three copies of two recent, gestetnered newsletters written in English and French. The title was a single word in Kinya-rwanda. When I asked what it meant, Emmanuel said it was a word meaning *When will it ever end*? They were likely copies of the Interahamwe newspaper, *Umucunguzi*, printed to publicize the rebels' aims. Emmanuel waited while we read through the pages. Fortunately, even without my glasses, the sun was bright enough and the print clear enough that I could read most of it. On the covers were drawings of war scenes that Emmanuel explained were meant to represent Hutus victories in the war against the Rwandan government. One showed a plane with USA and letters for the Rwandan government painted on the side being shot down from the ground by hand-held mortars. I wondered if the drawing with the mortars and airplane was President Habyarimana's plane being shot down in 1994.

The English part of the paper contained diverse articles, translated repeats of what was printed in French. A woman's letter told of soldiers stealing her household goods and breaking or defecating in her cooking dishes. There was an article about how the Rwandan government had ignored and humiliated a UN delegation that was there to ensure war crimes and human rights violations were dealt with properly. Another article written by the People for the Liberation of Rwanda (PALIR) listed twelve points related to issues of security, democracy and equality before the law. I said, "These are the points you made when you talked to us yesterday. Are you this group, the PALIR?"

"Yes! That is us! The PALIR. This is what you must take out to the world. These are our demands." Finally we knew who had captured us and what they wanted. It had taken six days.

The PALIR, People in Arms to Liberate Rwanda, came to the attention of the international community two years earlier in July 1996. The PALIR was made up of ex-FAR Hutu soldiers from the Rwandan army and the Interahamwe. Their goals were to overthrow the Tutsi-led Rwandan government and set up a government controlled by the Hutu. In its first 1996 tract, published in Nairobi, Kenya, the PALIR promised to reward anyone who killed Americans working in Rwanda to help with the country's recovery from genocide.

Obviously the information in the newsletter was important to Emmanuel, so it became important to me. "We will each take one copy to our countries. There are many people there who can read and write in French. They will help translate the French sections so we can understand them completely, too." I looked at my fanny pack and decided I shouldn't jam my copy in there. "Doug," I said, "you have the most room in your pack. Would you take the papers so they won't get tattered?" He nodded and slipped them in his pack.

Emmanuel smiled. "Tomorrow the Head Commander will come to talk with you. Once he has spoken with you, you will be taken to see with your own eyes where the houses are burned. After that," he said, "you will be released."

It was hard not to roll my eyes. I'd been hearing that same line for six days and I was still on the mountain. Jens suggested again that our cameras would be a great way for us to take images back to our countries. Emmanuel replied in a small, distracted voice that he didn't have any cameras for us. I figured he'd discovered the men above him had taken them. He didn't mention being ravished or returning our things.

After he left there was another outbreak of gunfire and explosions—grenades or perhaps mortars. The sounds seemed close, but not as close as the first gunfire. I thought about all the women and babies who had come to the clearing. Emmanuel's voice echoed in my head. "Women and children! All murdered by the soldiers yesterday." I shuddered. None of us said anything during the gunfire. Isolated in my thoughts, I waited, watching for men with guns to come bursting into the clearing.

About 4:00 p.m., the Commander in Chief strode back in camp. After his usual greeting, he announced, "We are moving to another camp. This camp is too old."

At his direction, the men sprang into action folding and tying tarps in bundles, retrieving the sleeping bags and other belongings from the bushes, gathering pots and dishes. It took less than five minutes for the camp to be dismantled.

Reluctantly we emptied our shelter. From the edge where they had lain forgotten for three days, Jens pulled out the plastic bag of fried bread rounds. Dozens of little black ants swarmed over his fingers from the bag which was now peppered with chewed holes. Doug and I flicked the ants off the bread with our fingers. After Jens shook the bag to free any hiding ants we put the bread back in the bag. The others slipped on their packs and we head out of the clearing in a line interspersed among the men. Doug brought his walking stick. "It's really too heavy," he said, "but I want to keep it." Anxious about how far we had to walk, I placed myself in front of Doug and behind Jens with a request that he try not to go too fast.

Feelings of relief alternated with dismay as we headed higher up the mountain into the pass; we were going away from the gunshots, but away from Kisoro, too. There was bamboo everywhere. High stalks poked out of the canopy of green, looking like topiary trees or an Alice in Wonderland garden. As before, I could see nothing but the person in front, the path and the bamboo. I was alert, listening in case we ran into soldiers with guns.

We didn't walk very fast or very far. In what seemed like a random place, the men stopped and some of them bushwhacked up through the bamboo on the left side of the path. Though I couldn't see anything, I could hear their machetes slashing and chopping above us. A few minutes later we were herded up through the bamboo thicket. We emerged in the middle of a new clearing and were left with only Richard and Oscar to guard us. At Jens' suggestion we sat down and waited.

After talking for a few minutes, Richard and Oscar began to chop bamboo poles and construct a shelter similar to the one we had been using. "Just wait," Jens said. "Let them do it." We sat and watched. When they had the frame up and bamboo foliage over the sides and top, curiosity got the better of us. One close look was enough to show us the shelter wasn't right. The uprights were too high and the ground dropped down at the back and left side of the shelter.

"This isn't going to work the way it is," Jens said. He took his knife and began to saw off the uprights. "We have to cut off the back two supports and slope the roof."

"Bloody hell," Doug said to me as Jens was working. "Just who does he think he is giving orders?" Doug's growing irritation with Jens was obvious. "Cutting it down won't help. It's on a bloody slope. We have to build up the back corner or we'll be sleeping with our head downhill and to the side." Doug began cutting bamboo leaves to pack down on the floor. "I know who will be the one in the worst place," he said. "It won't be him."

Although Doug and I managed to get the floor a bit more level, we realized that because of the slope we would have to lie sideways in the shelter. Jens volunteered to sleep at the open front edge because he had the most weather-proof clothing. With Ann-Charlotte and me in the middle, that left Doug on the lowest part of the slope at the back. We used the tarp to line the top and back of the shelter, leaving the front and half the floor uncovered. As we worked, I could see the tension between Doug and Jens.

On the other side of the clearing, Richard began to prepare supper. "Couteau," he said to Doug, holding out his hand for the knife so he could peel potatoes.

"I think I'll give him the knife when we leave," Doug commented as we watched Richard begin to peel a big bag of potatoes, "but not until then."

The new clearing was ringed with a thick, lush matt of green bamboo stalks from eight to twenty feet high, but no dead bamboo. As a pile of potato peels mounted in front of Richard, Oscar left to hunt for bamboo to burn. When he and another young man pushed back through the brush balancing huge bundles of gray, dry, dead bamboo on their heads, a picture flashed in my head of all the women walking on the roadside carrying bundles of bamboo that I'd driven past. I think that was the first time I realized how far those women had to walk carrying heavy bundles from the distant mountains down dusty roads and winding trails so they could cook their food at home.

The Commander in Chief came back a short while later and came over to see us. "Ça va, Mama?"

"Ça va, bien. Merci." I was a pleasantly surprised when he handed me another pop bottle filled with murky liquid, slightly cloudier and thicker looking than the banana juice. Cautiously I smelled it—yeast. The taste was a curious mix of sweet banana and new fermentation. We named it banana beer. I'm sure each of us could have drunk the whole bottle though we shared it fairly equally. I tried to get Ann-Charlotte to drink a bit more because she was eating so little.

By this time it had been dark for quite a while. The Commander in Chief came over and told me he was sorry that dinner was so late. I knew Richard and Oscar had been busy making the shelter and cutting wood. I replied, "Pas de problem, mon ami." The Commander in Chief went back to the cooking area where he and the other men were also drinking banana beer.

Our dinner arrived shortly after. Rice and sweet potatoes. There was no escaping the fact that we were not only being closely watched but listened to as well. The milk, beer and sweet potato proved it. Someone had noticed my reaction to the sweet potatoes being put in the coals the day before and made sure we got some today. Rather than being upset by their scrutiny, I was touched. It seemed, in their own way, they were trying to make up to us for our loss of freedom, searching for some way to please us and show us they weren't bad or dangerous people. Banana beer *and* sweet potato; two treats in one day. "Merci. Asante sana."

The potatoes were a warm brown contrast to the white rice. Unfortunately they didn't taste the way they looked. I cut through the brown skin with my spoon, anticipating the moist, deep yellow-orange flesh of our yams. The flesh under the brown skin was white with a mealy, desiccated texture. I don't know which was worse, my disappointment or the taste. However, they had given me a gift and didn't deserve to be insulted because it wasn't what I had expected. I was determined to eat everything I'd been given. I managed to swallow the last mouthful of sweet potato and rinsed my mouth with water. Unfortunately the others weren't able to eat theirs and soon I called out, "Nous sommes fini. We're finished. Merci, ça suffit. Thanks, that's enough."

As the men waited for their food to cook, we sat talking quietly. Jens said, "They're obviously watching and listening to us very carefully. I want them to overhear us again discussing who we'll talk to when we were released and how we'll let the world know about the Rwandan problems."

Suddenly, the Commander in Chief strode over and squatted down directly in front of me. He was visibly upset and angry. "Demandez à les autres ... *Ask the others...*," he began firing questions at me, pointing to the other three. Why I was the only one who was friendly and talked to them? Why I was the only one who ate the food? Why weren't the others like me? Flabbergasted, I sat with my mouth open. I'd been living my decision to make each day the best that I could. I'd been making choices about how to act and interact that made life more pleasant; I ignored the things over which I had no control. I didn't want what I did to be seen as 'me against them' or that I was better than they were. I hadn't meant to make myself different.

I started to explain, but the Commander in Chief cut me off. He pointed again to the others. "Demandez à les autres ... . *Ask the others...*"

I turned my body slightly and looked back at them over my shoulder. "He's upset because you're not acting happy or eating all your food." I knew Jens had studied French in school, though I wasn't sure how fluent he was as he'd never said anything in French. I hoped he understood enough of what the Commander in Chief and I were saying and would consider how he could make relations between our captors and us smoother. Although the other three didn't respond, the Commander in Chief seemed willing to listen as I tried to explain. Without worrying about my grammar or using the exact French words I talked about our differences. "I am the only one who can speak with you. These two, Doug and Ann-Charlotte don't speak any French. I've been in Africa before. This time I've been here for five weeks. These two, Jens and Ann-Charlotte, have been here only three days before they came to see the gorillas. I am a different personality. The others are quieter, shyer." What I couldn't say was, You captured us with guns and brought us here under force—don't expect us to act happy about it. I didn't want the Commander in Chief to blame anyone for what they were feeling.

When I stopped, he began to speak again, his voice cracking with emotion. "I am not a bad man," he told me. "I have no more family. My family is all dead. My wife is murdered. My child is murdered. My child is murdered. My child is murdered. My child is murdered. I had four children. All are dead. Murdered."

I felt the force of his voice in my chest. I closed my eyes against the image his words evoked. He was my jailer and I was filled with compassion for him. I put my hand on his arm and told him how sorry I was, how my heart ached for him. He dropped his eyes, turned away, and walked back to sit at the cook fire. I watched him in the firelight, then explained to the others what he had said. "His family was all killed. He had four children. It upsets him that we aren't all acting happy." It sounded bizarre. Have compassion for your enemy? Pretend that this is a camping picnic? I knew part of the reason he'd come to speak to us was the banana beer.

We spread the sleeping bag out and settled down to try and sleep.

Still waiting for their food, the men set up their tarps for the night, one suspended from poles and the other one on the ground under it. As they finally began to eat, the sky exploded. Unseen in the darkness, a wild storm had advanced directly over us. The first blast of wind sent the men, food in hand, scurrying under the suspended tarp.

Simultaneously the skies opened and the air turned to water extinguishing both fires almost immediately; it was pitch black. We hauled the sleeping bag in and squeezed as far back from the open front as possible. I could feel the others tugging and pulling on the tarp and sleeping bag in a futile attempt to keep dry, but saw nothing. Within seconds the lashing rain and a stream of water flowing over the ground settled in pools in the low loop of the tarp soaking the sleeping bag and us. Torrents of water ran into the shelter. Rather than a shelter, the lean-to had become a funnel for the rain-water, directed right at us.

As the tropical downpour advanced over us, the wind whipped every-thing in powerful gusts. In a series of brilliant white lightning flashes I saw the men's tarp balloon into a giant, blue parachute, rip loose from its lash-ings and dance in the air, flapping violently. Flash! Boom! Thunder fol-lowed hand-in-hand with the lightning. The men raced to grab the tarp and resecure the corners to the posts. Flash! Boom! Our ears vibrated with the volume and the hair lifted on our arms and the back of our necks. In the strobe-like, continuous, white light flashes we watched the men struggle to deal with the blasts of wind, the waterfall of rain and their dinners. Flash! Boom! The Commander in Chief was standing in front of us like an appa-rition. He stared at us, four white faces peeking out from under hats and hoods, eight white hands clutching the edge of the tarp pulled up high under our noses. Flash! Boom! He was gone.

Eventually, the front passed and the wind and lightning stopped, though the heavy rain continued through most of the night. We lay like ducks in a row covered with the wet bag. Jens lay in the opening and Doug at the back. It was a toss-up who was wetter. Jens kept the front of the bag pulled down to the ground and that kept him warm, if not dry. Doug lay behind me, at the back where the tarp curved from the back wall onto the ground. Trickles of water ran down the tarp under my body until they reached the back where they gathered in a growing pool where Doug was lying. I kept kicking at the bottom side edge of the tarp trying to push it down so the pooling water would drain away. With my top hand I gripped the sodden bag and reached back over Doug's body, holding it at least partly over Doug's back. There was no way any of us could sleep. Some-time in the blackhole of night Jens gave the bag a big tug and ripped it out of my hand. "Bloody hell!" Doug yelled. "You've got all the cover."

"No, I haven't. I have no cover." Jens yelled back.

There was a moment of silence broken only by the sounds of rain drum-ming the ground and tapping rapidly on the tarp above us as it dropped through the bamboo roof. Something had happened, but what? We could see nothing. The bag couldn't have shrunk. "The bag's turned sideways," I said. It was the only possibility. I could hear Jens moving around and tug-ging on the bag.

"Yes," he said in a calm, rational voice. "The bag got turned." We repositioned it, pulled it down over our bodies and rested.

That was the hardest night. Although my back and hips weren't aching as much, I had developed sharp needle-like pains that would suddenly shoot down my legs. If I lay just right, I was fine for a few minutes, but the slightest shift and the pain was back. Moving as slowly as I could, I pulled my fanny pack out from under my head, fished in it for the film canister, pried the top off and swallowed my last two aspirins. We lay and waited for dawn.

NINE

The morning air was cool, and mist, heavy with moisture, hung low over the trees. As soon as we were up, the men lighted our fire. It was the first time we'd had a fire during the day. We stood close to the flames and rotated slowly as steam rose from our drying clothes. Later, when the sun broke through the overhead mist, clouds of water vapor rose from everything. We hung the open sleeping bag on the shelter in the sun so the air could get at both sides and hopefully dry it before night.

Everything in my fanny pack, which I had been using as a pillow, was also soaked. The water had stuck the layers of my folded flight schedule together. I held it in front of the fire, opening it carefully as the paper dried. Though the ink had run and stained the front in a checkerboard of lines, it was readable. Entebbe—London / Gatwick AWYS 2066M 17 AUG 98 1030P 455A OK. OK? Not OK. Dan and I were supposed to fly home today. I was sure Dan was still waiting in Kisoro.

When my fanny pack and the paper were dry, I carefully slipped the folded schedule back into my fanny pack. I went over and stood by Doug, resting my head on his shoulder. "Oh, Doug! Today is our going-home-day."

He patted my back. "Now don't get too upset." As he patted me, I realized how melodramatic I was being. Since my capture I'd been pretending that everything that happened was ordinary and normal. I had been trying to act as calm and in control as I do at school when everything falls apart and it's my job to put it back together. I was getting tired, though. What I wanted was someone strong to put their arms around me so I could suck some strength into me. But no one else had any more strength than I did. The strong person I was looking for had to be me.

The Commander in Chief came over as usual and asked me, "Ça va, Mama?"

"Ça va ... mais ... " I told him I was fine, but my hips were very sore and I didn't know how many more days I would be able to sleep on the ground. After our encounter the night before, I decided to play on his sympathy a little. I was being truthful about my sore hips, but exaggerating how debilitating they were becoming. I explained that I was afraid that I wouldn't be able to walk out when it was time for me to go home. He answered that he had to go talk with his commander and went off down the mountain.

Around 9:30 a.m., a smiling, excited Emmanuel arrived. "Good morning, good morning," he said coming over to stand close to the fire with us. "The Head Commander is too busy come," he began. Before my heart had time to drop all the way to my feet, he continued. "The assistant to the Head Commander has arrived. He wants to talk to one man, and that man is you, Mama." My heart gave a jump. I was instantly energized. If only one person was able to go, I was glad it would be me. After waiting six days for something to happen, I wouldn't have to wait any longer. Emmanuel looked so happy about his news that I was sure nothing bad would happen to me.

"How long will it take you to be ready?" he said.

"I have nothing to get ready. I *am* ready. Now."

Emmanuel looked at the others. "We will be gone about one hour and a half. Then you will come join us. Your guides will take you out of the jungle and you will be released."

"Emmanuel," I reminded him, "when we're released, we need to go to Kisoro." He didn't answer.

I shoved my water bottle in my pocket and followed Emmanuel as he pushed down through the brush and bamboo to a trail. As we loped down the slopes he explained over his shoulder that he was taking me to see where the soldiers had come and burned all their houses. "When you see them," he said, "you will know what I have told you was true."

We hurried downhill for about thirty minutes before we reached the edge of the forest and broke out into the open. "This is my village," Emmanuel said. "I will show you the houses and what the soldiers have done."

The widely spread, rural African villages bear no resemblance to North American towns. In the poorer rural areas like this, small houses surrounded by large, dusty, dirt yards are scattered sparsely over the hillside. Each house consists of one room, one door and one small, unglazed, shuttered window. Built of mud bricks or mud plaster over a wooden lath frame, the house is used primarily for sleeping and storing the family's belongings. Although many houses have a firepit on the dirt floor inside, the cooking fires are outside in the yard or in tiny lean-tos adjacent to the house. Food is cooked over an open wood or bamboo fire in pots supported by three stones. Where charcoal is available, braziers are sometimes used. Most of the basic food, like corn, beans, vegetables and grains, is home grown, though their garden plots may be some distance from the house.

I looked across the mountain slope at Emmanuel's village. Although I knew I was in Rwanda, the cultivated area below us looked identical to the terraced fields and houses in Uganda around Kisoro. In fact, where I was standing was less than ten miles from Kisoro.

I followed Emmanuel along a well-packed, narrow, dirt trail undulating across the hillside. At regular intervals we passed young men with guns posted along the trail as lookouts, standing guard on the hillside in case soldiers came up the slopes. In the distance, as far as I could see, tiny houses dotted the grassy hillside and spread far down the steep mountain slope.

In a little over a kilometer, I saw twenty-five buildings with varying degrees of damage. Many of the burned houses lining the path were reduced to charred wooden post stubs. Some were less badly burned; one was roofless, one had two standing walls, and several with corrugated tin roofs had huge holes in the wall or sections that were being repaired. Through gaps in the wall of some of the more intact houses, I could see women and men inside gathered around fires while children stood or played outside.

Pointing down the mountain at the roof of one house, Emmanuel said, "Ten people in that house were all murdered one night by the soldiers. From that time no one sleeps in any of the houses you can see down there. All the people live near the edge of the forest. They come out during the day to work, to cook their food and to do small chores. Each night they gather their belongings and go back into the forest for safety. They sleep there with no houses or proper shelters so they will be safe from the soldiers." I imagined hundreds of women and children in the forest last night while it rained, huddled under tarps or nothing, waiting for morning and the end of the deluge.

The path ended at a small cluster of buildings around an open courtyard. Emmanuel pointed to two men seated a short distance away on a bench in the courtyard. "These men are my Commander, my boss, and the Head Commander's assistant." OK, I thought. Let's get this meeting done and get going home. I took a deep breath and stepped toward them. "Not yet," Emmanuel said stopping me. "First, I want to show you more."

I cast a regretful look back over my shoulder as Emmanuel lead me across the courtyard away from the Commanders toward another group of men who were standing watching us. He asked if I remembered the three ethnic groups who lived in Rwanda. I was a good student. I responded: Tutsi, Hutu, and Twa or pygmy. He pointed to one man who was quite different in appearance from the rest of the group, shorter, less than five feet tall, broad, with a deeply wrinkled face. Slung over his back was a bow and arrows. "This man, he is a Twa." I didn't ask if any of the rest were Tutsis.

A voice called from behind me. "Mama!" Pascal appeared with a wide, bright smile. "Mama, I am pleased to see you today. I was not able to come to see you yesterday. It was Sunday. The priest was here and I went to Mass.

"My mother and father are here, too. I have told them of you and they would like to meet you. Please come with me this way so you can meet them." I didn't look at Emmanuel standing beside me. I was unsure of the hierarchy among the men, but was reasonable positive Pascal was not one of the leaders. I was curious about his family and would have been interested to meet them, but my sole aim was to follow directions and get out of there as fast as possible. This was not the time to wander off and go visiting.

"Thank you, Pascal, for your kind offer. I am honoured your parents would like to meet me. But, I must go with Emmanuel. Please take my greetings to your parents." I did a lot of head bobbing and smiling as I spoke.

"Our priest is here." Pascal said, looking past me over my shoulder. "I would like you to meet him." I turned and faced a slim, thin-faced man dressed in the same dark worn clothing as the other men. If I accepted the stereotype of Tutsis being thin and finer featured than Hutus, I'd have pegged the man as a Tutsi. Though he had no outward symbols of his vocation, I accepted he was a priest. "He was here to say Mass," Pascal explained.

Suddenly I was nine years old, standing on the steps of the church, looking up at the priest. As I had been prompted so long ago by the nuns, I greeted him, "Bonjour, mon Père," and extended my hand. I thought fleetingly of kneeling down and asking for his blessing, but that would have been overboard, even for Africa.

During the genocide, many members of the various religious communities throughout Rwanda took an active part in the killings. Rwandan Tutsis, who gathered at churches hoping they would be protected, had found themselves corralled into easily accessible groups for the *génocidaires* who systematically murdered all who had sought refuge. Given that he was high in the mountains among the Hutu militia, I wondered what role this priest had played in the genocide.

Pascal exclaimed, "Ah, you are a Catholic!" The priest looked at me intently. Without saying anything, he reached out and shook my hand. I nodded my head in return.

"Come," Emmanuel said. I glanced at the priest again, then turned and continued at a slow stroll down the path past more burned houses. I recognized two of the women who had come to our shelter working in the dirt yards beside their houses. I felt a burst of excitement seeing someone I recognized. My face lit up, split with a big smile.

"Hello. Habari?" I called, waving. They smiled back, seeming pleased that I recognized them. Outside another house we passed three women kneeling on the ground in front of flat blocks of rock. Methodically, they were grinding sorghum into flour by pushing a grinding stone back and forth in a deep groove worn in the base block. Without stopping, they looked up and watched as we passed.

The path skirted a small grassy knoll where three or four people had spread small tarps on the ground. On the tarps they had set up displays of small plastic bags of rice and beans, a few bottles of something liquid and packages of deep orange cooking fat. In the middle of one tarp was an elaborate, old, brass balance beam scale set. "This is our market. It is not big. Many people cannot go to town to shop. These things are brought here for them to buy."

"Is this where Pascal came to get our food?"

"Yes."

Close by, a group of men squatted on the ground around an anvil, trying to mend an old gun with primitive woodworking tools, a few screwdrivers and hammers. "These men fix our guns," Emmanuel said. "We do not have many new guns. Most of our guns are old and they are hard to keep working." Although I had seen a few semi-automatic guns that I learned were AK-47s or Kalashnikovs, most of the guns looked well used and often had wire or tape around the stocks.

The path dead-ended at a rocky outcrop where Emmanuel said the women gathered to do the laundry. The face of the outcrop was a six foot jumble of stacked boulders. "There is nothing to see there," Emmanuel said. "You don't have to climb up."

I looked at the rock face and the grass hanging over the top edge. In a flash of stubbornness, I thought, If the African women can climb up there in bare feet, I can make it. The rock face had numerous flat steps and hand holds. I scrambled up without difficulty and stood gazing over the hazy scene below me. It was impossible to imagine the social upheaval that had taken place in that beautiful, pastoral setting. The idyllic Noble Savage living-at-one-with-nature seemed more appropriate than hate-crazed men chopping women and babies with machetes. As I climb down from the outcrop, Emmanuel asked, "What will you say when people ask you about this?"

I paused. Here we go again! Indoctrination session twenty. I knew what I had to say about peace and security and helping the Hutu cause. But I had met the women face-to-face in my shelter. As terrible as my capture had been, I could go home. I was going home. Today. The Rwandan women had to stay here.

I answered Emmanuel, speaking with my heart. "I will say, 'I am just one person. I have been away only one week. My story is not important. The real story is about the women of the Rwandan forest. They live there. I am the voice of the women. *They have killed my husband. They have killed my children ...* '" I will speak for the women—they are me and I am them."

"Good."

We gradually worked our way back to the group of buildings where the Commanders were sitting. Before taking me over to them, Emmanuel explained, "There are some papers we want you to take back. I have given you three copies of everything so each of your countries would get one. As well, the Assistant to the Head Commander will give you some papers and two of the newest copies of our newsletter."

With Emmanuel standing slightly behind me, I walked over to the Commanders and bowed. In my most formal French I greeted them with a sentence I'd learned in Ottawa twenty years earlier during a French conversation class. "Je suis enchanté de faire votre connaisance." *I am pleased to make your acquaintance.* I wasn't sure if they would think I was being cheeky, but I was certain I'd never use that greeting for a more important event than this. They didn't say anything, just stared at me. After a minute, one of them handed me the papers. Even without my reading glasses I could see that the typewritten sheets were written in French.

"Do you understand what they say?" Emmanuel asked. I squinted and studied them carefully. In the bright sunlight I could see that the main sheet was a repeat of the twelve points from the PALIR that had been in the newsletter. The second sheet was a French version of the English article I'd read about the UN being treated badly by the Rwandan government. The third was a letter asking us, or our countries, to help spread this information.

"Yes. These are the things you want—peace, security and an equal role in governing your country. These are the same as in the newsletter. They are from your group, the PALIR." Emmanuel nodded and seemed satisfied that I understood.

"When I am in Canada, I will get all the French translated."

"Who will you give this information to?"

"We have talked often about how we can help you. When we are back in our countries we will tell the newspapers and talk to the men in our government." I repeated the list we had devised. I carefully rolled the papers and slid them sideways into my fanny pack next to my itinerary.

"Come," Emmanuel said. Finally we're going to get the others, I thought. As we retraced our route, everyone we passed, including more of the women who had come up to the clearing, stopped and stared. Among the people were two young boys less than ten years old who had been wounded. One had his calf wrapped with a dirty bandage wet with pus and suppurating fluids. Emmanuel said he had been shot. He said another boy with a bandage on his cheek and a red, angry, scabbed wound on his upper lip had been cut by a soldier with a knife.

"Look, look there. See that man. See that woman. They are not soldiers. That one has a gun, but he is not a soldier. He is a guard to keep everyone safe when the soldiers come. He will not attack anyone."

A line of ten women with babies and a handful of children and teenagers wound past us. Everyone, no matter how young, was carrying something balanced on their head, giant bundles of household goods—pots, rolled mattresses and blankets. "These people have left their homes in the villages at the bottom of the mountain because they are afraid. They are coming here to join our group so they can hide in the forest and be safe." I rubbed my underarms remembering being pulled and lifted up the steep slopes. I might be able to climb onto the little knoll, but I'd never be able to even lift one of their bundles leave alone haul it up the mountain on my head.

On another nearby grassy knoll, scattered groups of men were sitting close to an older woman with a large jerry can. Emmanuel pointed at the woman. "This woman makes beer from sorghum and sells it here. The men come to drink and she earns money. Would you like some sorghum beer?" I was surprised at the suggestion. Although we had been walking slowly, I thought we were headed directly to the forest to get the others. Obviously Emmanuel had other plans.

Intrigued because I'd likely never get another chance to taste sorghum beer, I was none the less wary. The banana beer had been wonderful, but the sweet potato was a disaster. "I'll try a little bit," I said. I held my fingers about two centimeters apart to show what 'a little bit' meant. The old woman picked a battered enameled cup from a pile at her feet, slowly tipped the jerry can and filled the cup to the brim. Emmanuel handed it to me and motioned that I should sit.

Another line of women filed past, singing softly. The sweet, rich harmony floated through the air. "That is so beautiful. What are they singing, Emmanuel?"

"Hymns. When we are sad and everything seems impossible, we sing hymns to God." I watched them disappear down the path to the forest, their music hanging in the air after they could no longer be seen.

Emmanuel left a few minutes later, but I wasn't alone for long. A man dressed in slacks and a golf shirt sat down. He was lean and muscled, somewhere in his mid thirties. There was no softness about him. A prominent vein on the right side of his forehead pulsed as he talked. When he greeted me in English, I realized that he was the man who had taken our cameras and the men's watches. I shivered as though a cloud had passed in front of the sun and a chill wind slid down my spine. Everything around me faded and I focused on him. His name was Steve. He was an Interahamwe soldier.

"One time I went to University and studied languages and mathematics." I complimented him on his English, which was excellent. He took a small coil bound notebook out of his breast pocket and leafed through the pages. "In this book I have written many things that I must remember. You see here," he said showing me a page. "You cannot have a rose without the thorns. You cannot make an omelet without breaking an egg. " I nodded, hiding my bewilderment about why he had recorded such trite sayings and why he thought they were so profound. Then it struck me that the sayings were his way of justifying the violence in which he was involved; the end justifies the means.

He asked what I'd studied in University and then wrote a mathematical sign from calculus or trigonometry in his book questioning if I knew what the sign meant. I shook my head. "Oh, my friend, I went to university, but I only learned how to teach arithmetic to young children, not how to do difficult math like you are able to do."

"Write your name and address for me in my book." He handed me a stubby pencil and his notebook. As I wrote, I thought to myself, In about five years I'll start getting letters from all these people I've given my address to, asking me for something—money, help to build a house, sponsorship to Canada.

Steve talked about the problems in Rwanda. His tone was strident and his anti-Americanism evident as he spoke. "The United States is the enemy of the Hutu. They are working with the Rwandan government, influencing them against the Hutu.

"The President, Mr. Bill Clinton is a bad man," Steve said. As our safari group traveled around Uganda, we had seen several billboards erected in places where President Clinton had taken part in official functions during his visit to the area earlier that year. Almost spitting his words, Steve told me, "President Clinton is a womanizer. He procured white women for the President of Congo. When Clinton came to Congo, he was given black women for his sexual tastes. I know this because one of my family saw it happen and he knew the women. The United States is run by a pimp and fornicator." He showed me where he had this written in his notebook and made me promise not to forget it. When I later read about Monica Lewinsky, his words seemed prophetic.

A second English speaking man, wearing a red and black crocheted hat like Richard's, sat down with Steve and me. He had a wide gap between his front teeth and was quite homely, unlike most of the Hutu men I had met. I didn't think I'd met him before. He asked about my family. "I have a son twenty-seven. He has one son who is eight."

"I am twenty-seven, too," he said. "Do you have only one child?"

"I have a daughter who is twenty-five."

"Is she married?"

"No."

"Would you let her marry me?"

Not bloody likely. "My daughter is still going to school," I explained politely and patiently. "She won't marry anyone until she's finished. Then, she will have to be the one who decides. In my country we don't tell our children whom to marry." I was back in my 'tell the truth but don't make waves' mode.

"Why do women in your country have so few children? You have so much money and could afford to have big families," Steve said. "My mother had seven children and all her children honor her and take care of her."

I tried for a few minutes to explain about Canadian families, but quickly gave up, unable to explain how I felt about the population explosion, overuse of resources and conspicuous consumption. Given that I had enough discretionary money to fly around the world to see a wild animal, nothing I said would seem legitimate. "It's a different culture." I knew he didn't understand me any better than I understood him.

I sipped slowly on the sorghum beer as we talked; the two men each drank several large bowls of beer. "Why are you drinking beer?" Steve asked. "White women don't drink beer, they drink Fanta."

"Ah," I said, "When you get to be my age, you drink whatever you want. I have been drinking beer for a very long time. At home I drink beer with my husband every day. I wouldn't usually have an opportunity to taste the sorghum beer. It's very special." I got a sense that, although we both spoke English, words were inadequate to explain our different cultures.

Emmanuel reappeared and stood looking down at me. "Now we can go," he said.

Obviously he'd been talking with someone and waiting for them to OK us leaving. I jumped up, eager to go immediately. I was so glad to be going I wanted to do something in thanks for being free. I looked down and noticed the guardian angel pin on my fanny pack. "Emmanuel, would it be appropriate for me to offer my guardian angel pin to these men?" I asked.

"No." From his face and glum demeanor it was obvious that it was not a good idea.

"OK. I won't."

I said good-bye to the other two men and left with Emmanuel. He led me on a leisurely stroll back toward the edge of the forest. He seemed withdrawn and uncommunicative in contrast to the relaxed friendly way he'd been earlier. I was puzzled about the change in his mood.

"We must go up to get the others," Emmanuel told me as we walked. I cringed at the prospect of having to climb back up the hill. It had taken half an hour at a steady, fast trot to get down the mountain. Though I had no watch, I was aware that I had been on my tour of the village for a long time. The others would be waiting impatiently.

"Emmanuel. It's hard for me to go up the hill. I'll take a long time. Perhaps I could wait here and someone else could go up and bring them down?"

"That won't be possible." His tone said the matter was closed.

As we neared the forest a motley group of armed men carrying a man on a homemade bamboo stretcher passed us. The injured man, who had a bandage on his thigh, raised himself on one elbow as they went by to get a better look at me. Emmanuel took no notice of them nor gave me any indication of who they were or why the man was being carried. I decided he'd been shot. I was glad they were going in the opposite direction. They didn't look like the kind of men I'd have wanted to meet alone on the mountain path. They frightened me.

At the edge of the forest, the Commander in Chief and a group of young men joined us. "I must go now," Emmanuel said. "These men will take care of you." He turned and, without a backward look, disappeared back toward the village.

I followed the Commander in Chief a short distance to a large clearing in the forest. I was psyching myself up for the walk uphill when the Commander in Chief said, "Restez ici. Stay here. Asseyez-vous. Sit down." A huge weight lifted off my shoulders. I didn't have to go back up the hill.

"Thank you, mon ami. Merci beaucoup." He sent one of his men up to get the others.

I settled myself on a slight rise along the edge of the clearing which seemed to be the grassy bottom of a dry seasonal waterhole. The lush, green grass grew in an irregular donut shape around a central clump of bamboo and brush. The sun, still high in the sky shone through the thin surrounding foliage and cast a dappled, dancing pattern of light on everything. The only thing missing was the trill of a songbird. I realized suddenly that I hadn't heard any birds at all during our week in the jungle.

It seemed only a minute until Doug, Jens and Ann-Charlotte appeared. "What happened?" Jens asked. "You were gone so long."

"What time is it?"

"Just past 2:30."

"It's a long story. It took a lot longer than I expected for whoever was in charge to say we could go. I had to wait." As we were talking, Brother *Something* appeared. This was the first time I'd seen him since the day we were captured.

He spoke quickly in French. I didn't understand everything. "I think he said we're going to go out in a line with spaces between us."

"No," Jens said, "he said we'll go out one at a time with about twenty minutes between us. It's something to do with security." I was surprised. Jens had never indicated he understood French that well.

Then I realized that meant we would be separated. "Would it be OK if I go first?" I asked. "I always get out of breath, and I'm the slowest." Brother *Something* must have understood what I said to them because he asked if I had asthma. I recognized the word in French and said, "Yes. Oui. Asthme." There was no problem. I went first.

Brother *Something* said we would all be searched, one at a time. I didn't understand why; we had already been searched several times. Brother *Something* had me taken around the bamboo island out of the others' sight. With him watching, they had me open a small pocket on the breast of my jacket where I had a plastic squeeze bottle of Deet mosquito repellant and 50 USh. The day before, in the new clearing, I had seen a mosquito. With nothing else to do, I'd taken the bottle out and put on some Deet before offering it to the others. Someone had obviously been watching. It was the first time they realized it was a pocket not a decoration. A man checked all my other pockets and my fanny pack. He motioned me to raise my arms and began thoroughly patting down my middle and lower body, back, front and all sides of my legs. I had nothing on under my trousers for him to find. He straightened up. I held my breath, waiting for him to start patting my upper body. Fuck. When he finds Doug's money in my bra they'll think I lied about not having any money. He turned away, not checking that area at all, perhaps because African women don't wear bras. So I kept Doug's $100 US tucked safely away.

As I was zipping my pockets back up, they brought Doug around and began rifling through his backpack. Having finished with me, the men took me back to the others. With a few rapid sentences in Kinya-rwanda, the Commander in Chief appointed two men I didn't recognize to go with me. In my head I named the first man The Man With The Gun, and the other, a young man who walked behind me and carried my water bottle, the Young Guide. As we got ready to go, the Commander in Chief told Jens to give me some of the fried bread that he was still carrying in the tattered hole-filled turquoise bag. I put one round into my pocket. Bread and water. I was set.

As I left there was a lot of commotion in the clearing; men were milling around, calling to one another. I don't know if I said anything to Doug, Anne-Charlotte and Jens. I hope I said goodbye.

TEN

We set off at a fast steady pace, one that required me to stretch my gait to the maximum in order to keep up without breaking into a jog. The narrow, well-trodden path climbed gently at first, then leveled off. To my relief, I was able to keep pace with the men, only stopping once on a steep incline.

I began to recognize places I'd seen spotlighted by the flashlight on the day we were captured—a rounded log embedded in the path, a set of steps formed by twisting gnarled roots, a dry stream bed with rounded rocks.

Today the path wasn't soft and velvety. It was a line of squishy mud dotted with puddles and cut by the trench with two inches of gummy mud and a skim of water in the bottom. As I hopped from side to side over the trench and tiptoed around the puddles my boot treads became clogged with mud. I began to slip and slide, teetering on packed mud platforms. After I nearly fell, for the first time since the day we were captured, the voice in my head started talking to me again. *Why are you trying to keep clean? To hell with the mud.* I took a breath and slowed down, concentrating on planting my foot straight and firm, no longer avoiding the mud.

We walked on higher ground around the edge of the two boggy areas. At the second bog, about thirty rag-tag armed men stood talking together in small groups. The Man With The Gun joined one group, leaving me with the Young Guide. Everything around me was dark brown and muddy, the ground, the men and their clothes. As I stood there, I felt everyone's attention focus on my white face under my white hat. I stayed very close to the Young Guide as he led me a few paces further around the edge of the boggy area and then stepped behind him so he was between the men and me.

The Man With The Gun came toward us talking intently to an old man dressed in worn, tattered clothes. His jacket was faded and dirty; the shoulder stitching on one sleeve had ripped, exposing the torn lining and shredded inner fill. His knit pants, the elastic long gone, were held up with a twist of twine at the waist and stuffed at the calf into big black rubber boots. His battered navy baseball cap was pulled low over his gray, curly hair. Under his arm the Old Man carried an old, well-used gun.

When they reached us, the Old Man began talking to me. His words mixed with the powerful yeasty smell of sorghum beer washed over me in waves. I stared at his face, trying to understand what he was saying. He had intense almost black eyes under eyebrows peppered with white wisps. His wrinkled sunken cheeks were covered with a scattering of fine corkscrew white hairs. He had obviously never been to a dentist. What does he want? *Get away.* As the Old Man stepped toward me, I backed away, ducking behind the Young Guide again as we all started walking up the path. I wanted to escape from the Old Man but he kept pace with me, talking all the time. The more I tried to hurry away, the more I slipped; my feet threatened to slide out from under me and my arms wind-milled for balance. The Old Man grabbed my arm and held me tight under the elbow, steadying me. I looked at his face right beside me, his hand gripping my arm, and the mud on the path. There was no way he was going to leave or let go of my arm. *Don't panic. Stay in control.* I took a deep breath, returned to walking firmly and let him help me. What I couldn't change, I needed to accept.

We eventually reached the end of the path where it opened into the large clearing at the summit. It was nearly the same time of day as when we'd been there the day we were captured. Like then, scattered groups of people with their bundles were resting in the clearing. The Old Man, still gripping my arm tightly, led me over to the bamboo bench. The people in the clearing, particularly the women and children, watched us closely. I'm sure it was the first time they'd seen a white woman sitting in their clearing talking intently with an old black man. I wasn't sure where my two guides had gone, but the familiarity of the scene and the number of women who were nearby comforted me. The calmer I became, the more I was able to understand the Old Man. He was talking French.

"I am Bernard. Do you understand the problems my people are having?" I had the line about security, democracy, equal government and justice down quite well by this time.

In my fractured French I began, "I have read a list from the PALIR. You want to have peace and security. You want the government to be for all the people, not for just the Tutsi. I have seen the women and the children. They have no homes. Their husbands are dead. They live in the forest.

They need a place where they can live and raise their children safely. When I am home I will tell my country about the women." He seemed to understand what I said, nodding and smiling with each thing I added. When I finished, he took my hand in both of his and shook it firmly. When he stood up, I thought he was leaving. "Au revoir," I said.

Bernard strode over to one woman who was standing a little apart from the others. Her son, a toddler perhaps eighteen months old, was leaning against her leg, holding tight to the fabric wrapped around her waist and staring at me. Bernard reached down, grabbed him tightly around the upper part of one arm and swung him into the air. Bernard carried the toddler, screaming at the top of his lungs, across the clearing toward me suspended by his arm. The closer he came, the louder the boy's screams became. I called to Bernard in English, motioning for him to stop. "No, he's afraid. Put him down." Bernard swung his arm forward and held the boy suspended over my lap. With amazing strength and dexterity, the toddler, still hanging by one arm, bunched his body into a ball, twisted his legs up and nearly succeeded in inverting himself.

"Stop, Bernard. Stop. He's afraid." Laughing, Bernard slowly lowered the boy onto my lap, letting him drop the last few inches. I made no attempt to hold the boy, but slid him feet first toward the ground. Like a cat, the little boy was instantly on his feet and dashed back to his mother who was rooted motionless. The toddler ducked behind his mother, his wails instantly ending when we disappeared. Bernard continued to laugh, a deep, hearty belly laugh I associate with a good joke.

I reached into my pocket and tore a chunk off the bread round. In a slight crouch I edged toward the mother, the bread held out in front of me as far as my arm would reach. In a soft singsong voice I called, "Hello little one. I'm sorry you were frightened. I have some bread for you." From behind the woman's leg one eye, still brimming with tears, peeked out and monitored my approach, focussing alternately on my face and the bread. I glanced up and smiled at the mother, squatted low in front of her with my arm outstretched and waited. Slowly a tiny hand crept around her leg and reached for the bread. His fingers touched it tentatively at first and then tugged it out of my fingers; he disappeared behind his mother. I stood up right away and returned to the bench. One teary eye followed me. When I sat down, the toddler inched around his mother's side staying partly shielded, lifted the bread to his mouth and began to chew.

For about fifteen minutes Bernard and I sat on the bench. I spotted the Man With The Gun keeping watch back down the path we'd come up. He waved at Bernard and called something. Bernard stood up and took my hand in his again. "Au revoir, Madame," he said. "Bonne Chance." The Man With The Gun motioned and we headed out the opposite side of the clearing, down the path toward Congo. *The next person has caught up. It's their turn to rest for a while.* I accepted what my head told me. That explanation seemed as good as any other.

I rarely saw the rationale behind what the Africans did that week. I simply accepted it. Why would Bernard haul that boy over and drop him in my lap? A joke? Because I was a female? Because of what I'd said about the women? I could understand their expectation that I'd carry their message to the rest of the world, but it wasn't rational.

After we had been walking for about ten minutes, the Man With The Gun signalled me to stop. He stepped off the path and disappeared into the thick brush. I thought perhaps he had to pee. The Young Guide and I stood there waiting for a much longer time than necessary for a pee break. Suddenly, with no warning, Doug, Ann-Charlotte and Jens appeared on the path behind me. I was astonished to see the three of them together since I'd imagined we were strung out across the mountain with a long distance between each of us. But, here they were, all together in a group, with eight or ten men guarding them.

"Hello! What are you doing here? What happened?" I said.

"They searched us all thoroughly, our clothes and packs. They took our wallets and removed all our money," Jens said. He stressed the word *all* several times. I wondered if this was one of his strategies, a coded message. I couldn't figure out if he meant they found the money in his shoe or that he still had it. I couldn't say anything about them not finding the money in my bra. After all the 'coincidences' I knew someone understood at least some of what we were saying in English. *Too bad you can't speak Swedish.*

"The men who took our money said it would be returned when we are released so we can pay $20 US to the men for a tip," Jens said. *Why take it and give it right back? That doesn't make sense. They won't get it back.* Jens made sure the men around them heard what he was saying. "Doug and I are going to give the men all the money we have left when we're released. We'll pay for you, too."

I nodded. "Thanks."

From behind me, the Man With The Gun reappeared. He said something to the rest of the Africans, gestured, and pointed up and down the path. With a jerk of his head to tell me to follow, he hurried down the path leaving the others behind. It was about 4:30 p.m. and would soon be dark. There was a long way to go. Fortunately the trail was all downhill and we moved at a near jog.

Suddenly pandemonium broke out ahead of us—loud voices yelling and calling, the snap and crash of branches being broken and brush trampled. *It's an ambush. There's a battle.*

I looked closely at the men with me to gauge their reaction. They seemed more interested than frightened. There were no gunshots. The Man With The Gun stepped off the trail toward the noise and disappeared through the brush. The Young Guide stood on his toes and stretched to peer over the heavy undergrowth. When he, too, started through the bushes toward the commotion, I felt my stomach churn. I had no idea where he was going or what was happening. I needed them to get me out of the forest. I might be walking into danger, but I was afraid to be left alone. I took a deep breath and followed.

At the bottom of a short, steep slope, I broke through the brush into a small, flat, open grassy area not much bigger than a large room, similar to the clearing where we'd been searched. On the other side of the clearing a group of men were shouting aggressively and cautiously poking spears into an impenetrable thicket of bamboo and vines.

"Est-ce que c'est un gorille?" I asked the young man.

"Non," he said, "un couchon de la forêt." They were hunting a mountain bush pig, not a gorilla. The men with spears were understandably wary. Spears would offer little protection against a bush pig's razor sharp lower tusks, backed by powerful forequarters on a one hundred thirty-pound body.

To my left, at the edge of the grass, a group of women and children stood watching. One of the toddlers looked me, screamed in terror and buried his face in his mother's kanga. I was more frightening than a bush pig. "Pole sana. I'm sorry," I said. His mother smiled at me, put her hand on his head and gently turned him so he could see me. *Try the bread again.* I tore off another chunk and held it out. His mother whispered something and he held out his hand, his palm a flash of pink in the deep shade. His face was awash with tears, but he began eating as soon as he got the bread.

Suddenly a man wearing a red sweater appeared at the top of the slope behind me and began shouting at my two guides. He motioned for us to get moving, now. The Young Guide took my arm and led me out of the clearing, pushing through the bamboo underbrush toward the path.

In the midst of the thick forest growth we passed two old people standing soundlessly beside a pot suspended over a small smoldering fire in front of a tiny shelter. So this is where the people live in the jungle. Three or four more steps pressing through the thick bushes and we broke out onto the path. I glanced back over my shoulder. The forest had closed in behind; there was no sign of the shelter or the people.

We immediately headed down the mountain at an even faster pace. I wondered who the man was that shouted at us. Perhaps one of the men guarding the others. That would mean they had passed me while I was off the path looking for the pig.

It got steadily darker. We passed several long lines of people hauling huge sacks up the mountain on their heads. The Man With The Gun stopped for a hurried conference with two of the men we passed. There was lots of pointing; they appeared to be sharing information or directions with him.

The path eventually ran along the edge of a cliff; it wasn't as high or steep as the one I had been carried up on the first day. In any case, we didn't climb down the cliff, but continued travelling along the crest and onto another path, a new, different path. We weren't returning to where the trucks had dropped us off. Perhaps this path went to Kisoro.

All I had been told was that we were going to be released. No one had ever answered my questions about where this would occur. "Are we going to Djomba? Bunagana? Kisoro? I need to go to Kisoro. My husband is there." The protected forest area of the Virunga Mountains was shared by three adjacent countries, Uganda, Democratic Republic of Congo, and Rwanda. Although I knew there were formal border crossings in the settled town areas, I thought there might be an indirect network of trails in the forest between the three countries. Perhaps the path we were on bypassed the border, crossed into Uganda through the forest and went directly to Kisoro.

As I hurried along the mountain path, I kept my eyes focused on my feet. I didn't want to stumble on the uneven path or slip into the deep, center rut. When I was first captured and again as I was coming down, I kept noticing a scattering of dried cornhusks along the path and at the bottom of the rut. Like many things in Africa, I couldn't figure out why the husks were there. They seemed an anomaly. In the clearings, there were fire circles with cornhusks and debris scattered around them. I considered the possibility that people ate corn while they were walking up the path, dropping husks as they went, but that didn't seem likely. None of the people I passed was eating. I considered whether the husks might provide traction or keep peoples' feet out of the mud. But there were too few for that. I could think of no reasonable explanation for the scattered cornhusks.

In the fading light, the cornhusks began to stand out starkly white against the dark, wet earth. They appeared luminescent. I was quite drawn to those white beacons, fascinated by them, almost mesmerized. As darkness deepened, the whiteness of the cornhusks increasingly defined the path, light against dark.

We left the confines of the forest and began to cross open countryside. On both sides, fields of corn and high growing plants edged the path. The Man With The Gun stopped. "Au revoir,' he said, explaining that they would go no further. He held out his hand. "$20. Tip," he said. I didn't know which was more upsetting, his request for money or his statement that they weren't going any farther.

"I have no money." I said, thinking of the $100 in my bra. I considered trying to get $20 out and give it to them. *They might be angry you lied about not having money. If they see all that money they might kill you for the rest.*

"You must ask the other men. They have money for me," I said firmly, hoping Doug and Jens had left some money for me when they were dropped off. I felt guilty that these men had led me out and they weren't going to get paid. I reached up and felt the tiny zircon studs in my ears. *They can sell them.* I indicated the earrings but the Man With The Gun shook his head. The Young Guide handed me my water container. It was still over half full of water. I was almost home. They had a long trek back through the forest. I held the water out to them. Perhaps they could use it. The Young Guide shook his head and turned to go.

I glanced around. I had no idea where I was. "Attendez! Wait," I called. "Où est Kisoro? Where is Kisoro?" One of the men waved vaguely toward a line of trees growing on the horizon.

"Kisoro est là. Vous pouvez suivre le chemin." The road? What road? I watched as they melted into the darkness.

ELEVEN

I stood alone in the rapidly deepening darkness; my heart pounded. I whispered, "I don't know where to go." *There's no one here to help you. Kisoro is over there. Follow the path.*

I took a deep breath and wetted my lips. I turned my back to the forest so the dirt path was straight ahead. I scanned the horizon, a line of trees silhouetted faintly against the dark sky. There were no lights anywhere. I stood immobile as the vestigial light faded and a million stars burst across the sky. I looked up hoping to see the moon, but there were only stars.

Where was Kisoro?

My head dropped in despair. There, against the dark earth, a scattering of cornhusks glowed softly. The cornhusks marked the path. Breathtakingly simple. I would follow them to freedom.

I walked slowly and carefully. Soon it was darker than any place I had ever been. I was surrounded by a tapestry of black against black. On the ground I could still find the faintly lighter cornhusks. Staring down intently I would take a few steps, searching for a variation in the darkness, any spot that seemed fractionally lighter. When I saw a place that appeared lighter, I stepped cautiously toward it, pausing between each step. Every five steps I stopped, took a deep breath and looked around. Had anything changed? Were there any lights yet? Time and distance had no meaning. How long had I been walking? How far had I gone? How far did I still have to go? I looked for the moon. It hadn't appeared in the five minutes since I last looked.

It became increasingly difficult to see the cornhusks. I realized that my white hat, which I had been carrying in my hand, and the cream top on my water bottle were so light colored that they were interfering with my night vision. They overpowered the cornhusks; I needed to see cornhusks to find the path. I argued with myself about whether I should throw the hat and bottle away. As soon as I focused on the bottle I became aware of how dry my mouth was. I hadn't had anything to drink all day except sorghum beer. Although I had offered to give the water bottle to the men, I was grateful they'd refused. I took a mouthful of water and swished it around slowly before swallowing. I needed my water. Who knew how long it would take me to get to Kisoro? I looked at my hat. I knew it would get colder. I'd need my hat. *Why are you carrying your hat? Put it on.* Of course! With my hat pulled down firmly, I covered the bottle top with my hand and waited while my eyes became accustomed to the darkness again. I followed the cornhusks.

When I thought I saw the faint lightness of cornhusks, I would take a step forward with reasonable assurance. I knew I was on the path when my boot landed on packed dirt. In other places, thick, knee-high grass had fallen across the path obscuring both the path and the cornhusks. Nothing looked different. Everything was black. I had no idea where to go, but I had to keep going. I had no alternative.

Whenever I lost the path I stopped. First I needed to make sure that I hadn't turned my body or that the path hadn't turned. I took tiny side-by-side steps in a semi-circle around my base position feeling for the smooth, packed earth. When I found it and reestablished where the path was, I shuffled forward, lifting my feet only fractionally, inching through the grass. Several times I moved too quickly and tripped, snared by the long grasses. Like a pendulum I fell forward, landing heavily. When I recovered from the jolt, I pushed myself back up and began again, stepping slowly back and forth, tapping and sweeping with my boots. Where are you? Damn grass. *Don't look. There's nothing to see. Feel for the edge.* Ahh-hh-h! There! I always found the path again and kept walking. Only the tiny pinpoints of starlight assured me I hadn't gone blind.

When I stopped to rest and looked around were the only times that I became aware of anything besides the black space in front of my feet. I rested often. Though visually there was nothing around me, the air fairly shrieked with magnified sounds. A million amorous cicadas competed for each other's attention, their humming chirp cutting through my head like a chainsaw. The rasp as my feet and legs brushed through the sandpaper dry grass raised the hair on the back on my neck. Once I heard a sound to my right, a heavy rustling like dry corn stalks rubbing together as something pushed between them. I froze and listened, tracking the movement with my ears and the raised hair on my arms. I quickly dismissed the thought that I call out and ask for help. I was certain that if I was aware something was there, whoever or whatever it was knew where I was. Having lived most of their lives without bright lights at night, Africans have superb night vision and travel with ease through the dark. A wary person might have gone through the field to avoid me. I didn't think a person trying to avoid me would pay attention to anything I said, assuming that they even understood me. But, the noise could have been made by something besides a person. I listened until the rustling died away, and then listened some more. Then I continued walking.

The soil under my boots changed from packed dirt, to packed dirt and rocks, to pans of rocky outcrop, to the crumbly volcanic soil I remembered around the Kisoro area. The path squeezed between stacked walls of heaped volcanic rock that stretched like black specters beside me.

I began to fantasize about what Doug, Ann-Charlotte and Jens were doing. I was certain they had passed me while I was stopped looking for the wild pig. With their greater speed they would have travelled farther before dark and would have been closer to town; I was sure they had already reached Kisoro. Would they be eating? Or having a beer, maybe? I wasn't concerned that I was walking slowly and would get in much later than they had. They knew I was coming. They would be waiting for me. I wondered whether they would send someone with a light to guide me in.

The longer I walked the more charged with adrenaline I became. The intense attention I needed to stay focused kept my fatigue at bay. Whenever I stopped, my body would begin to droop and my head hung forward. I would search the blackness by my feet for the cornhusks, lift my head and take the next step. I had no idea how much time had passed. A minute could have been an hour. I remembered having seen the moon from the lean-to in the middle of the night, high in the clear sky. Moonrise would be late. Even knowing that, I checked the sky frequently, hoping the three-quarter moon would somehow magically appear so I could see better and travel faster. I dismissed the thought that I sit down and wait for moonrise. I had to keep going.

I walked each step deliberately, checking the sky—no moon yet; checking the horizon—no glow in the distance from the lights of town yet. Keep walking, look for the lighter spots and feel for the rocks. I didn't allow myself to think about Dan. I had a job to do first. I had to walk home.

Finally I reached an area where, no matter how hard I searched the ground I couldn't see any cornhusks or the line of a path. I tapped with my feet and every place seemed equally hard. *You've lost the path.* I don't know where to go. Now what do I do? I looked up in bewilderment. My mouth fell open. Off to my right, about twenty feet away, were the solid square shapes of buildings. I almost laughed. I had been so focused on watching the ground that I had come to the end of the path. I'd reached a village. *Someone here will help you.*

A faint light was visible inside one building, a house. The soft, warm, yellow-orange glow of light drew me like a moth to flame. Cautiously and hesitantly I made my way up to the house, mesmerized by the soft light that outlined the edges of the shuttered window and the closed door. I tapped gently on the door and called softly, "M'aidez. Help me. Je suis perdu. I'm lost. Où est Kisoro? Where is Kisoro?" Inside the house I heard a chair scrape as it was pushed back and footsteps hurry to the door. I waited, anticipating the door opening and seeing someone silhouetted half behind the door, looking at me and asking what help I needed. With a sharp click I heard a bolt slide in place, locking the door. From the faint sounds of breathing and the lack of any other movement, I knew someone was standing behind the locked door, waiting. I stood there for a few seconds awash with disappointment, but not surprised. If I lived in an isolated building, high up on the mountain slopes in an area filled with bandits, shooting and violence, I wouldn't open my door at night to a stranger. I whispered, "Merci. Au revoir," turned back to the road and walked on.

Not much farther down the road, the door on another house was open and inside I could see a candle flickering on the table. A man, his white shirt glowing in the darkness, walked toward me. "Où est Kisoro?" I asked, hoping he'd understand my French and I'd be able to understand his reply. "I'm lost and I'm trying to walk to Kisoro."

"Kisoro is about seven kilometers away. Keep walking down the road you're on," he responded in French. I looked into the darkness where he was pointing. I couldn't see anything, no path and no road.

"Please, can you help me?" I mumbled something about following the cornhusks and not being able to see them any more. "I can't see where the road is." In a few seconds there were a number of men milling around me. Where they had come from, I had no idea. Most likely they were from nearby houses, ones I hadn't noticed because they weren't lit in any way. Several of the men touched my arm hesitantly, guiding me and walking with me down the road. I couldn't tell where the road was or where I was going, so I stayed in the middle of the men, confident I'd at least avoid walking off the side of the road. Could I trust these men or would I be captured again? I looked at their faint dark shapes moving around me and remembered the nice young man who had taken me back into the forest. I decided I had to trust them. I couldn't find my way to Kisoro by myself.

The men were all chattering. I wasn't paying attention since they were talking to each other, not to me. A couple of French words, something about the radio and people being captured caught my attention. I got quite excited. "C'est moi! That's me! Je suis libéreé. I'm free. I am going to Kisoro to see my husband." There was a burst of excitement that continued to ripple through the men as we walked. Inside me eagerness began to grow. I really was going home.

In the distance, I watched a light bobbing toward us. As it got closer, I saw it was a flashlight held by a man in a light coloured shirt, one of six young men. I was thrilled. Doug, Ann-Charlotte and Jens had sent these men to find me and guide me back to Kisoro. The light would make walking the rest of the way much easier. Before they were close I called to them. "Bonjour! Hello." Thank goodness. Someone to take me to Kisoro. I was thrilled Jens, Ann-Charlotte and Doug had thought about the light. I called to them in French again, my delight obvious in my voice. "Hello. You're looking for me. I need to go to Kisoro. You are looking for me, aren't you?"

"I will take you to Kisoro," the man with the flashlight said, "but the border is closed for the night. We have to stop at the border to see the military Commander." Another commander. But this commander was at the border. I shrugged. As long as we were heading to Kisoro and not back to the forest, I was content to let the young men lead me.

I stayed in the middle of the throng, surrounded by the village men, following the leading beam of light from the flashlight. The young man in the light shirt had a tight grip on my hand. I supposed that he was trying to help me, but he was holding my hand with my wrist bent back at a sharp, awkward angle. It didn't feel helpful; it felt uncomfortable and confining. My stomach began to quiver and my chest tightened with the beginnings of panic. I tried to tell myself that he wanted to help me walk on the uneven ground and that his grip was not to confine me. I couldn't convince myself.

I pulled my hand away and unscrewed the top of my water bottle. "I need a drink," I said so that he wouldn't be offended. After my drink, I kept the bottle in the hand beside him and said I was fine, I'd walk by myself. My independence ended when I stubbed my boot against a protruding boulder and fell like a board. Although I managed to get my hands out in time to save my face, I split my water bottle open. I lay there for few seconds wanting to curl up and rest. I was more tired than I'd thought. The young man in the light shirt reached down and pulled me up. When he took my hand again, I adjusted his grip so I was comfortable and continued walking, unwilling to protest further.

From the edge of the group, someone passed forward a small kerosene lantern. Everyone stopped as they attempted to get it lighted. There they were, a large group of men squatting in a circle around the lantern, all chattering away, pointing and gesturing, obviously discussing how to open the chimney and get the wick lighted. I began to grin, thinking of a variation on an old light bulb joke. How many young men does it take to light a kerosene lantern? They got it lighted before I thought of a suitably descriptive answer. The man who had come to find me took the lantern and turned off his flashlight. Kerosene is cheaper than batteries.

Walking in the lantern light was strange. Unlike the flashlight that shone a directed beam in front of us, the circular lamplight shone not only on the road, but also on my face. The chimney supports cast black bands of shadow that seemed to hang in front of my eyes. Several times I reached up to brush a nonexistent object away so I could see better before I remembered and ignored the shadow.

The longer we walked, the more exhausted I felt. We walked slowly. The air temperature was cool, but I was hot and dripping sweat. With difficulty, I peeled off my jacket, which was wet from the inside and plastered tightly against my skin. The cool air and evaporation quickly chilled me. Shivering, I pulled the jacket back on again. The soaking wet fabric stuck to my skin and made it even harder to put back on than it had been to take off.

"How much farther?"

"Only two kilometers."

I kept searching the sky for a glow of lights to signal we were nearing the border. The telltale glow never materialized. Suddenly we were among dark, solid shapes, dark buildings seen faintly in the black of night. There were no lights anywhere. The buildings appeared to be deserted.

We trudged down the road and stopped by a building where two men were on guard. The encroaching darkness nearly overwhelmed the faint light from a lone light bulb on the porch. There was a sign over the door—Customs / Immigration. There were no other lights in the surrounding buildings; the border was closed. The man guiding me spoke to the guards, one of whom stepped in front of me, slung his gun onto his shoulder, switched on his flashlight and shone it directly into my face. I put my hand up to shield my eyes. "Ann-Charlotte?" he said.

"No," I replied shaking my head, "Donalda Reid." Why would he call me Ann-Charlotte when she was already out with Doug and Jens? As I puzzled through his question, the man guiding me and the guards spoke rapidly. He's just a border guard, I decided. He has no way of knowing if the others crossed the border in the hills and went directly to Kisoro.

The guard pointed back up the hill in the direction we had just come. "We must go back up the hill. The military Commander is there," the man guiding me said as he turned around and began to lead me back up the hill. I pulled my hand away. Was he like the nice young man?

"I won't go back. I'm too tired." The darkness pushed in closer; nothing felt safe. Where else could I go? My body drooped with weariness and despair. Then I sighed. I didn't believe him. But this time I was at the border. "How far up the hill is it?"

"It's not far. Just a few steps." I'd trust him enough go a little way.

Fortunately, we stopped after a minute or two. As I searched the darkness, a man with a gun appeared in front of us. While he and my guide talked, I stared into the blackness; slowly my eyes made out a solid black shape with faint lines of light hinting at a window and door. A house. Someone was inside. This must be the Commander's house. We could easily have passed it unseen on the way down.

Inside I was directed to sit on a wooden sofa against the wall. After a few minutes I gathered enough energy and curiosity to look around. I was in a small room, about twelve by fourteen feet, with wooden board walls bare of pictures or decorations. Along the outside wall, a small crowd of people was squeezed into the room watching and listening, though no one seemed to be paying attention to me. The lone window beside the door was tightly shuttered. In front of me, two candles stuck in puddles of congealed wax on the top of a large, long coffee table cast flickering shadows around the room. The warm yellow light reflected off the glass of five open bottles of beer and glistened wet in a pattern of interlocking rings and puddles of liquid spilled on the tabletop.

Facing me, at the opposite end of the table, was an unprepossessing man sitting in an upholstered chair. He was small in stature and slight in build, of an indeterminate age—no longer smooth cheeked, but not yet grizzled and gray. Only his uniform, camouflage fatigues, showed he was a soldier. I assumed he must be the Commander.

He was talking with two young soldiers who were sitting in chairs to my right. On a sofa to my left were two young, pretty, well-dressed women. Unlike the colorful lengths of printed cotton fabric the women in the countryside had worn wrapped around their bodies, these two ladies were dressed in African style tailored dresses, one a heavy deep burgundy polished cotton and the other a midnight blue. The neckline and sleeves were embroidered with filigreed gold line patterns. The lady in burgundy had intricately braided hair that swirled in precise rows around her head rising to a wide knob at the crown. She was very pregnant. I wondered if either of them was the Commander's wife. The Commander set down his beer bottle, turned to me and began asking me questions in French. "What is your name?"

"Donalda Reid."

"Where are the others?" Doesn't he know? He's the Commander.

"I don't know. Maybe in Kisoro. They walk faster. They must be ahead of me. Didn't you see them?" How could he have missed them? They had to be here somewhere.

"I know nothing about them," he said shortly. If he didn't know anything about them, they must have been delayed somewhere and were still coming. He signalled the pregnant lady and pointed at his bottle, which was now empty. She gathered the empty bottles and went into an adjacent room. Through the open door I could see three wooden crates of twenty-four bottles sitting on the floor, half of them without caps. This wasn't the Commander's house, I realized. It was one of the local drinking places.

"Where are the rebels? Are they near here?" Was he going to send soldiers out right then to try and catch the men who brought me down the mountain? They'd led me out and maybe didn't get paid. I didn't want them caught.

"They left me when it got dark, about 7:30. They were near the edge of the forest and went back. What time is it now?" I asked.

"It is 9:45." So early. I thought I'd been walking half the night. But enough time had passed that even if the soldiers left immediately there was no way they could catch the men. They were long gone.

But, 9:45? Where could the others be? There was no way it would take them that long to walk out. They had to be in Kisoro.

"I am pleased you are free. Your husband is still in Kisoro. We will tell him about your release tomorrow." A little flame of excitement burst through me. I smiled. I knew Dan would still be here. Just wait till I see the others. I'm going to stick it to them. They *are* waiting for us. I was right.

"Every day your husband came to the border. He begged me to give him a gun so that he could go in and look for you himself." The Commander puffed up like a macho pouter pigeon as he spoke. I couldn't imagine Dan wanting a gun, but I wasn't going to argue. I was almost back. Just a few more hours to wait. The Commander signalled for another beer for him and one for each of the soldiers sitting beside him.

The soldier closest to me got up and opened the outer door. The candle flames danced in a gust of wind; one, nearly extinguished, spluttered weakly. The Commander looked at the open door. "Why is the door open?"

"It's for fresh air," the soldier replied, adding something I didn't understand.

"Shut the door," the Commander ordered. "I don't want to have the cold air come in." The soldier shut the door and sat back down. From his sideways glance, I was sure he wanted fresh air because of me.

The flames on the tabletop steadied and burned tall. "I'm sure you must want an opportunity to get washed," the Commander said. Without waiting for my response, he spoke to one of the men by the door who immediately left, only to return in a few minutes to speak with the Commander.

"None of the charcoal burners are still lighted. We cannot heat the water for you to wash. We have only cold water. If you would like, you can wash in cold water." I smiled and nodded. After wearing the same clothes day and night for a week, I didn't care what temperature the water was; anything to be cleaner.

I'd begun to relax the moment I sat on the sofa. I no longer had a sense of being unsafe; I didn't need to be on guard. These men knew Dan. They would take care of me. Waves of fatigue rolled over me, washing away my ability to think and talk in French. A gray curtain of incomprehension slowly dropped. "Pardonez moi? Je ne comprends pas." I looked at the seat of the sofa, fighting the urge to curl up and close my eyes.

When he realized I wasn't able to answer his questions in French, the Commander brought in an English-speaking soldier to translate. It was soon clear that his English was only as good as my French. At first I tried to cooperate, but soon I couldn't think in any language. I felt I was going to melt and flow onto the floor in a puddle. If I no longer understood, they'd stop. "Je suis trop fatigué."

The Commander had continued drinking steadily as we talked. He signalled the Lady for another beer. "You can't tell us any more information tonight. We will continue in the morning.

"Would you like a beer?" he asked.

I didn't answer immediately. I was thirsty. I'd finished the water that survived in my split bottle while I was walking. But I wasn't sure how I'd handle beer. The last food I'd had was rice early that morning. Reluctantly I shook my head. "Non, merci."

"Chai?" he said. I smiled and nodded; tea sounded wonderful. Almost instantly someone placed a huge silver thermos, a red chipped enamel tin cup and a bowl of sugar on the table in front of me. When I unscrewed the thermos top and poured the liquid into the cup, it was white, obviously not tea.

I turned to the English-speaking soldier beside me. "What is this?"

He looked surprised. "Milk and sugar, of course." I nodded, too tired to explain my confusion about chai.

I dumped another heaping spoonful of sugar in the cup and gave it a quick stir. Steam drifting up from the top of the foamy surface warmed my nose as I lifted it to my lips. Everyone was watching me closely. I took a sip. It was steamy hot, sweet, rich, creamy and thick. It was utterly delicious; it was ambrosia. "Mmm-m-m!" Everyone burst into laughter. I sat quietly nursing the cup of milk, savoring each sip, the cup cradled between my palms and held close to my nose so I could smell it and feel the rising heat. No longer required to answer questions, I sat, watched and listened.

I couldn't follow all of the discussion, but I recognized a few words now and then. " ... lit ... ce soir ..." They're deciding where I'm going to sleep.

The group of young men who had guided me to the border came into the room. "... shillings ... brought her to you ..." They were asking the Commander to pay them for bringing me to the border.

The Commander began to laugh. " ... too much ... only five or six kilometers ... " He handed them some money. I'm not sure how much, but not as much as they asked.

The Commander and the two soldiers continued to drink Nile Special Lager beer, new bottles fetched by the woman from the wooden crate in the next room as soon as the last were empty. The two soldiers sitting to my right began horsing around, pushing and wrestling with each other. I leaned away from them, sliding along the sofa. With a crash, one chair tipped over backward and the two soldiers jumped to their feet, teetering unsteadily as they tried to stay upright. One of them hit the coffee table with his foot and sent everything on it flying. In a blink the thermos and beer bottles lay smashed on the floor. The English-speaking soldier picked the thermos up and shook it. In the swish of liquid was the crunching abrasion of broken glass. Protectively I nestled the half-cup of milk I was holding against my chest. As one woman picked up the large pieces of broken bottle, the pregnant lady brought more beer. The Commander shouted at the two soldiers, berating them. " ... poor impression ... don't behave in my presence." He insisted they stand at attention and salute him. "..show respect ... others ... fear me ... " The two soldiers barely stifled their laughter as they stood up and saluted lazily with limp hands. It was like watching a Marx Brothers comedy routine.

"Do not fear," the English-speaking soldier whispered in my ear. "This is not serious. The Commander does this for you. He worrying you think bad about them soldiers doing. He want you think he is good leader and soldier men afraid of him."

The outer door opened and a man carrying a large, brown plastic basin brimming with water walked through the room and disappeared somewhere out the back of the house. The pregnant lady signalled me to follow her. By flashlight, she led me to a small, square, bamboo enclosed dirt area in the corner of the back yard. It reeked of urine. I had seen a similar walled area where men went to urinate beside the outhouses at the Virunga Hotel. I was standing in the bar's *pisser*. It was at least private. The basin of water had been set on the ground in the middle of the four-foot square enclosure. The Lady said something, then handed me a pair of rubber thongs, a bar of heavy, dark green soap and a length of brightly coloured fabric.

As she returned to the house, I stood there, my arms filled and the flashlight dangling from my fingers, trying to decide how to manage this. I hung the flashlight pointing downward from one of a line of nails pounded in the top edge of the wall. In the indirect light, I stripped everything off except my boots, hanging my clothes and the Lady's cloth on another couple of nails. I peeled Doug's money off my bra and tucked it in the back of my fanny pack.

I wanted to wash my hair first, but the only way I'd be able to get my head in the basin was by kneel in the urine saturated dirt. Instead I squatted down and bent over, dumping handfuls of cold water over my head. I rubbed the soap into my hair until I got a bit of lather and rinsed, shivering as rivulets of water trickled down my bare body. Not wanting to waste any water I let the rinse water drop back into the basin. Next I washed down to my hips, splashing water on my skin, rubbing with the soap, and splashing more water to rinse myself. Covered with goose bumps, I stepped out of my unlaced boots and into the basin. After I'd washed my legs and feet, the basin water was a scummy, dark brown. I stepped into the thongs and stood there wet and shivering. I had no towel. I needed to wear the Lady's fabric since there was no way I was going to put my filthy clothes back on. I decided my t-shirt was the least dirty and wiped it lightly over my skin. Unwilling to dig in my fanny pack among the papers from the Hutus with my damp hands to find my comb, I finger straightened my hair the best I could. Then I wrapped the fabric around my body from underarms to knees like a sarong. Hoping the cloth would stay securely tucked, I gathered my clothes together in a floppy bundle under my arm and, with the flashlight in one hand and my boots in the other, I shuffled across the yard into the house.

No one had moved from around the table. There were fresh full bottles of beer on its top. I stood awkwardly in the doorway, waiting, unsure of what to do. I certainly didn't want to sit down on the sofa again. The Lady signaled me to leave my clothing and boots in the corner and then led me by candlelight into an adjacent room.

A bedroom. The only furniture was a wooden double bed. On the bed the foam mattress loosely covered with sheets had been folded in half lengthwise leaving the back half of the bed slats uncovered. On one wood wall was a small open shelf with a small pile of folded clothes stored on it. The Lady handed me a long, fuzzy, nylon nightgown from the pile. The nightgown sliding over my body enveloped me in a feeling of warm, caring comfort. Before she left the room, the Lady handed me a blue bottle of body lotion. I looked at it, inhaling the baby-sweet scent from another world. I didn't feel clean enough to put it on. I wasn't home. I set it carefully on the shelf, crawled into bed, blew out the candle, and pulled the sheet up under my chin.

Even after the voices from the next room quieted and everything was still, sleep was impossible. I kept worrying about Doug, Ann-Charlotte and Jens. I didn't understand why they weren't here. They should have been. I tried unsuccessfully to convince myself that they were in Kisoro. They'd been right behind me. We'd met on the mountainside. I was certain they'd passed me. The alternative didn't make any sense. I could only think of one reason they wouldn't have been released—leverage. Emmanuel had made a big deal about hearing the announcement on the radio. The radio was the key. If the others weren't in Kisoro, then the rebels must be waiting to hear something on the radio about their twelve demands before releasing them. I had to get their message out.

Huddled under the blanket, I tried to imagine talking to reporters, repeating the Hutu demands and describing the Rwandan women and children. I shivered.

All night the same thoughts circled through my head. Where are Doug, Ann-Charlotte and Jens? Why aren't they in Kisoro? If they're not in Kisoro, where are they? What can I say to reporters? I don't want to talk to them. Where are Doug, Ann-Charlotte and Jens?

TWELVE

As soon as the faint light of predawn became visible through the curtained window, I began to hear people passing outside, talking and calling to each other. It seemed a long time until I heard movement in the next room, someone coming and going, doors opening and closing. I got up, wrapped the cloth I had worn the night before over my nightgown, slipped on the thongs and stepped hesitantly into the main room.

Almost immediately the Lady appeared. Without knowing the words, I seemed to understand her. "Today I have hot water. Do you want to wash again?" As we crossed the dirt yard to the bamboo enclosure, we passed a central, open-sided, kitchen area covered by a reed-thatched roof. A few pots, used on a charcoal brazier or a central open fire, were stored on the ground under a simple work surface of rough planks.

The smell of urine was still strong, but the water was *hot*. Before she left, the Lady handed me the lotion. Following the same sequence, I finished washing before the water got cold. This time I rubbed the soft baby powder scented lotion over my body, intensifying my clean feeling. When I stepped out of the enclosure, I was startled by a young man standing in the yard. I recognized him as one of the Border Rats hanging around our truck at the Ugandan border the week before. Seeing someone I knew, even so slightly, reinforced my feeling of almost being home. I smiled. "Good morning," I said as I walked back to the house.

From her small pile of folded clothes on the bedroom shelf, the Lady handed me a Tommy Hilfiger t-shirt and another fabric wrap for a kanga. Dressed, I went into the main room, sat in the Commander's chair, and waited. Facing me, a man sat on the sofa where I had been sitting the night before. "Je suis une garde, une Ranger. I'm a guard, a Ranger," he announced.

Puzzled why he was telling me who he was, I none the less responded politely, "I'm glad to see you." It wasn't until weeks later that I realized he was one of the Congolese Rangers from the gorilla trip. He, too, had been taken hostage and had been released that morning. He was likely waiting to speak to the Commander.

I sat passively, isolated from my surroundings and waited. Outside the open door to my left, I could hear people passing in a steady stream. Someone placed a delicious smelling omelet and a cup of hot, steaming, sweet milk on the table in front of me. The omelet, the size of a bread and butter plate, was a rich, deep yellow, flecked with golden pieces of onion, crunchy, wavy and brown at the edges, glistening with frying fat. I swallowed quickly before I drooled, chopped a piece off with my fork and shoveled it in my mouth. I almost moaned.

I was savoring that first mouthful when a white man sat down beside me. It was Jens and Ann-Charlotte's tour organizer, Niclas. That morning, as soon as the border opened, one of the Border Rats had run the seven kilometers to Kisoro and told Niclas and Tony, another European living in Kisoro and working with Dan, that a white woman was free.

Tony and Niclas drove directly to the border without telling Dan. They confirmed a woman had been freed and Niclas hurried to the house where I'd spent the night. He was both excited and anxious as he sat beside me. I sat calmly chewing another mouthful of omelet and smiled at him.

"How are you? Where are the others?"

"I'm fine, but I don't know where the others are. Maybe they're in Kisoro," I said hopefully, realizing as I said it that it was a ridiculous statement. Niclas had just come from Kisoro. I shoveled more omelet into my mouth.

"Let's go. Dan's waiting in Kisoro."

I looked down at the omelet in front of me. It tasted better than anything I could have imagined. And the Lady—she'd taken care of me. She got me hot water. She let me use her nightgown and clothes. She gave me body lotion. I couldn't offend her by leaving without eating my food. After a week in captivity I couldn't get up and leave. I had survived by being passive when I had to be, enthusiastic when demanded, and avoiding anything aggressive. I was unable to change. I took a big swallow of milk and concentrated on the omelet. From the corner of my eye I watched Niclas talk to the Lady and give her money.

I'd finished half the omelet and most of the milk when someone darted in the door and set an open loaf of white, sliced bread in front of me. African store-bought bread is bone white fluff, totally lacking in substance and nutritional value. I was used to white food. I took a slice. All the joy the omelet brought disappeared with the faintly sweet, powdery taste of the bread—the taste of everything unpleasant, everything to be avoided in Africa. Overwhelmed by an immediate need to leave, I jumped up, dropping the fork and bread on the table.

"I have to go, *NOW*." I grabbing my boots, bundled my filthy clothes inside my jacket, and hurried outside with Niclas.

Women carrying bundles, boys with water containers on scooters, children on their way to school—everyone on the road stared at us as we hurried to the Immigration building. Niclas kept his arm around my shoulders while I juggled my bundle of clothes and slopped along in the flapping thongs. Not tucked securely, my kanga slowly began to loosen; the faster we moved, the looser it got. I tucked my elbows in tight to my waist gripping the edges and prayed it wouldn't drop to the ground leaving me naked below the t-shirt.

Tony, who was waiting at the border, went into one of the buildings with us. My passport appeared, retrieved from Immigration, and was stamped with an exit stamp. "Before you're allowed to leave, you have to answer some questions," Tony said and stood with his hand on my shoulder as they brought me a chair. I nodded. Behind the counter, a man, the Recorder, carefully counted and tore three legal size sheets from a pad of forms. He turned them over to the blank back and began to question me. A Congolese man who may have been the same man who had translated the night before repeated the questions in English. I was glad I didn't have to answer in French. My translated responses were recorded in tiny meticulous script. I answered in detail at first, but as the long page filled up excruciatingly slowly, my responses became shorter and shorter. The Recorder paused as he reached the end of the first long page. We'll be here forever I thought as I looked with dismay at the other two sheets. The Recorder must have had the same thought. He looked at me, slid the single sheet across the counter and made a motion telling me to sign and date it. As I passed the sheet back, Tony grabbed my elbow, lifted me to my feet and sped me out the door.

At a near jog, the three of us crossed 'no man's land', me still clutching my bundle of clothes and boots, trying not to step out of the thongs or let my kanga fall off. Tony turned the truck around while Niclas and I went into the Ugandan Customs. More forms. My shoulders drooped. *Do what you have to.* I stood there blinking slowly, almost numb. After a short discussion, my passport was stamped. Niclas explained I'd been given a two-week visa so I would have enough time to leave the country.

As we stepped out of the Customs' building into the bright sunlight, a man in a Ugandan police or military uniform stepped in front of us.

"I need to talk to this lady," he said. Before I comprehended what the uniformed man had said, Niclas stepped like a wall between him and me. I pressed tight against Niclas's back, trying to be invisible.

"Nothing happened in Uganda," Niclas said. "She doesn't have to say anything to you or anyone in Uganda. It's none of your business." Half of me wanted to pull Niclas's arm and warn him not to make the officer mad. The other half said, Oh, good, no more questions. Niclas pushed past the man, lifted me into the truck beside Tony and climbed in still arguing with the official who was holding tight to the open truck door. Tony hopped out from behind the wheel, hurried around the truck, wrenched the door free and slammed it. Hopping back in, he immediately drove off.

As we rounded the last corner I could see Dan sitting alone on the patio in front of the Virunga Hotel. Dan looked up but didn't move as the truck skidded to a stop. "I don't think he's seen you yet," Niclas said as he jumped out, holding the door open. I slid across the seat and began waving as I climbed down.

"Danny, Danny, it's me."

For a second he didn't move. Then he jumped up, raced over and pulled me so close I could feel his heart pounding. He kissed my lips, my cheeks, and my lips again. He wrapped his body around mine, loosening his grip only far enough so he could tip his head back and make sure it really was me. I knew I was home, safe. We spent the rest of the day in Dan's room hugging and talking.

It took several hours before I could give Dan even a summary of what had happened. I watched his face closely while I was telling him about the men trying to rape me, trying to gauge what he was thinking. I didn't know how he would react and braced myself for anything. When I was done he knelt on the floor in front of me and pulled me close, stroking my hair and kissing me softly.

"I love you," he said. "You can't imagine what I thought might be happening to you. It got more horrible every day." He straightened his arms, held me a bit away and looked at me. "You look great!"

It was a good thing he hadn't seen me right after I got to the border. I sent a mental Thank You to the Lady. When I was finished talking, it was Dan's turn.

THIRTEEN

Dan's seven-hour long-walk trek had been demanding. Although his group had seen about thirteen gorillas, with the crush of sixteen tourists and the guards, porters and Rangers, many of the animals had stayed half hidden in the brush. At the end of their hour, rather than return to the trucks, they bypassed the drop-off point and went directly to Bunagana, the town on the Congo side of the border. As they wound their way down the mountain, they passed a fully dressed, desiccated corpse lying at the side of the path. No one said anything; they kept walking.

Dan was surprised that I wasn't there when he reached the border. We should have arrived back by truck hours earlier and been waiting at the border with a cold beer; no one had any idea where our group was. The long-walk guides explained that we'd likely had a hard time finding the gorillas and had to stay longer and walk farther than usual. They assured Dan that we would arrive soon. As the sun set, he was still waiting.

Before the border closed our assistant driver took the rest of our group back to Kisoro in Uganda. Dan, Charles and Niclas stayed on the Congo side in a small house bar run by the sister of the man who owned the trucks that had taken us to the drop-off site. While they were in the bar, someone brought word that the trucks had been burned. Something had gone terribly wrong. Dan wanted to contact the Canadian Embassy immediately, but Charles and Niclas convinced him to wait in case we showed up later that night.

Hours later, long after dark, Dan and the leaders were still waiting. Suddenly dancing headlights and the roar of an unmuffled engine filled the area in front of the bar as a large military transport truck rumbled into the open square at the border. Before the squealing brakes had quieted, a stream of soldiers holding semi-automatic guns jumped out of the back and formed a crouching circle around the truck.

Dan jumped up. "Maybe they have some information." He hurried out of the bar, but before he could go down the steps Charles grabbed him and pulled him back inside.

"Don't go out there. It's not a good place to be." While Dan watched from the doorway, Charles went out and, in Swahili, explained the situation to the Commander. With a great show of theatrics and bravado, the Commander strutted back and forth in front of his men shaking his fist and talking to Charles.

"I told him something happened," Charles told Dan, "and he's going to take immediate action." But, as Dan watched, the Commander dismissed the soldiers. In spite of his words, during the next week the Commander made no genuine effort to locate us.

The soldiers, gesturing with their guns and talking loudly in Swahili, swaggered over to the bar. Shouting and pointing with their guns, they ordered Dan, Charles and Niclas back across the border. "You have no permission. Go back to Uganda."

African border guards don't have a reputation for being reasonable. No one crosses the border at night. The three walked cautiously through the darkness that filled no man's land. Would they be shot? Fortunately their reception was open and friendly. The Ugandan guards knew something had gone wrong and reacted with uncharacteristic flexibility.

The rest of the night in Kisoro was interminable.

As soon as the border opened, Dan returned to the Congo bar. As he sat waiting, the air was suddenly filled with the thud and boom of mortars and grenades, sounds he knew from his years in Zimbabwe.

That morning the second Swedish couple I had seen racing down the mountain when we were captured made their way out to the border. They had escaped capture by hiding deep in the brambles lower on the mountain. All that day and through the night they huddled among the thorns, bitten by ants, afraid to move or talk. When it was light enough for them to see they crept out from their hiding place and headed down the mountain, only to emerge in the middle of a local skirmish. Surrounded by gunfire, running and crawling when necessary, the two worked their way to a small nearby village.

Surrounded by a swarm of local people, the Swedish couple finally reached the border. The man, dressed in shorts and a t-shirt, sat down in the middle of the dusty road, untied his boots and handed them to the boy who had guided them safely to the border.

The news they gave Dan horrified him. They had last seen me walking or standing with my hands up and the other Swedish couple crawling through the grass. Not only had we disappeared, but all our African drivers, porters, Rangers and guards had also disappeared. There was no hint of where we were or who had taken us. They didn't know whether I was alive or not. Only the Swedish couple at the border managed to avoid capture.

With our capture confirmed, Dan and the tour leaders immediately contacted the Canadian, New Zealand and Swedish Embassies, as well as the heads of the companies with whom we were travelling. The police in Kampala released a list of mixed up names to the press, a mish-mash of our first and middle names. In the Ugandan paper, Sunday Vision, on 16 Aug 1998, we were reported as Mrs. Donaldo Joan, Douglas John, Mrs. AnnCharretta Jorisson and Mrs. Jenns Olsson.

For the next three days Dan maintained his vigil at the border, sitting on a bench, a log, the steps, in the bar, waiting and watching until he simply couldn't sit and watch any longer. The town was a constantly changing surreal kaleidoscope of colours and people. Hour by hour the scene outside grew more bizarre. Military trucks screeched up and roared away again. Drunken soldiers, as full of their own importance as they were of beer, swaggered and bullied through the border area. Streams of people carrying huge bundles on their heads poured across the border. Charles explained that this was not the usual cross-border movement, since people were carrying all their family and household belongings with them. They were afraid. They were running from war.

As the rebellion or insurrection spread, Congo transformed from a country of relative calm to chaos. The army build-up at the border increased, though the military didn't stray far from the safety of the built-up areas. A contingent of soldiers was sent to try to track us or find some trace of us. All they brought back were some candy wrappers and other inconsequential scraps of paper found in the long grass. They didn't go into the forest. In the absence of fact, rumours abounded.

On the morning of the third day, our tour group had to leave Kisoro. Everyone was upset because they had to leave Dan to wait alone. Many were in tears. As they hugged him goodbye, Dan told them to treasure each day they had, because, in a moment, everything could be different and they might never get back what they had before.

With the truck and tents gone, Dan moved into a room at the Virunga Hotel. Each room was named after an African animal. Dan got the Gorilla Room. Fortunately, Paul, the head of the Kenya operations of our tour group, arrived from Nairobi that day to stay at the hotel with Dan.

On the fourth morning a meeting was held in Kisoro to strategize ways to contact our kidnappers. The group included Dan, Paul and Niclas (the heads of the tour groups) and two Europeans including Tony, who were full time residents in Kisoro. They drafted a note in Kinya-rwanda, French and Swahili asking for the names of any whites being held captive. The note was wrapped around one of Dan's Bic pens, a type he always uses but we hadn't seen in Africa. He hoped that I might recognize it as being from him. The problem they faced was getting the note to the right people. Tony gave one of the head Border Rats $100 US to go into the hills and get the note to the rebels. When there was no response from the rebels over the next few days, the planning group assumed the Border Rat had not done his job. Tony was very harsh and only reluctantly agreed with the others to let him keep the money. That was the same day I was asked to record our names and addresses—with Doug's pen. Perhaps the Border Rat was successful.

Each day as the sun traced its path across the sky and daily torrential rains dumped a river of water over the land, Dan waited at the border and in Kisoro, imagining the unimaginable. Rumours reached Kisoro that the *wazungu*, white people who had been captured, were to be released. Tony, who knew the area best because he lived there, traveled at some risk to the border between Rwandan and Uganda where the rumour originated. He was unable to verify the information. Was that the border crossing where Pascal had gone?

It was impossible to phone out of Kisoro; the two land telephone lines that served the town were down, a frequent occurrence. On the fifth day, while Tony was at the border checking the rumor, Dan and Paul drove seventy kilometers to Kabale to make an International phone call on the radiophone in the corner of the lobby of the Highlands Hotel. After an involved process getting a line to Canada, Dan stood waiting impatiently as the phone at his sister's began to ring. He heard the click of the phone being answered. "Hello, hello. Nadine, this is Dan."

Their answering machine responded, "You have reached…" In frustration he left a long message. When he next called the Canadian Consulate in Kampala, he found they were aware of our capture. Everyone knew something had happened, but no one knew who was responsible or where and why we were being held.

On the seventh day, Dan and Paul went to Kabale again. Paul left Dan in Kabale to phone while he continued to Kampala to pick up Martin, the London head of our tour company, who had just arrived in Uganda. They arranged for a taxi to take Dan back to Kisoro.

This time Dan's sister was home. She told him that Canada's External

Affairs department had been in continual contact with our families and was working to get me released. Dan looked around the wood paneled lobby of the hotel. Africa was so far from Canada. How could External Affairs find someone half a world away? It seemed futile to even try.

Dan was anxious to get back to the hotel to see if any more information had surfaced while he was gone. The taxi ride back on the twisting road was slow but uneventful. Suddenly, as they entered Kisoro, a bicycle shot from a side street directly in front of the taxi. With no time to swerve or brake, the taxi smashed into the bike sending it and the rider flying. As Dan and the driver untangled the man from the bike, they realized, from the uniform the man was wearing, that they'd hit a policeman. Between them, they got the injured policeman into the taxi and hurried him to the hospital in Kisoro. Though the hospital admitted the policeman, they held Dan responsible for the policeman's hospital costs. No amount of reasoning or explaining that he was a passenger made any difference. He was white. Until he paid the total amount of the estimated bill, they wouldn't let him leave. He paid.

With a receipt for the costs tucked in his pocket, the taxi driver and Dan next went to report the accident at the Police Station. The Police Station was bizarre incarnate. Once again, it was Dan who was required to fill out the police report. As he sat at the counter filling in forms, the prisoners, most of whom were being held for treason according to the ledger, kept shouting a barrage of advice and comments from their cells. The police went about their usual business, seemingly unconcerned that one of their colleagues had been injured.

When Dan finally got back to the hotel, there was no news of any kind. In spite of all their efforts, there had been no word or sign of us for a week.

Dan's despair had been growing daily. Before my capture, he had had two strong premonitions that something would go wrong on our trip. About three months before we were to leave I'd been checking the travel updates posted on the Canadian External Affairs website. None of the areas on our itinerary were close to or listed as major trouble spots. However, as I always did, I showed the cautions to Dan.

"I think we should cancel the trip," he said. "We should just cancel the whole thing." His reaction had astonished me. He couldn't explain why he wanted to cancel, so after rereading the information and checking the problem areas again, he reluctantly agreed we should go.

On the day we went for the gorilla trek, just before he left with the other group, he was hit with similar strong negative feelings. As he had the first time, he ignored them. Sitting in Kisoro waiting, and at the border waiting, he wrestled with the knowledge that he had let me go alone when he had had such strong feelings that something bad would happen.

People who had lived in Africa for a long time told Dan that hostages are released after seven days; a week was the magic time period. In July, less than a month before we were captured, the Interahamwe Hutu militia had kidnapped two groups, three Catholic nuns including one Canadian, kidnapped on July 7, 1998, in Ruhengeri, Rwanda and two Belgian priests from Ruhondo commune, Ruhengeri, Rwanda, kidnapped on July 22. All of them were released within seven days. I reached the border house in Bunagana on the seventh night.

Dan stopped every few minutes as he told me his story and smiled. "You look great. I love you."

After leaving us alone for a couple of hours, Niclas, Paul and Martin, the London head, came in several times to talk briefly with Dan and me. I told them what I had been thinking all night in Bunagana. "I'm afraid the others are being held until the rebels hear something on the radio. They want to hear their demands. That's all they talked about all week. I have to get something broadcast on the radio—on the BBC overseas news broadcast. That's what they listen to. I think." The radio broadcast was all I could think of. Waiting to talk to my government when I got home wouldn't help anything. Whatever happened had to be now.

"I don't think you should be talking to the press," Martin said. I was relieved. The thought of talking to reporters made me shiver. "Let Niclas and me write something to give to the press. Just a short statement. What do you want to say?" He took out a pencil.

The others' freedom rested with me and what I did. "It has to be positive. I don't want the men to get angry and hurt them."

"But I'm worried that if they hear their twelve demands being broadcast, they'll have what they want and the others won't be free. Say something vague like I was released unharmed after being held captive for a week, that I was well treated."

On the mountain, when I imagined passing on the Hutu demands, I'd always pictured the four of us together. "Say, as soon as the other three hostages join me, we'll make a joint statement." I didn't hear what Niclas and Martin gave to the press, although I was told it was broadcast that day.

Dan and I remained closeted in our room. A string of people kept trying to talk with me. A camera crew in town to film a documentary on the gorillas requested an interview. The Ugandan police came several times hoping to question me. The manager of the hotel, John, ran interference.

"She is sleeping. She is not available." At one point John brought us a message that there was a phone call for me. "Someone has come to say that your wife is getting a phone call from Canada."

"Are the phones back in operation?" Dan asked.

"No." John said. "The call is on a radiophone at the guesthouse. They want your wife to come there and talk with them."

"Who's calling? Who in Canada would already know that she's here?" Dan asked. John shrugged. He had no idea.

No one knew who this mysterious Canadian might be or how they knew where I was. I was afraid to leave the shelter of the room or let Dan leave me. We decided that we would ignore the phone.

We spent the rest of the morning repacking. We wrapped our African carvings in the few clothes we were keeping and stuffed them in Dan's backpack. The culled clothes including all of the clothes I had worn in the forest went on a pile in the corner of the room for the manager, John.

When the rest of the tour group had left on the third day, Dan kept Doug's things in Kisoro. We wrapped Doug's gifts in his folded clothes, making sure Doug's $100 and the food money I owed were buried deep inside his pack. As soon as Doug arrived he'd be able to grab his pack and be on the plane immediately. Dan left the pack with Martin in case we were gone when Doug arrived.

About midday Shaun Hughes, from the Canadian High Commission in Nairobi, landed at the airport in Kisoro to fly us immediately to Kampala. We weren't at the airport; we were in our room with all our belongings and Doug's spread everywhere.

"Didn't you get a phone call from Canada telling you I was coming?" he said when he arrived at the hotel.

Dan and I looked at each other. "No. We didn't know who was calling. We didn't take the call."

"Right now there are trauma counsellors in Nairobi," Shaun said. "They've been working with the Canadian Embassy staff since the US Embassy bombing. I recommend you fly to Nairobi and spend some time with them."

I reached out and grabbed Dan's hand. "No. I don't want to go to Nairobi. I don't want to talk to some stranger. I just want to be with Dan and go home as soon as I can. We can fly home from Kampala."

"The press will be waiting to talk with you when you get to Kampala."

"I don't want to talk to reporters." I shuddered. Reporters push microphones into your face after a tragedy and ask what you're feeling. Or, they ask the victim to tell what happened. I didn't want anyone asking me questions like that. "What I should do, Shaun?"

"It's up to you."

Never tell someone who's still half in captive mode to do what they want. It had nothing to do with what I wanted—which was for it to be over or for it to have never happened. What I did hinged on one thing —whether it would help the others. Whatever that was, I'd do it.

"If I talk to the reporters, will that help free the others?"

"I'm not sure that anything you might say would make any difference." I took that to be a no. I didn't want to think about the meaning underlying his statement. "OK. No reporters."

"Unfortunately the plane that brought me has already left. We have to drive to Kampala," Shaun said. "Be ready to leave early tomorrow morning. I have a reservation for you at the Fairway Hotel. The Sheraton was fully booked."

That evening we ate in the little hotel dining room with Martin, Paul, Niclas and Shaun. All my calm detachment, my sweet politeness vanished. I was manic. I smiled and laughed and snuggled close to Dan.

It was like a party. I sat at the table in a real chair. There were electric lights, napkins and more than two utensils. I had a cold beer, Nile Special Lager. The menu was exciting. I could choose any of the six things on it. Whatever I wanted. I remembered how my mouth watered when I saw Richard holding the goat meat. I chose goat stew. It was almost as delicious as the omelet I'd had in the morning. When my beer was gone I had a second. Goat and beer; a gourmet feast. I was so alive.

Suddenly, I felt as though I'd slammed into a cement wall. I set the bottle down and lay my head on the table on my folded arms. "Time for bed, I think," Dan said. I was so tired I could hardly stand up and walk the few steps back to our room. While I stood with my arms dangling straight at my sides, Dan undressed me. He put his arm around me and guided me to the bed. After I was tucked in, he undressed and slipped into the narrow bed beside me. We slept without moving, curled tight against each other.

FOURTEEN

At breakfast, Niclas brought news that all the drivers, Rangers, guards and porters who had been captured with us had also been released the day before and were back safe in Bunagana. My heart leapt. If the Africans were free, then the others would be, too. We could give Doug his bag before we left. I wondered if he would bring his walking stick. I didn't know how he was going to take it home, but he had it when I saw him on the mountain. "What about the others? Are they there?" When I saw the look on Niclas's face, I knew the answer. There was no word at all about Doug or Ann-Charlotte and Jens.

Around eight a.m. two cars pulled up in front of the hotel. We were to travel with Martin, while Shaun and Annette, the owner of Niclas's tour company, followed in the other car. I climbed in the back seat; Dan got in the front beside Martin.

On Wednesday, the ninth day, we left Kisoro. I'm never going to be here again, I thought. Good-bye Virunga Hotel. Good-bye volcanoes.

The drive from Kisoro to Kabale was spectacular. A warm, fuzzy glow of happiness at being free, being safe and being with Dan filled me with benevolence toward everything I was seeing. Steep hills; breathtakingly beautiful scenery; treacherous, winding, potholed road. Good-bye hills. Good-bye Africa. I lay my head against the seat back and tried to imprint all the images into my mind so deeply that I would never lose them. Looking out the window, I felt the same closeness to that place as I have for my home. I knew I could never forget what happened, but I wanted to take some visual image back with me. "See," I wanted to say as I showed the photo, "this is what it was like." I had Martin stop twice. However, as I looked through the viewfinder of Dan's camera, I realized no photo could capture what I was seeing. I was filled with a sense of loss. Doug should be here. We started the trip together. We should end it together. I sent him a mental message. Good-bye my friend. Keep well until you get out. Please get out.

Niclas had asked me to call his camp on Lake Bunyonyi when we stopped for coffee at the Highlands Hotel in Kabale and talk with the other Swedish couple who had escaped. Niclas was concerned because they were feeling frightened and guilty. I called from the same radiophone in the hotel lobby that Dan and Paul had used to contact Canada and Nairobi. As I talked, black faces would peer around the doors and then duck back quickly; it seemed everyone working in the hotel was watching and listening.

I repeated everything first to the man, then the woman. "Don't feel guilty or depressed about escaping. You did the right thing by hiding. There was nothing you could have done to help us. If we could have hidden as well as you, we certainly would have done it. Just be glad you got away. You were lucky."

They were afraid that we'd been physically tortured. "No one hurt us," I said not wanting to upset them further. "We were well treated. We had enough to eat, and even a sleeping bag. I'm sure your friends will be released soon." I wasn't sure how well they knew Ann-Charlotte and Jens or whether what I'd said was helpful.

With only one short stop after that for gas and a sandwich, Martin drove slowly and cautiously toward Kampala. He was anxious to get to the Fairway Hotel and confirm that his London office had arranged seats for us on the 8:30 p.m. flight to London at that evening. By the time we reached the outskirts of the city, it was dark.

The traffic around Kampala was horrendous. The equivalent of eight lanes of traffic jammed onto a four lane road riddled with potholes so deep and wide that the undercarriages of the cars scraped and tires thumped down with a horrendous bang. Without warning large groups of people crossed unexpectedly in every direction through the middle of the traffic. The air overflowed with sound—squealing tires, a cacophony of horns, whistles and shouts as people flagging down taxi buses that picked them up in the middle of the road. Everything was sooty orange from hundreds of candles and kerosene lamps and wildly swinging car headlights. We drove mile after mile through this chaos.

"I've never been to the Fairway Hotel," Martin confessed as we inched our way around a gridlocked traffic circle. "I'm not sure which way we should go." My heart dropped. How could he not know where to take me? He was supposed to be in charge.

I scrabbled on the car floor for the Ugandan travel book I had looked at earlier in the day. Even in the dim light I was able to locate the Fairway Hotel on the map of Kampala. However, when I looked out the window, there were no directional mileage signs, no landmark indicators, just a solid river of cars. I kept pouring over the map, trying unsuccessfully to make some sense of where Martin was going as he squeezed around the traffic circles through the lanes of gridlocked cars. He pulled onto a pitch-black side street close to where he thought the Fairway Hotel was and stopped.

"Where the hell are we?" I said. With my nose against the window I tried to see anything in the blackness that might tell me which way to go. All I could see were our headlights shining down the curb of a long curving road. We were lost.

A man appeared out of the darkness and began to walk toward us. I slouched down in the back seat and followed him with my eyes. In Swahili, Martin called out the window to the man. In a long, incomprehensible explanation, the man pointed in several directions. As he walked away and Martin pulled away from the curb, I let out a long held breath.

We arrived at the Fairway Hotel at 7:00 p.m. "Just leave everything in the car. If you're confirmed on the flight, we'll head directly to the airport." If? I thought we had seats. We followed Martin through the heavy brass doors to the front desk.

There was no message from the Nairobi office about a flight and no telephone lines available for Martin to call Kenya. Martin was beginning to act as anxious as I felt. He hadn't known how to find the hotel. I stood as close to him as I could, listening carefully to make sure he knew what he was doing, my eyes riveted on the front doors. Whenever they squeaked open I braced myself, expecting a crowd of reporters to rush in. The woman behind the desk responded to Martin's requests with glacial, polite slowness and a deadpan face. Finally he got a call patched through his London office that confirmed Dan and I were at the top of the waitlist for the 8:30 flight.

"I'll need the sheets from the PALIR," Martin said. "I'm meeting with the press again tomorrow, and we'll start publicizing them. The group here in Kampala that's been working on contacting the rebels and getting you all released will keep looking for Doug and the others. They'll need the information, too." The sheets were in my fanny pack, right beside my flight itinerary. They were the only things I had that linked Doug and me together. They were all I had that showed where I'd been for the past week. The Hutu had given the sheets to me. No way was I giving them to someone who couldn't find the hotel.

After an interminable wait of ten minutes, Martin got photocopies made and handed the originals back to me. We had a little under an hour left to get to the airport. When a taxi driver outside the hotel assured Martin he could get us there on time, we threw our bags into the taxi and roared off—through Dante's Inferno into the pitch-black night. It took almost forty-five minutes to go thirty kilometers to the airport.

The driver screeched up outside the Entebbe International Airport terminal building and, before the car had stopped rolling, Dan and Martin were out, racing for the check-in counter. With detachment I watched them through the back window. After only a minute at the counter, they hurried through the terminal and disappeared. I huddled in the back seat while the driver sparred verbally with Airport Security personnel demanding he move the taxi from the No Parking area.

Dan and Martin reappeared about twenty minutes later. Martin shook his head. "The flight tonight is about fifty people overbooked. There's no way you would have gotten on. The next flight is in two days. It's already a hundred people overbooked. Everyone's trying to get home after their holidays. But, we've got you confirmed seats on that flight." I looked at Dan. He nodded. Somehow, upstairs at the customer service area of British Airways, Dan and Martin had arranged assured seats on the next flight. I have no idea whether they said something about my capture or if it was the pull of a tour company that books thousands of flights a year, but we got seats.

I began to shake as the taxi engine started. The benevolent numbness I'd felt that morning and my cheerful detachment was gone. I was exhausted. On the drive to the airport I had held everything together with the thought that I would be getting on a plane and leaving in a few hours. Even two days rest in Kampala before the flight couldn't push down the Oh, No! thoughts that bubbled up. I faced another nightmare ride and reporters lurking in wait at the Fairway Hotel with their flashing cameras and impossible questions. My stomach heaved.

Earlier in the trip, Doug had told Dan that he and his wife had made reservations after the end of the safari at the Imperial Botanical Beach Hotel right on the shore of Lake Victoria close to the airport in Entebbe. "Martin," Dan said, "it seems ridiculous for us to go all the way back to Kampala. We're going to fly out from Entebbe in two days. Why not take us to the Imperial Botanical Beach Hotel?" After a mercifully short taxi ride Martin got us registered and paid for our room before he headed back to Kampala. We were finally alone.

I felt like a zombie, but I needed to eat. Fortunately, the dining room was still open, though, at 9:30, we were the only customers. This wasn't the little Kisoro hotel. White, stiff, linen tablecloths, a long line of cutlery, beer that cost more than our meal the night before—President Clinton had stayed at the Imperial Botanical Beach Hotel on his African trip. Fancy hotel or not, I knew I was still in Africa when a dozen little black ants skittered out of the basket in which my fish and chips were served. The replacement dinner was presented on a nice, white, china plate.

Full, clean and safely locked in the room, we curled up together and slept.

Early the next morning Dan connected with his sister and my brother in Canada on a conference call. He handed me the phone. "You better talk to them so they can hear you're all right." As wonderful as hearing their voices was, telling them we'd be home in two days was better.

Later, at the end of a leisurely breakfast, Shaun Hughes paged me from the Sheraton in Kampala. "Thank God I finally found you. I was driving behind you most of the way into Kampala. Suddenly, you disappeared. You weren't anywhere. I tried to reach you at the Fairway Hotel, but they said you weren't there." He sounded both exasperated and relieved. I was perplexed. I had expected Martin would talk with Shaun and tell him about the flight and the hotel. Who was in charge? Anyone?

"You know," Shaun said, "the trauma counsellors are still in Nairobi. Let me make arrangements for you to fly to Nairobi to talk with them." That was the third time he'd brought the trauma counsellors up. Through the balcony patio doors I could see wide green lawns flowing down to the glassy water of Lake Victoria. I had been in downtown Nairobi. It was crowded, dirty and unsafe. I explained we had assured seats on the next flight.

"Don't you worry about getting home," Shaun continued. "We could always look for space in First Class if that was all that was available. Or we could even fly you back to Entebbe in time for the flight you're book on." The prospect of two days flying back and forth in Africa, packing and unpacking, dealing with immigration and visas, unsure when we'd get home, made me shudder. Not even the carrot of First Class was enough to get me back to Nairobi. I didn't need trauma counseling. I needed to be with Dan. I wasn't flying anywhere but home.

Martin arrived at noon. "I never did get to hear what went wrong on the gorilla trek. Do you mind telling me? We're still working to get the others out, and something you tell me may make a difference."

After I told him an abbreviated version, I said, "Martin, I was wrong about not saying much on the radio. The Hutu didn't release the others after the broadcast about waiting until we were all together. Maybe they won't be released until the Hutu hear their demands on the radio. I think there needs to be another broadcast, and soon."

I looked at Martin, frustrated that all I knew was what he was telling me. I didn't actually know what, if anything, was being done. I didn't doubt Martin was concerned; it was his employee who got us in this mess. From what he said it sounded like a lot of people were involved, but I had no idea who was doing what. Much as I wanted to forget the whole capture, I wanted the others released. Choking down the urge to scream, Do something! Get them out! I took a deep breath. "Did you give the photocopies to the press? Maybe if I talked to them…"

"Don't worry about that," Martin said. "I'll pass everything on and make sure it's printed and broadcast."

Shortly after lunch, Helen Harris from the Department of Foreign Affairs and International Trade phoned from Ottawa to ask if I'd be willing to meeting with Kaj Persson, the Swedish Chargé d'affaires from Nairobi, and talk on the phone with Doug's wife Mary in New Zealand. Finally there was something I could do though I wasn't sure what I could tell them that would helpful. I knew though, if it were my family, they'd want to know anything, everything. What they'd imagine was worse than what I had experienced. I pushed away the thought that I had no idea what was happening to my friends now. I spent the afternoon sitting on our balcony making notes. I didn't want to forget anything that might be important.

As nice as it was being by the lake, it wasn't a holiday any more. I couldn't reconcile my need to keep away from reporters with my desire to be actively working with anyone who could help Doug. However, what I wanted didn't seem to be important. Other people were making the decisions.

In the early evening Kaj Persson met with Dan and me on the main verandah at the hotel. He wanted information for the Swedish government and Jens and Ann-Charlotte's families. I told him about our capture, where we were held, and where I had last seen the others. It was bizarre, sitting in a glamorous hotel sipping beer and talking about the mountain.

The phone call from Mary came about midnight Uganda time. Although Doug had talked about Mary with me and I felt as if I knew her, to her I was a total stranger. She had a soft accent like Doug's. "Thank you for agreeing to talk with me. I know how difficult this must be for you." I could hear her hesitation. I didn't want her to feel she had to tiptoe around asking me questions.

"Mary, I'm fine," I said, trying to sound strong. "When I last saw Doug, he was well, not sick or anything." I wanted to reassure her, convince her and me that Doug would be out any time.

"The men who captured us never treated us badly. We had enough to eat. It wasn't great cooking, but it was the same as they had. I'm sure he's still being treated well." How could anything bad happen? Doug was with Richard, Emmanuel and the Commander in Chief. He'd given Richard his lighter.

Mary said little. I pictured her sitting in a chair with the phone held tight against her ear in a white knuckled hand. She murmured, "Thank you for telling me that," and, "Oh, that's good to hear." She had traveled with Doug in southern Africa several years earlier. She knew what Africa was like without me having to say much.

Then she asked the impossible question. "Do you have any idea why they still have Doug?" My heart pounded. That was my constant question, too.

"I have no idea. I don't know what happened." No matter what I told her about how well we'd been treated or how many ways I tried to assure her Doug must still be fine, I knew nothing. I could hear the drop in her voice. She was so far away. Except for an accident at the beginning of the trip, she would have been with Doug. I shuddered. She might have been with Doug now, too. Dan was safe because he'd gone with the other group. I knew how he'd worried. I knew Mary was doing the same.

On Friday, our last day in Africa, my anxiety level soared into the red. By 4:00 p.m. we were already at the airport waiting for our 8:30 flight.

Entebbe is a very small airport. There is absolutely nothing to do there, not even a place inside to sit. I sat on a luggage cart outside watching people come and go. Dan and I were first in line when the check-in counter opened and checked in without any problems.

We landed in London, Gatwick, at 4:15 a.m. after a nine-hour flight. As we disembarked, the flight crew handed me a note from someone at the Toronto Star asking me to call him as soon as I was able, ' … bearing in mind the time difference between London and Toronto.' I couldn't figure out how he got my name or had known I was on that flight. "Look at this, Dan. A reporter wants me to call him."

"You're not going to, are you?"

"No."

We transferred to Heathrow and waited twelve hours for our flight to Canada. Heathrow was like a giant carnival. Flashing lights, constant announcements over the PA, people rushing everywhere. I needed to keep moving. Dan and I walked up and down the terminal, end to end, over and over. It was as though each step was taking me closer to home.

Suddenly I stopped. "Dan, do you think the reporter might have heard Doug was released and wanted to tell me about it?"

He shook his head. "Martin or someone from the government will get in touch with us when they know something. We have to wait."

FIFTEEN

We landed in Canada on a Saturday evening, four days late. Our family crowded the exit corridor. My daughter, my son and his wife. Dan's mother, sister and brother-in-law. Dan's nieces and nephew. My brother, his wife and family. My aunt and my grandson. Everyone was there. There was a momentary hush as we walked through the glass doors into the Arrivals area. Everyone's eyes were on me. Was I OK? Obviously relieved by what they saw, they swarmed over us, hugging and kissing, smiling and thrusting flowers at me. I felt like a movie star. As touched as I was, it seemed to be a lot of fuss over nothing. I wasn't aware of the tension everyone had been under since Nadine listened to Dan's first message on her answering machine saying I'd been captured by someone and had disappeared. My brother told me all week he'd gone to work, sat at his desk and waited for calls from Ottawa. He would pick papers up, but couldn't concentrate enough to make sense of what was written on them. He made a pile to deal with later. It grew several inches tall before his secretary stopped bringing anything in.

Only four people came back to the house with us: my brother and his wife, Dan's sister and her husband. I don't know who made that decision. Dan and I told them a short version of what had happened. My brother gave me the notes of his conversations with Helen at DFAIT and articles from the Vancouver newspaper. One article said, 'Canada has asked for help from the British High Commission in Kampala as well as the governments in Uganda, Rwanda, Congo and Kinshasa. ...The tourists' vehicle was travelling through thick, bamboo-forested mountains when it was showered with gunfire.' Interesting. It didn't matter that some of the facts were wrong. I was comforted to see how many people were involved in helping find the others.

"Someone from Ottawa is going to contact you tomorrow. They want to set a time for an interview with the BBC to be broadcast on overseas radio. The BBC will aim it at Rwanda and the people who captured you. Helen is being very careful to preserve your privacy. She won't give the BBC your address or phone number. Anyone who needs to contact you will have to go through Ottawa first." Like me, none of our family had spoken to the press, though obviously, from the note I got on the plane, some reporters knew who we were. One reporter had called Dan's mother, but she hung up.

All Sunday I waited, trying to remember everything I needed to say. The whole purpose of the broadcast was to help Doug, Jens and Ann-Charlotte get free. When I was a Vice-Principal I'd taken part in workshops on talking to the media. The workshops stressed that the answer you gave didn't have to exactly match the question. I remembered the Rwandan women and children and how I said I would speak for them. I remembered the warnings I'd had from Shaun about giving terrorists the publicity they sought. During the interview, however, everything I remembered became irrelevant.

The BBC interviewer in London began by setting the scene. "For some time now ethnic conflict and political upheaval have made the border between Rwanda and the Democratic Republic of Congo a volatile region in central Africa. Two weeks ago four foreigners from New Zealand, Canada and Sweden were returning from the Virunga Mountains at the Congo border with Rwanda. They had been taken there to see gorillas in the wild. Returning to their vehicles they were seized by a movement calling itself 'People for the Liberation of Rwanda'. Armed, but not uniformed, one of the hostage takers' aims is, it seems, to protect their communities from attacks by military forces in the area. A week ago one of the four tourists, Canadian Donalda Reid, was released with a list of the movements' demands. From her home in western Canada she has been telling me how they were captured."

OK. How were we captured? "We were returning from having visited the gorillas in the Virunga Mountains in the Democratic Republic of Congo. We were just coming down the mountains to go back to our trucks when the guides saw the trucks at the foot of the mountains were burning. They took us on another path to bring us to a different village. The men came out of the mountain and shot over our heads. Some of us were taken captive." Fuck. This isn't important. He already said all that. I was rambling. I wasn't going to be able to summarize something as complex as being held captive for a week in a few sentences. I couldn't tell everything.

"And how were you treated after you had been taken hostage?"

This is going to be broadcast to Rwanda. The men are going to hear it. I have to be positive. I wouldn't let myself even think of the rape. "Other than the first day when we were all understandably upset and worried and they were getting us up the mountains into Rwanda—that was the only day that we were really frightened—after that, even though we were held captive, we were treated well." They don't need to know about the rest. They won't broadcast everything if I talk too long. Remember the 30 second sound bite.

"Just over a week ago you were released by the group. But you were the only one released. How did that take place?" I can't explain. I didn't do anything wrong. They should have been with me.

"We were told their High Commander had OK'd our release that last day. He said that he would take me as a representative down to show me the problems they had been talking about with my own eyes. After that I joined the others and we started out of the mountains. At approximately four o'clock the others were having a rest and I carried on. I didn't see them after that. I don't know what happened."

"It must be a bit difficult for you now realizing that you were the only one released and that your companions are still being held."

My eyes filled with tears and I grabbed a Kleenex. After a few seconds I managed to say, "Yes, it is." My throat closed. I couldn't talk about the others. There was a long pause as though he were waiting for me to say more. I couldn't.

"The region is a very troubled one at the moment; there are lots of problems politically, militarily. Are you hopeful that the situation can be resolved?" Fuck, no. They're grabbing innocent people and holding them as pawns. Why are you asking this? Don't you know we need to keep the Rwandans happy so they treat Doug and the others well? I'm not going to say anything that might upset any of those government officials or give the rebels a lot of sympathy.

"I don't know a lot about politics. I do know that the people I was with didn't seem to be soldiers. I met women and children. They spoke to me and asked, 'Please let the world help us'. That for me was the most…" I choked again as I saw the women crowded in our shelter under the blue tarp. The woman stared at me, wiped her tears and asked me to help them be safe in their homes again. "That was something I will never forget. All of them had had their husbands killed by people coming up to attack them." I had no idea what had really happened when we heard the guns and mortars. I was careful not to say soldiers. "Their houses had been burned, I saw the burned habitation. This to me is proof that the women and children are being targeted in that area and they shouldn't be."

I was relieved when he said there were no more questions and thanked me. I wasn't sure what I had expected him to ask, but I thought my answers were horrible. I hadn't said anything important apart from mentioning the women and children. One of my British cousins listened for the broadcast on short wave Overseas BBC and called to say it had been aired. I don't know if anyone in Rwanda heard it.

The next day was Monday and finally my family doctor's office was open so I could have him check me for sexually transmitted diseases: HIV, syphilis, gonorrhea and anything else he might think of. I was confident he would find nothing. There had been no penetration, nor had the men ejaculated. But I had to be sure. My doctor was aware of everything that had happened because my son had seen him to make arrangements for the necessary shots so he could fly to Uganda and be with Dan. When the doctor finished the tests, he leaned back against the wall, with his arms crossed on his chest the way he always does when he's going to say something important. "What about some trauma counselling? I can arrange an appointment with a psychiatrist that treats Post Traumatic Stress Disorder."

"I don't need that."

He nodded slowly. "Well, if you ever think you might like to talk with someone, come in to see me and I'll set it up for you. Have you thought about writing down what happened to you?" My brother had mentioned I should write a book, but Dan kept urging me to forget the whole thing. I shook my head.

"I already wrote the main things in my journal. I wanted it written down in case I might need to tell someone something that had happened. I didn't want to forget." I crossed my arms, too.

"That's super. You might want to keep writing, maybe fill in some of the details. Writing is a helpful tool after a trauma. If you want, think of writing it for your grandchildren," he said. "It'll have great interest for them one day." He had found the one reason that I couldn't counter. For thirty years I had been working on genealogy and my family history. After the thousands of hours I'd spent ferreting out bits of information and checking obscure resources, I understood the personal historical value of my experience. Though I had mental reservations, I began writing that night. A few days later all my tests came back—negative.

For the first three weeks after we arrived home, the phone rang constantly; External Affairs, CSIS, and the FBI—everyone wanting information, everyone working to find and free the other three; calls from England and Africa; interviews with officials from everywhere. Everything upset and interfered with my attempts to get back to life the way it used to be. I didn't talk with my family and friends about what had happened. "Don't worry about me. I'm fine," I told them. "I'm not going to let a few days dictate the rest of my life. Everything is fine. I'm fine."

A week after we landed in Vancouver, it was time for me to start back at work. One of the women from the safari group had contacted our School Board to let them know that there was a possibility Dan and I wouldn't be back for the beginning of school. When I called the Superintendent's secretary to say Dan and I had made it home and we'd be at work on time, it was obvious she had no idea what I was talking about. The message hadn't reached the Superintendent's office. Shortly after, the secretary returned my call to say I could have all the time off I needed. I didn't want time off. I was glad to get back to work. I was the Principal of an elementary school. Although I'd been transferred and was starting at a new school, my job was a known, predictable activity. I needed that.

However, my first two days at the new school were anything but normal. The first day, shortly after noon, Helen from DFAIT called. "Hello, Donalda. I'm in a meeting with my boss, Gar Pardy and two men from CSIS—that's the security branch. I know you're at work, but we hoped you could give us a detailed summary of what had happened in Congo and Rwanda. I've got my computer here, and I'll make notes as we go. Tomorrow I'll fax the notes to you to check and make any changes. Are you all right with that?"

Finally, someone with some power. This was my government. They'd been looking for me and they'd help look for the others. I didn't want to forget anything. It didn't matter that I didn't have my notes with me. Every detail was burned into my memory. I had no idea what might be important, so I told them everything—except the rape. When I hung up after two hours, I wanted to run away someplace. It was as if I had been captured and taken up the mountain again. I was exhausted by the energy it had taken to focus and describe what had happened logically and sequentially. Fortunately it was time to lock up the school. I went home to Dan.

Helen's fax was fourteen pages. That evening, a Friday, I went through it and drew detailed memory maps of the areas through which we travelled, the trails we walked, and where we were kept. I added notes on the landscape and geography, descriptions of the various people with whom we were in contact.

"Why are you doing that?" Dan said. "Come to bed and forget it for a while."

"I can't. I have to get these done." Would my maps help them find the area where we had been held? As I drew and described the various locations, I wondered if this was the bit of information that would help them find Doug. When I later checked the maps I'd faxed to Helen against maps in a guidebook, I was surprised how accurate my maps were. There was no way to mistake where we had been.

In spite of being given a clean bill of health earlier in the week, by mid afternoon Saturday, I was feeling dreadful. I was familiar with what my body felt like when I had pneumonia. Shivering and weak, a hot coal burning in the middle of my chest, I called my doctor at his home. He phoned in a prescription for antibiotics and told me to come into the office first thing Monday morning. I swallowed the medicine as soon as Dan brought it and collapsed on our bed.

That night, Saturday, a huge family party had been planned to celebrate Dan's aunt's 90th birthday. When the time came to go, I was feeling so horrible that I told Dan to go without me. I was too sick. "You don't have to do anything," he pleaded. "You can sit in the corner. I know it's supposed to be for Aunt Maureen, but it's really so everyone can see that you're fine." Fine was the last thing I was feeling, but I agreed to go, with the understanding that I would sit quietly in the corner.

That wasn't so easy. "You must have had a terrible time." No kidding. "That was quite a holiday. I guess you won't be going back there again." Good guess. I pulled a chair into a corner behind the table. Dan stood beside me and deflected questions. It wasn't long before the message that I wasn't going to talk got around. Part way through the evening as I sat sipping a glass of water, a familiar searing pain started in my chest near my shoulder. I sat straight and still, breathing shallowly so my lung wouldn't rub on the inflamed part of my chest.

"Dan, that's enough. I have to go."

Tylenol 3 kept the pain in check and on Monday the doctor confirmed I had pneumonia. He told me to stay home in bed until my temperature was normal. Fortunately the antibiotics worked fast. The next day my temperature was normal and I went back to work. I needed to be busy.

The phone calls from Africa and Ottawa continued. Martin phoned me at work from Kampala on Tuesday. "We haven't had any news at all about the others since you left. Doug's son has arrived from New Zealand. He's in Kampala right now.

"It's getting quite unpleasant in Kisoro. There are streams of people crossing into Uganda from Congo, running away from the fighting. It's almost impossible at the border. There are so many soldiers.

"I've sent Paul back to Nairobi. We both don't need to be here, and nothing's happening. It was risky, but we've sent a man into Rwanda with letters from the New Zealand High Commission about Doug. He got back OK, but he bought back no news of any kind."

On Wednesday I got a phone call from Niclas from his camp near Kisoro. "Kisoro's still safe, but the Congo's in turmoil. There are hundreds of refugees crossing the border every day.

"We've got people in Kampala working full time to find and free the others. They have to try to deal with the rebels because there's no real government in that area of Congo any more.

"We printed a letter to the rebels. It's being distributed everywhere. We hope we can set up a meeting to arrange the others' freedom. All the newspapers have been printing a copy of the rebels' press release. People from New Zealand and Sweden are arranging to have the rebels' twelve points published there. The consensus is that the points need be published soon if they're going to be helpful. We had an unsubstantiated report that some rebels, accompanied by white people, had stolen medicine from a Congolese hospital."

Niclas said there was a TV crew with a satellite phone with 'them', though it was unclear whether 'them' referred to the rebels, or those searching for Jens, Ann-Charlotte and Doug. In one of the debriefing interviews I'd mentioned that Jens was wearing contacts but didn't have any cleaning solution in his pack. Niclas said, "Dozens of small bottles of contact lens liquid for Jens are being sent into the mountains with everyone possible. Since we don't know where he is, we're trying everything."

Helen contacted me. "The Swedish government has hired a British company whose business is finding and securing the release of hostages. The company would like to send a representative from England to interview you." The representative arrived on Saturday. We sat at the kitchen table for two days and went through all my notes. One thing he asked was that I refrain from saying anything about the company or revealing any strategies they used in their search for the other three. I completely accepted this restriction, since in future hostage-taking incidents it might make the difference between someone being released or killed.

Dan took one look at my face after the fellow had gone and lost it. "When is enough enough? What else do they expect you to do? This is just making you sick and upset. It's time to forget it and get on with life. All this talk and drawing maps and writing is a waste of time. Nothing will do any good now."

"It doesn't matter. I have to do this." Doug wasn't home yet.

Meeting acquaintances for the first time after my release became a pain. I soon recognized 'the look' as they wondered if they should say anything and what I'd tell them. I waited for their predictable comments.

"How horrible!"

"How exciting!"

"I knew if anyone would be freed, you would be."

"What happened?"

"You need counselling."

"Tell me all about it."

"You must have felt … " This phrase was the lead-in for a list of things they would have been afraid of.

The most common greeting was, "And how are you?" with major emphasis on the word 'are'.

"I'm fine."

After the initial three-week barrage, I became quite adept at changing the conversation. The man delivering our mailbag asked, "I just heard about your summer. Who are you going to get to play you in the movie?"

"Mia Farrow, but she'd have to dye her hair. I like her better than the other actresses who work with Woody Allen. Have you seen his latest movie yet?" And we discussed Woody Allen movies. Much better.

But not having any real information didn't stop some people from developing imaginative interpretations based loosely on the few facts that were available. Some teachers from my former school told me they'd heard I was released because I spoke French and was able to convince the rebels to let me go and be their spokesperson. That explained a couple of comments from my colleagues at a local Principals' conference. As I sat down at the front of a bus driving us back to our hotel, a voice called out, "Donalda, take us to Africa." For a second I wondered if I'd heard accurately.

Then a second voice added, "But don't leave us there." I didn't turn around to see who it was.

My close friends, however, were wonderful. They didn't ask anything. I was skittish about going to the first meeting of my book club. One woman came into the kitchen and threw her arms around me. "Oh, Donalda!" she said as she hugged me close. I could see the tears in her eyes.

"I can't talk about it," I said turning my back to her. "Just pretend that nothing happened. I need some wine. Let's talk about the book." For the rest of the evening we all pretended nothing had changed.

I went out for beer with my best Principal buddies, John, Ted and Liz. We sat around and talked about work. No one even hinted that I'd been to

Africa. After an hour and a couple of pints, I relaxed, "OK, you guys. Thanks for not asking anything. You've been great." By treating me exactly the same as they always had, they made it safe for me to talk. I told them what I like best about the week—being released and coming down the mountain following the cornhusks. That was all I could handle. A few months later I discovered my story had made an impression when John talked about running after dark and noticing the shades of black.

I began calling the three of them my Angels because they kept watch over me. With several hundred people talking and milling around at the beginning-of-year Superintendent's meeting, I became quite anxious and wanted to crawl under a table and hide. My Angels surrounded me and ran interference, fielding questions and comments sent my way. I was surprised by the number of people who made what they thought were funny comments about guerillas and gorillas. I wanted to tell them to fuck off, but I said nothing.

Every day during the first few weeks I expected to hear that the others had finally been freed. Whether I was talking to External Affairs, the owners of the tour companies, or others working to affect their release, I was convinced that something I said, or something I did or didn't do, might be the single thing around which their freedom revolved. On the days I got calls from overseas, I ignored the school and focused on doing whatever was needed. When I hung up the phone and looked around, my head was back on the mountain in Africa. My office was a foreign place. I knew that if I hadn't been released, someone else would have been sitting in my chair. It made my job meaningless.

In our elementary school, when a child does something wrong or breaks a rule, they come to see me. All fall I worked with students to help them develop problem-solving skills and increase their ability to manage anger. Their conflicts mirrored the world's. I wanted to build empathy and help them learn better ways to interact. If I couldn't help them settle their personal conflicts, what hope was there to find solutions on an international or global scale?

The efforts to find the others continued. In mid-September, Niclas phoned from Kisoro. He told me there had been another BBC broadcast, but didn't say what it had contained. "You know the drivers and guides who were captured at the same time as you? They had a very rough time. They were blindfolded the whole time they were captives. Although they got released at the same time as you, they weren't taken to the same place as you. They had to walk for almost fourteen hours to get home. And then, the Congolese authorities held them for over a week more for questioning." I remembered the man who had spoken to me at the Lady's house. So that's why he told me that he was a Ranger. When I heard about how the Africans had been questioned, I sent Niclas and Tony a mental thank-you for how quickly they'd gotten me across the border.

At this time the Vancouver newspaper was reporting that Goma and most of east Congo was under attack by the Interahamwe. Niclas said, "I have a bunch of men that are trying to make contact with the rebels for us. One of them got badly beaten up by the Congolese. They thought he was working with the rebels. It was a big mistake.

"We've been trying to find the man that guided you out. I'm not sure, but maybe we made contact with him. I need to verify whether the man is telling me the truth or not. He said he was paid $20 for bringing you out. Is that right?"

"No. No, it isn't. I didn't have any money. What I told the men who guided me was that they would have to get money from Doug or Jens. I offered them my earrings and my water bottle. They wouldn't take them." I hoped that might help Niclas question anyone who claimed they had information.

In October, Dan and I got a letter from John, the manager of the Virunga Hotel. He sent greetings and thanks. "What a lucky couple you are. Sorry for everything (problems) you met in Uganda-Congo but again praise God for you are blessed. The other people you left still missing are still missing. So you were only lucky."

Later in September my mother-in-law asked, "Has there been any word of the people who were captured with you?"

"No, nothing."

"Maybe they will be let free at Christmas." My heart dropped through the middle of my body. I could hardly breathe. It had never crossed my mind that they might be held that long.

I got a fax from Doug's son, Rob. A New Zealand journalist who wanted to trace our trek in Rwanda and try to contact the rebels who had captured us had approached him for help contacting me. I refused. I told Rob to tell the reporter he had no idea the danger he'd be getting into. He was crazy to even think about it.

At the beginning of December, Doug, Ann-Charlotte and Jens were still somewhere in Africa. There had been no contact of any kind from their captors. Every phone call from Africa brought me running to my office. In the beginning, as I picked up the receiver, I hoped the call was about them being released. Then, I feared I would be told they had been proven dead.

I finished writing every minute detail about what had happened from when we got to Kisoro until we left. I waited to feel calm and normal, but it didn't happen; I felt frightened all the time. I would leap at any loud noise. It took all my control to stay calm and deal with union problems and angry parents. I tried to keep busy all the time so I didn't have time to think about Africa and Doug, Jens and Ann-Charlotte on the mountain. The only place that felt safe was at home with Dan.

In January, Helen from DFAIT went through town on her way to some exotic place to save some poor Canadian in trouble. We met at her downtown hotel. She explained, "I told Guy Pardy that I wanted to stay in Vancouver overnight if I was ever flying through. I wanted to meet you in person." I'm not sure what I expected—the middle-aged mama meets the hotshot savior from Ottawa. But, she was a tiny, delightful woman, only slightly younger than I was. She amazed me with stories of the work she had done around the world at Canadian Embassies, Consulates, and as Director of Emergency Services for Canadians, like me, who got into trouble overseas. Though fortunately most Canadian tourists never need help, it was comforting to know how Canada takes care of her citizens in need. I offered to send her a couple of my better African photographs and gave her a copy of the completed story of my capture.

I also sent a copy of the story to the British company with a query about any new information. They replied, "We are still getting a mixture of rumours, none of which can be confirmed. Our major proviso to anyone arriving with 'the latest' information is that we require a minimum of 'Proof of Contact', which nobody has been able to provide at the present time. We have followed up and investigated all rumours and stories, but with no positive results. We will continue to do so until something positive is found. Recently the rumors have tended to be less optimistic and we are now receiving more rumors indicating they are dead rather than alive. Bearing in mind the area involved and the occurrences over the last months this may well be the case … " I didn't want to hear that. I knew what the fax said was right, but I didn't want to believe that I was the only one released. If I thought that, I would have to think about what had happened to the others.

I decided to read about Rwanda, to put what happened to me in a broader context. Were there bad guys and good guys, or, was what Helen said the truth? "There are no bad guys or good guys. The real question is, who are we supporting today?" What I read paralleled what Emmanuel had told us. The facts were the same, only my interpretation was different.

As a colony of Germany and then Belgium, the fluid relationship between the Tutsi and Hutu remained much as it had been historically until the Belgians issued identity cards around 1930. When the fluidity between groups disappeared and the Belgians supported the Tutsis, who dominated all areas of power and privilege, the resentment between Hutu and Tutsi escalated. In 1959, there was a massive Hutu uprising against the Tutsis in power which resulted in about 20 000 Tutsis being killed and many thousands more Tutsis leaving Rwanda to lived 'in exile' in the neighbouring countries.

In response to the Tutsi drive for independence, Belgium switched its support to the Hutu, increasing the discord between the groups. In 1962, when Rwanda was given independence, a Hutu majority government, the Parmehutu, was set up. This set the stage for on-going periodic clashes between Tutsis and Hutus over the next 30 years that resulted in tens of thousands of deaths and as many as 100 000 fleeing as refugees.

In 1973, Juvenal Habyarimana, the Hutu commander of the Rwandan army, took over the leadership of the country in a coup d'état. Over the next twenty-one years he gathered power and money into his hands. His Presidential Guard was responsible for assassinations and massacres of anyone, Tutsi or Hutu, who opposed him. He trained two Hutu militia groups, the Interahamwe, "Those Who Attack Together", and the Impuzamugambi, "Those Who Have The Same Goal". Bolstered by foreign aid from the French government, money in Habyarimana's hands was used to build up the Rwandan army.

In 1990, children of exiled Tutsi refugees who had been living in Uganda organized the Rwandan Patriotic Front (RPF). Led by Paul Kagame, they began attacks on Rwanda. In response, the Rwandan army murdered thousands of Tutsis and moderate Hutus in Rwanda.

By 1993 the Hutu Rwandan government had instituted a systematic program of promoting dislike, fear and resentment against the Tutsis who remained in the country. On government radio they broadcast hate propaganda against the Tutsis and any Hutus who opposed Habyarimana. Murders of moderate Hutus and Tutsis increased. France ignored the growing abuses and continued its military assistance to Habyarimana.

After long negotiations, the Rwandan government and the RPF signed a peace agreement, the Arusha Accord. United Nations troops, UNAMIR, under Roméo Dallaire, were sent to Rwanda as peacekeepers to assist the set up of a transitional government with shared power between Hutus and Tutsis. Delays in setting up the transitional government continued through the early months of 1994. French forces in the country continued to provide training, leadership and arms to the Hutus. The government-supported radio continued to promote the killing of Tutsis—with machetes, bow and arrows, swords and spears, since guns were scarce. UNAMIR personnel, aware of what was happening, attempted to get assistance from the UN, the USA and the world community generally, to contain the increasingly volatile situation and prevent the impending massacres. No one listened.

When Habyarimana was killed on April 6, 1994, widespread killings began. As Dallaire feared, the moderate Prime Minister, members of Habyarimana's cabinet and Belgian UN Peacekeepers were murdered. As predicted, Belgium withdrew its troops. When the UN reduced its troops and refused to broaden the UNAMIR role to include the protection of the population and prevention of killing, the UN forces were helpless to avert the killings.

In the next three months, between April and June 1994, between 800 000 and 1 000 000 people, including women and children, were systematically murdered, hacked to death by Hutus with machetes as they attempted to flee or sought refuge in churches. Their bodies were left to rot or thrown into the rivers.

Throughout the genocide the RPF made forays into Rwanda and in July took control of Kigali, the capital of Rwanda, setting up a Tutsi-dominated government. Over 500 000 Hutus, afraid that they would be killed in reprisals, fled into Zaire. By August, two million Rwandan Hutus had fled into Zaire, Uganda and Tanzania. Among them were the *génocidaires* who were directly responsible for the planning and execution of the Tutsis. In the refugee camps the *génocidaires* operated with impunity, continuing to murder, loot and control the distribution of food. By mid August there was a virtual state of war in the refugee camps. None of the UN member nations would provide troops to restore order. Cholera and disease killed over 60 000 refugees. Those Hutus not involved with the genocide were too afraid of the Interahamwe to return to Rwanda. For two years it remained this way.

In 1996 Paul Kagame forcibly closed the camps. Hundreds of thousands of Hutu refugees flooded back to Rwanda. The *génocidaires* hid in the forests of Rwanda and Zaire and waited.

A UN International Tribunal on war crimes was set up in Arusha, Tanzania, and by 1998 was beginning to hold trials for some of the leaders responsible for inciting the genocide. The news articles about the efficiency and effectiveness of the Tribunal are less than complimentary. Hundreds of thousands of other Rwandan Hutus were still being held in Rwandan jails waiting for overwhelmed, inadequate courts to deal with them.

On August 11, 1998, the day we went to see the gorillas, we walked into the beginning of a civil war that would ultimately involve the majority of the countries of eastern Africa.

SIXTEEN

After I got home and recorded every detail, the question 'Why?' remained. Unable to separate myself from the experience, I accepted I needed professional help.

After six sessions with a psychiatrist I was left with a diagnosis of PostTraumatic Stress Disorder (PTSD) and an understanding that seemingly innocent events could 'trigger' intense feelings of upset and distress. Unfortunately, there was no reduction in my symptoms. I was still bothered by recurring thoughts about my capture and a whirlwind of feelings —anxiety and fear when I was exposed to anything reminiscent of the capture; a general depression, sadness and low energy; irritability, anger and resentment. Although I was easily startled and overly alert, I was emotionally numb and withdrawn.

I haunted the library looking for information about PTSD and trauma. I learned PTSD was a 'condition fear' that had bypassed the conscious areas of my brain and was etched into my amygdala. No amount of thinking could change it. Every time anything related to the capture came up, my amygdala sprang into action sending hormones and neurotransmitters raging through my body flooding me with dread, fear and anger. *Beware, beware! There's something dangerous here.* I became hyper-alert, searching unsuccessfully for what was making me uneasy. Every place became unsafe. Even when I recognized I had been 'triggered', I had no idea how to avoid it in the future.

While I was seeing the psychiatrist, I continued to look for other ways to treat my trauma. The most promising was a relatively new therapy, EMDR, Eye Movement Desensitization and Reprocessing, which had been used to treat survivors of the Oklahoma bombing quickly and successfully. Fast and easy appealed to me. At the beginning of March 1999, I got a referral to see Ian Macnaughton, a psychologist who, among other therapies, did EMDR.

When Ian opened his office door, it was like being greeted by an off-duty, slim, sophisticated Saint Nicholas with a head wreathed with white hair and a companion white beard and mustache. His sparkling eyes and welcoming smile only enhanced my impression. His room resembled a comfortable den. Two leather chairs and a footstool were grouped on one side of a small oriental carpet, and a wine-coloured armchair with a light bar behind it on the other side. I sat in one of the leather chairs with Ian opposite me in the armchair.

I explained the problems I was having and showed him the bound pages of my writing. "I thought that if I wrote it all down it would go away, but it hasn't. I've seen a psychiatrist. He says I'm doing well, but it doesn't feel like I am."

"I'd like to read what you've written, if you want to share it with me." I was relieved and grateful. By reading it, he would know what happened, everything, without me having to talk about it. I handed him the copy.

"I understand you do EMDR."

He nodded. "We don't know exactly how EMDR works in treating trauma, but it can be quite successful." I was confident, if it worked for the people in Oklahoma, it would work for me. The hour was up too soon. We agreed to meet again in a week.

At our second session, Ian returned my story and encouraged me to keep writing and record my therapy. "Can you tell me what happened the day you were captured?" he said.

I began calmly describing the men coming down the hill, shooting at us and ordering us out of brambles. When I said, "The men forced us to go up…" I panicked, terrified, and began to cry.

"You can leave that part out if you want to," Ian said. The terror disappeared instantly. I skipped the men hauling me up the mountainside and continued talking. Nothing else upset me, not even telling him about the rape attempt.

We focused on my memory of going up the mountain in our first EMDR session. It, and each subsequent session, began with a set of questions.

"On a scale of seven, how high would you rate your discomfort around the incident?" Ian said.

"Seven out of seven."

"On a scale of ten, how high would you rate your ability to deal with the incident?"

"Two out of ten."

When Ian moved the light panel in front of me, I panicked and burst into tears again, too distraught to use the EMDR lights. Since I was unable to deal with my trauma head on, Ian began to teach me how to become a detached observer. "I want you to be able to identify the feelings and body sensations that come up when you get upset or anxious, and look for places in your body that change or react. Try to be non-judgmental about what is happening. I call it *being mindful.*" As long as I concentrated on my body changes I was able to follow the lights; the panic stayed manageable, never overwhelming me. When I left his office I felt stronger, more confident and able to cope.

At the next session I had no problem following the EMDR lights back and forth, left and right with my eyes, until I thought about the *guns.* Instantly, in my head, I was watching guns and shooting; men in long, dark coats ran down a hall shouting and shooting. Panic, horror and helplessness beat through me. It wasn't Rwanda; it was Columbine, only in my school corridor. Those images morphed into Dan and me holding each other. With his arms around me, the upset and fear washed down through my feet and out of my body leaving my skin infused with blood and life. I was filled with a deep, total calm.

I arranged to meet Ian every Thursday morning before school.

"I want you to call me if you're feeling shaky," Ian said as I left the office. I agreed, thinking I wouldn't need to. I was fine. I was strong.

In May I was in contact by fax with Doug's family in New Zealand. They were trying to find answers to their questions about how Doug could have simply disappeared. We exchanged information; I sent them a copy of my story about the week Doug and I were captives together and Doug's son sent me a translated copy of the PALIR demands. As I read them in English for the first time, I became explosively upset and angry. What had sounded so reasonable in Rwanda was suddenly inflammatory. I could see Emmanuel's smiling face and I wanted to spit. You want freedom? What about my friends? Where are they? Murderer.

In June 1999, headlines in the local paper screamed *Ugandan Tourist Massacre*. Another group of tourists who had gone to see the gorillas in Bwindi National Park had been attacked by a swarm of rebels, later reported to be Hutu. Eight American and British tourists were murdered and six released. Shortly after, because of the Americans killed in Bwindi, I got a call from Helen at DFAIT hoping to arrange an interview with the FBI. I agreed. When the woman from the Counter Terrorism Department in Washington, DC, asked what kind of uniforms the men who captured me were wearing, it was obvious that she knew very little about Africa.

At home the next day, I sat in my mother's big blue leather recliner downstairs with my eyes closed and visualized the bandits coming down the mountain. My body shuddered, my stomach dropped and my mouth dried. When I imagined walking through the grass, my feet began twitching alternately in a continuous short, rapid, running movement. I concentrated on breathing and tried unsuccessfully to swallow. A wisp of unease began to curl up in the back of my mind; I opened my eyes. On the wall in front of me was my photograph of a Chinese temple, incense spiraling up to heaven. Dried flowers in an old birch bark basket made a splash of colour on the antique table. I was home. My legs immediately stopped running. I took a deep breath and swallowed.

At the next session I told Ian how the grass had made my legs run. Keeping a positive image of grass in my mind—a field of Canadian wheat, golden shoots bending and waving—I thought about the capture and let my feet run. Ian said, "While you were processing those memories, except for your feet moving, you sat absolutely still. This is like the frozen state where the trauma was caught."

"I tried my best to keep up. The ground was uneven and my feet kept getting caught in the grass. I thought my arms would fall off from the pain of their shoulders on my arms. I couldn't do it."

When Ian and I met next, he suggested we try something new. I lay on a mat on the floor with my eyes closed while Ian cradled my head in his hands, moving it gently. As I begin to relax, waves of sadness and loss welled up from deep inside my body. Tears poured down my face. Then, a thought of my father who had been dead for nearly forty years appeared in my head. I hadn't known he was sick until I was called home from University for his funeral. I hadn't been able to say goodbye or hug him. He had disappeared. The muscles through my chest, diaphragm and abdomen tightened; I was crying and shaking. The skin on my legs and hands began to tingle; my skin felt ghost white. It was over fifteen minutes before I was able to stand up.

"What's wrong?" I asked. "What happened?" With Ian supporting me I swayed unsteadily on my feet, close to fainting.

"All the blood moved from your extremities to your body core to deal with the emotions and release the energy trapped in your muscles. It will pass, but you'll need to sit in the waiting room until you feel more solid." It was twenty minutes before I felt safe to drive to work. Somehow I made it through the day.

Though I had hoped the therapy would cure me quickly, I finally accepted that I had a long way to go. I was dealing not just with the African trauma, but with issues from my past.

The end of June finally arrived and school closed for the summer. I was worried about Dan. There were so many things we didn't talk about since we'd come home from Africa. They were like invisible bombs waiting to explode. Bone weary, I lay curled in a ball on the bed. *I can't keep you safe*, screamed through my head. I began to sob. Safe? Who? My father? Doug? Ann-Charlotte and Jens? I needed to know that I had been successful just once.

When Anne, one of my best friends, told me she had decided to go to Africa, I was compelled to give her a copy of my capture story. I told her about the intense feelings that had surfaced around my father. Anne said, "And you never got to say good-bye. You wrote in your story that you don't know if you said good-bye to Doug when you left the group the last time, but that you hoped you had." I hadn't made the connection between Doug's disappearance and my father.

The first anniversary of my capture was approaching quickly. I remembered the psychiatrist's cautions about anniversaries being 'triggers' and was apprehensive how I'd react. Dan and I left on a driving holiday with Ian's phone number and email address tucked safely in my purse, just in case.

At Jasper we rode the airtram to the top of Whistlers Mountain where the wind scoured the bare rock slopes and buffeted our bodies as we slowly climbed toward the peak. The 8000-ft. altitude was almost the same as the altitude of the passes in Rwanda. I kept thinking, If Jens and Ann-Charlotte had chosen to climb the Rockies, instead of Kilimanjaro, and look at bears instead of gorillas, they'd be alive today.

While we were driving Dan and I talked about being captured. He had always felt that we'd both have been released if we'd been together when the men attacked. He was sure many of the Africans in that area knew what happened to the other three because of the numbers of people who would have seen us during our capture. He wondered how much more Charles, the tour leader, knew than he acknowledged. But, there was no way we would ever know.

Although the capture anniversary was without incident, the first thing I saw when I went back to school at the end of August was an email from the British company asking me for permission to release a copy of what I had written to the FBI. I'd already talked with the FBI after the second guerilla murders. I knew the story I'd written of our capture contained nothing substantive for tracking terrorists. I refused. It had to end sometime.

By the middle of September a giant black cloud hung over everything I did; my back and neck muscles knotted, pulled and ached. For two weeks I struggled with no idea why things were so bad. It was only a comment from Dan that made me realize I'd been triggered. I had been following the news of a hostage taking in Ecuador involving kidnapped Canadian pipeline workers. "They won't be released for a long time. In South America, when there's a hostage taking, it can take months before they're freed. That's just the way it is there." I felt much better once I knew what made me feel so sick.

At my next session with Ian, we talked about the Canadian hostages. I began sobbing as soon as I thought about them. "Run away from the danger. Run toward Dan," he said. The muscles in my legs responded instantly, not with the big muscle running movement I'd felt in my mother's chair, but in a micro-movement deep in the muscles, just enough that I could feel it. I pictured running to Dan; he put his arms around me and held me, smoothing my hair; I tucked my head under his chin. I was protected. My sobs subsided, the running slowed, and my emotions calmed. Dan put his arm around me and we ran together. With calm detachment, I watched us run while my legs continued moving.

"I'm running with Dan," I told Ian. Together we ran down the mountain through the long grass, toward the houses below. I could see our house in Vancouver and ran up the stairs and shut the door. My legs ran.

"Find your safe place." I ran down the stairs and sat in my mother's blue leather chair. Instantly my legs stopped. I was safe.

For a split second my skin was a white light covering my body, separated from the flesh and muscle by a millimeter of space. The flesh beneath the skin released a wave that flowed down and out of my body, leaving intense relief. Deep sadness and loss flooded in. "I ran to the chair. The chair was my mother's spot, but she's gone, dead. She gave me unconditional love, no matter what."

Later that day I was struck by the beginning of a thought—I had been minimizing what happened to me in Africa, discounting the seriousness of my experience. I WAS BRAVE.

I had been scared, very scared, deathly scared the whole time I was captured. In order to keep going I took my fright and buried it so deeply that I wasn't aware it was there. I had continued to deny the fear, unable to confront it, believing I had only been traumatised when I collapsed going up the mountain. In fact, everything, the whole week, was ongoing trauma. Fight or flight … everything I did was a mental fight using all my skills and wiles, to stay alive, to survive.

I was scared, very scared, deathly scared the whole time I was captured. I felt my stomach knot and my chest tighten. I sat in the blue chair, hid behind my hands and imagined going to my safe place. My mind's eye saw me driving up to the hotel in Kisoro. Dan had his arms around me, kissing me. Instantly I was calm.

I continued seeing Ian once a week through the fall. I didn't dwell on fear or think about it much, but I was always aware it was there. At times I could feel it bubbling up through my body like the black ooze on the X-files, creeping under my skin and flowing through my body, visible only in my eyes. When I was at work or at home, things were normal. If I let fear out here, where things are normal, *here* became like *there*. I didn't want to be afraid. And what if the fear overpowered me? Could I survive it again?

In November Ian and I started on the terror again. It was time. We sat facing each other, with our knees almost touching. "I don't want to be lost!" I sobbed. Lost, dead? I didn't know. I went to the mountain in my head. *They waved their guns and shouted at us to hurry. Vite! Vite! They pushed and pulled me up the hill through the grass.* My hands and legs waved and jumped. When I held my hands together to find where the energy was coming from I noticed a very painful spot near my elbow on the arm the men used when they were hauling me up the mountain.

For support Ian moved his knee so it rested against mine while he squeezed my hands in a tactile form of EMDR. My body began to twist as though the left half of my spine was a strong magnet pulling sideways toward an iron object where Ian was sitting. I tried to resist but the pull got steadily stronger, pulling me sideways. When Ian moved his shoulder against my left shoulder, the magnetic pull stopped instantly, though my tremors continued. The buzzer rang. I put the sound away and let the cycle continue until the energy released. I didn't want to stop. I needed to keep working on the terror. I set up a second, longer appointment each week through December.

When I went in for my first hour and a half appointment, we worked slowly so I wouldn't lose the control we had been building for most of a year. I listened to alternating tones in earphones and concentrated on the feltsense; there was an unrelenting tightness in my shoulders, like a solid inverted triangle with the base across my shoulders and the point down my spine, a thick rope along my spine, and a feeling of warmth under my shoulder blades. Ian monitored my muscles. "Let it happen without trying to control or restrict it. It's like riding the edge between pulling back and falling in."

The voice in my head started shouting, "*This is stupid. Why are you doing this?*" I told Ian.

"That's what I was referring to. Just stay with the feeling."

"*He doesn't know what he's doing. Why are you listening to him?*"

Each session we built my strength and control. When I left the office there was a feeling in my body of something solid, a core of strength.

One morning I drove up to a cold dark school building, empty of children, with the staff standing outside on the sidewalk. Heavy winds at 7 a.m. had caused a power outage that left the school without heat or lights. While I was at Ian's, the Vice-Principal and staff closed the school and sent the children home for the day. Chaos. I experienced the same feelings I had had when I was in Rwanda—dry mouth, pounding heart, a feeling of being attacked and held hostage.

Later, during EMDR, I described how my body reacted similarly during my capture and the school closing. A voice in my head kept saying, "I need to keep them safe."

"Repeat after me. Keep the kids safe. Keep the others safe."

"Keep the kids safe. Keep the others safe." My eyes followed the lights. "Keep the kids safe. Keep the others safe." I had done all I could, but I had failed to keep everyone safe. I began to cry.

"I need to keep everyone safe. And I can't do it."

We began another round of EMDR focusing on the last time I saw the others standing on the path surrounded by the Rwandans. My thoughts immediately jumped ahead to the noise and commotion of the men hunting the wild pig. I had been terrified. "I can't stay here," I said to Ian. "I need to keep going down the mountain."

I went back down the hill, over the rocks and roots, moving quickly and steadily, down. The light faded and we were in the grasses out of the forest, following the path. I fell over rocks. It got darker and darker until it was as dark as sitting with my eyes closed. And then I was alone.

I was quite calm. I knew there was no one there to help. I didn't know where I was or where I should go. I couldn't see anything but the faint lightness of the cornhusks once in a while. There were lots of stars, but no moon or lights anywhere. So I walked out. It was black.

It was black. My eyes were closed.

"Were you relieved when you finally got to people?"

"No. The first day, the nice young man took me back into the forest. I had no way of knowing what these people would do. I didn't feel safe. I had to get to Kisoro to be safe; I had no choice but to trust them."

At school, there was an email from the British company saying there was nothing new to report from Africa. I typed my reply with tears running down my face.

Thanks for the message. If you are in contact with Anne-Charlotte and Jens' families please tell them I am very sorry that they weren't released too. I know that nothing I did could have made any difference. I hope they have found peace.

I thought about Doug's wife, Mary. I had been so certain the others would also be released when I spoke to her on the phone from Entebbe. I had failed. I didn't keep them safe.

As I hung the tinsel on our Christmas tree that night Dan and I talked about Africa. He told me about sitting around a table at the hotel in Kisoro planning what to send with the Border Rat into the mountains. "The only thing I thought you might recognize was my Bic pen. When the note was translated into French, Swahili and Kinya-rwanda, we wrapped it around the pen."

"I used Doug's pen." I didn't share my doubt that when I was on the mountain I'd have made the connection between Dan and a Bic pen.

At breakfast on New Years' morning, Dan said, "How long are you going to be going to Ian before you're cured?" Right then I wasn't sure what being cured would be like.

"I don't know."

Then he talked more about when he was waiting in Kisoro. Our conversation made me more aware of Dan's trauma. I had been a hostage, but he had to wait.

In January when our sessions began again, I knew it was time to start working on the fear, but even thinking about it frightened me. I held the pulsing EMDR paddles. "As I went up the mountain I remembered something I'd read by William Glasser about control. I was determined to keep as much control for myself as I could. Some things I did during the week were intuitive, but I was usually conscious of what I was doing and saying, working the edge between pushing for what I wanted and needed, and waiting passively."

An edge of anxiety crept in around the memories. I shut my eyes to cut out any distractions and seesawed between here-and-now and there-and-then, inching closer to the fear.

One afternoon in March when I got home, I heard the answering machine click on. As I listened, my ability to deal calmly with my life evaporated. "This is Constable Smith from the National Security section of the RCMP.

I'd appreciate it if Donalda would give me a phone call at her earliest convenience." The RCMP was passing on a request from the FBI who wanted me to sign a waiver giving the British Company permission to release written material to them. The RCMP couldn't tell me what material they wanted. Was it my story that I'd said no to a year earlier? Once again, I called Helen in Ottawa. From her I learned that the FBI wanted a sixty to seventy page document detailing what I had told the Company right after I was released. I want to see the pages before I gave my permission. I arranged to have a copy sent to me by courier.

As we talked, Helen told me about the work she'd done for the Canadian hostages in South America. Hearing how close they came to dying was almost more than I could emotionally handle. As I stretched to hang up the phone my body began shaking so hard I dropped the receiver.

My anxiety about Africa built as I waited for the couriered document to arrive. I couldn't ignore Africa any more.

"I want you to think about the hostages in Ecuador," Ian said. Instantly fear hit my upper chest tightening my breathing to short panting breaths, constricting my throat so I couldn't swallow. I felt as if I were choking. Fear surrounded my body like a cylinder under my skin, moving up from my hips to my shoulders and upper chest and then pushing down through the inside of my body to my core. My leg was running; I tried to go to my safe place, the big blue chair. My eyes moved back and forth.

"The men in Ecuador put one fellow who was very ill in a stream to keep him alive ... I couldn't keep the others alive ... I went first down the mountain ... If they had gone first would they have been alive?... If I hadn't gone first would I have been alive?... Did I cause them to die?... I don't want them to die!"

"Repeat after me, 'Better them than me.'"

"Yes, better them than me ... I want to live ... I don't want to die or disappear ... I couldn't keep them safe ... I can't do it all ... It's too hard."

The next day the long-awaited envelope arrived. It was so thin that I thought for a second there was nothing in it. I ripped the envelope open and pulled out a very thin coil bound report in a navy blue cover. The cover letter said, "...We agree with you that your full account need not be given to the FBI...In this synopsis, which went to the Foreign Offices ... (the interviewer) told them that much of your initial debriefing was personal and would not be of investigative advantage for them to have." I closed my eyes and sagged with relief. They agreed with me. The letter continued. "You might care to look at the synopsis to see whether you feel that this is the document that you feel comfortable to give to the FBI."

There were only three pages! Three pages for all that anguish. I skimmed it quickly, and then read it again slowly. It was accurate and comprehensive. I emailed my release consent and hoped I wouldn't hear from anyone again.

The three pages referred to me being indecently assaulted. That phrase kept niggling in my head. I thought I had already dealt with the attempted rape. After reading the report, however, it upset the calmness of every day and woke me up twitching every night.

"Ian, I need to work on the rape." We used the lights.

From a far distance I watched the men hauling me up the hill and laying me down. My body reacted strongly to the images. *Nothing... blackness... the relief of being on the ground, not having to move. Breathing again... the pain in my arms easing... breathing. Hearing voices but not caring what was said...* Then, suddenly, I was watching myself go up the mountain again. Ian slipped on earphones so I could close my eyes. My thoughts were intense and crystal clear. *Lay still... don't respond...* My senses were super acute. I could tell what was happening even with my eyes closed. *You should win an Academy Award for this acting... don't let them know how you really are...* I used every part of me to control what was happening without seeming to do anything but lie there in feigned unconscious non-compliance. *Survive!*

And I was so proud of myself for getting free. So proud that I had thwarted the rape! I was so sure that I was going to be free. What hubris! I knew I shouldn't go back to the forest. I knew the nice young man wasn't helping me get free. All of my instincts working overtime had saved me, and then I stopped listening. *I let myself be taken back to the forest.*

The thread of my thoughts wound back to the beginning, back to being captured. This time, when I walked down the path out of the forest and saw the grasses and the roofs of the houses below, I didn't go back with the nice young man. *I kept walking along the path, only it was daylight, not night. I went into the village and the people in the houses came out and met me the way they had at night, only it was day. And they took me down to the border where Dan was waiting. I was safe. Dan was there and he took me home. I was safe.*

When I was in the forest I used all my senses fully. I had one purpose—to survive. Anything that wasn't *there* and *then* didn't exist. There was nothing beyond the confines of those bamboo barriers. It took an enormous effort to remember that there was a world apart from where we were and ask them to take a message to my husband in Kisoro.

I tried to help Doug, Ann-Charlotte and Jens, but I was the most important. I acknowledged it without feeling guilty. Like any animal caught in a trap, I struggled to get free, to survive. I answered the way our captors expected. "What will you tell the world when you are released?"

Oh crap, here we go again! "I will tell them that you want peace and security. That you want justice and a share of governing the country." Mostly, though, I spoke from my heart, from my feelings of empathy and connection. I think that was what made the Commander in Chief tell me about his family being killed and prompted the woman to let me hold her baby.

At times my decisions were purely bravado and cheekiness, like walking up to the big commanders in the village, sticking out my hand and greeting them in formal French, "Je suis enchanté ..." I certainly *wasn't* enchanted to meet them!

At the end of the session we discussed my feeling that, if Dan had been with me, the whole incident would have ended badly. I couldn't have saved both of us. It took everything I had to save myself. If I had been worried about him, I couldn't have done what was needed to save myself and save him too. I thank God that he was with the other group.

At work I gave some resources to a parent whose adopted child had PTSD. I told her I understood because I suffered with PTSD. After she left, I wondered what I would have said if she had asked what caused my PTSD. I searched for words that would say what happened in the most accurate but economical manner.

I was kidnapped under gunfire with three other people, sexually assaulted, held captive in the forest for a week and then released. The others were murdered after I was released.

I told Ian my bare-bones description. As I spoke, I could feel the tension explode in my body.

"What do you see when you say what happened to you?"

"I don't see anything. A color. Black. It's all black ... evil, evil, evil." The horror and evil were visible to me.

Men with guns around us, shouting, prodding us with guns—swirls of black around their heads and shoulders ... evil.

Looking down on my body as they tugged my pants off—swirls of evil, black around their heads and shoulders ... evil.

Walking slowly up the mountain—swirls of black enveloping the bodies of the men who led me on ... evil.

Blackness all around—walking down the path between two men ... evil.

Sitting and sipping beer, responding politely that my daughter would choose her own husband ... evil.

Blackness everywhere ...

I looked at the evil over and over, acknowledging the fear I felt in each place—the walk up the mountain, the camp, with the men and guns, hearing the sounds. My body was braced and vigilant; my white knuckled hands gripped each other, my shoulders jerked, pushed and rotated, my head rolled from side to side, tears flowed down my cheeks.

"Evil, evil, evil! All that time I had to smile and ignore it to survive. And I did." My voice broke.

I continued to watch my body. "I feel like I could vomit." My stomach inched toward being sick and I felt the residue of our session throughout my body. When I was calm and grounded enough I left his office. I drove to the beach and sat for a half-hour in the blazing sun looking at the mountains. Then I headed back to work.

When I next saw Ian we were both excited about the amount of unwinding I had done, the major issues I faced, and the strength from which I had worked. "There was no dissociation or overload at all. You just kept with the feelings and remained in total control."

I thought it would be hard to find the blackness again, but in an instant my body reacted. Eyes closed, I noticed and watched my body. The muscle movements that usually came in the middle of the night began, slowly at first, then faster, more intensely. For a long time I monitored the movement. Then, hands thrown in the air, I froze. Without movement and minimal respiration I sat carved for several minutes. A tiny movement and I froze again. Ian waited silently. After four or five long sessions like this, I told him, "I'm watching." It was as though I was going down the path again, listening for sounds—hyperalert.

For about forty-five minutes I was an observer; images would flash in my head as my body reacted. *Heavy weight on my shoulders: walking beside the men.* A deep breath. *Remembering the strength I felt inside as I had stolen seconds of control for myself.* Spasms in my diaphragm, body twisting and face contorted. *Walking in the dark, seeing the flashlights going around the muddy area in the opposite direction to where the man was leading me, hearing or imagining his voice saying, couchez.*

"I'm walking in the dark and I can see the flashlights. I go through the mud to get back with the others. I don't want anything to happen to them. Without actually telling him what had happened to me I try to tell Jens to watch Ann-Charlotte, to stay with her at all times." Tears trickled down my cheeks.

I was kidnapped under gunfire with three other people, sexually assaulted, held captive in the forest for a week and then released. The others were murdered after I was released.

The three-page document had been pivotal in allowing me to look at what had happened separate from the conflicting emotions I had felt, the fear I had denied. That week, for the first time, I saw the evil alongside the fascination.

It was almost time for the buzzer to ring. My eyes were closed. From deep in my chest a force pushed up under my ribs, spreading to my throat, curling into my neck, and suddenly grabbing my legs in a rock-like contraction exactly like when I was being forced up the mountain, sending pain shooting up my body. When my muscles finally relaxed, several minutes later, I burst into tears and sobbed wildly. Almost as quickly as it came the uncontrollable outburst passed.

It was getting less difficult to talk with Dan about what Ian and I were doing and how seemingly innocent happenings affected me. We read a newspaper article about a reporter in Sierra Leone who survived a gun battle where two men had been murdered beside her. "She wrote calmly and objectively about it," Dan said, "but the horror of having two men executed beside her will hit home one day. They were killed right beside her. Not like you where there was shooting and all, but it was far away. Your time was more like a camping trip in the forest." He echoed the detached, dissociated tone of what I had first written.

Another newspaper article about airplane hostages in Indonesia said they had a 50% chance of survival. I wondered, if they had a 50% chance, what was my percent? 100% because I survived? Did the others have a 0% chance because they died? Or did I have a 25% chance? A 33.3% chance?

"How have things been going the last while?" Ian asked when we met three weeks later. I thought about Africa and waited. Nothing happened. I closed my eyes and pictured the capture, being prodded up the hill and falling. I watched the men on the path and how I walked out of the forest into the sunshine. I saw the nice young man draw me back into the forest as if I were a child's pull toy on the end of a string. The Bush Pig. The long line of cornhusks fading into darkness. The men. Smiling and being nice. It was like watching a movie. It was about me, but it wasn't ME.

I opened my eyes and looked at Ian. "It's gone." The blackness was gone. I no longer had to hide. I was in my safe place.

After eight days as a captive I had been physically freed, but it had taken almost two years of intensive work for me to reclaim my emotions, to get my Self back. I thought of the women I'd met on the mountain in Rwanda. They weren't able to escape from that hell. They may never be able to say that.

The second anniversary of my capture and release passed unnoticed. The stranglehold Africa had on my thoughts and feelings seemed to be permanently gone. All that was left was a feeling of loneliness for the all-consuming passion it had held.

I am the only survivor. The randomness of why I am alive and not the others is as incomprehensible as those TV images of 800 000 Rwandans murdered. Every evening from some distant part of the world we see horrific tragedies reduced to a two-minute announcement and a fifteen-second sound bite. We watch and then carry on with our lives, forgetting that, except for the vagary of birth, they are us; different cultures, different religions, different skin colours, but people, just as we are, sharing a common humanity. The women in Rwanda were the same as me. To survive, their basic physical needs for nutrition, shelter and health had to be met. To grow, however, they need to be secure, free and loved like me. The images of the week I was a captive were seared into my soul. For a brief time I had been one of the women of the Rwandan forest.

In 2001 Dan and I returned to Africa to celebrate my retirement. The physical effects of the trauma were gone. The memory was there, but surprisingly, no pain. It was like running my tongue over a big canker sore that I'd had for a while and discovering that sometime, when I wasn't aware, it had healed and no longer hurt.

The international news from Africa had been less than inviting; the continued war in Congo, Ebola in Uganda; bandits, kidnapping and murder in the Ruwenzoris and Virunga Mountains; Embassy bombings; floods in Mozambique; AIDS; war in Angola; murders, land appropriation and journalists jailed in Zimbabwe. I wanted to go back to Africa, but I wouldn't take chances. We went to Tanzania and Kenya, two of the most stable countries of eastern Africa.

When I was asked why I wanted to go back, I talked flippantly about the animal photos I took last time, about how a trip to the zoo would soon be the only way to see the animals that now roam freely in African game parks, and how it would allow Dan to climb Kilimanjaro. My other reasons were less easy to explain. Africa pulled me with a draw that exceeded the draw of animals or photographs or going back to prove something to myself. Richard Leakey spoke of the *genetic memory* we all have of Africa, the feeling of belonging there. When I thought about Africa, I was filled with an aliveness that was so intense I felt I was glowing. It was a mixture of newness, of ancient times and practices, the novelty of cultures so different from ours, the siren song of snuffling and howling around the night tent, some kind of affective core connection, of needing to be there. When I was a captive on the mountain, every one of my senses had operated at maximum, my instinctive responses perfectly in tune with where I was and the people I was with. I was fully there, in the moment. They were me. I was them. Nothing else existed.

While Dan climbed Kilimanjaro, I stayed with Anne who was working in Mshiri village near the starting point for groups climbing the Marangu route up Kilimanjaro. The two weeks in Mshiri village were warm, intimate, welcoming. I once again left the isolating truck cocoon where I was limited to staring at the African people, separated by a four-meter distance that was a vast uncrossable ocean of culture and privilege. As Dan reached Uhuru peak in a raging snowstorm, I was safe on the slopes of an African volcano among the African women. Africa was finally finished.

ABBREVIATIONS & ACRONYMS FOR RWANDA

DRC or Congo	Democratic Republic of the Congo
FAR	Rwandan Armed Forces (Hutu)
MDR-PARMEHUTU	Rwandan Democratic Movement/Part of the Movement of Hutu Emancipation
NGO	Non Governmental Organization
ALIR	Army for the Liberation of Rwanda (Hutu)
PALIR	Armed People for the Liberation of Rwanda (Hutu)—one of the translations
RPA	Rwandan Patriotic Army (Tutsi)
RPF	Rwandan Patriotic Front (Tutsi)
UN	United Nations
UNIMAR	United Nations Assistance Mission for Rwanda
UNHCR	United Nations High Commissioner for Refugees

Hutu 85% to 95% of Rwandan population
make up the ex-FAR, the former Rwandan military forces
make up the Interahamwe
make up the ALIR
make up the PALIR, People (Party) for the Liberation of Rwanda
the men who held us captive

Tutsi Watutsi (plural)
make up the RPF, Rwandan Patriotic Front
make up the RPA, Rwandan Patriotic Army
those exiled in 1959 to Uganda and Zaire
those currently in power in Rwanda

RWANDA'S HISTORY:
PREPARING FOR A GENOCIDE

1918	Treaty of Versailles sets Rwanda as a protectorate under the League of Nations governed by Belgium and administered under a Tutsi monarch.
1926	Belgians issue identity cards setting up Hutus and Tutsis as distinct groups.
1959	King Mwaami Rudahigwa dies. Uprising of Hutus against the Tutsi elite results in up to 100 000 Tutsi deaths and up to 200 000 Tutsis fleeing to exile in Uganda, Tanzania, Burundi and Zaire.
1962	Rwandan independence from Belgium sparks wide spread Tutsi killings and thousands more Tutsi refugees move to Uganda. Government restricted to Hutus.
1963, 1967	Renewed massacres of Tutsis and refugee movement.
1973	General Juvenal Habyarimana seizes power and sets up a one party state with ethnic quotas for Tutsis in the public service. Tutsis removed from Universities, more killings of Tutsis.
1975	Habyarimana forms political party MRND (Mouvement Révolutionnaire National pour Développement)
1986	Ugandan Rwandan Tutsi exiles support Yoweri Musaveni's overthrowing of the Ugandan dictator Milton Obote, and set up the Rwandan Patriotic Front (RPF) with a military arm, the Rwandan Patriotic Army (RPA)
1989	Severe economic problems in Rwanda due to the collapse of coffee prices.
8 June 1990	Habyarimana agrees to set up a multi-party democracy under pressure from Western aid donors.

30 Sept. 1990	RPA guerillas from Uganda invade Rwanda. French, Belgian and Zairean troops assist the Rwandan government. Cease-fire on 29 March 1991.
1990 / 1991	Interahamwe ('Those who stand together') civilian militia trained by the Rwandan army. Continued Tutsi murders, little progress in setting up the multi-party system.
Nov. 1992	Inciting to genocide commences with the first public appeals by Hutu activist Dr. Leon Mugusera to send Tutsis "back to Ethiopia" via the rivers.
Feb. 1993	The outskirts of Kigali reach by RPF guerillas who were fighting government troops receiving aid from the French.
4 Aug. 1993	Concessions to the RPF by Habyarimana in the Arusha Peace Accords to allow RPF and the Hutu opposition a share in the government and army.
Dec. 1993	UNIMAR (United Nations Assistance Mission to Rwanda) troops consisting of 2500 men sent to Kigali to oversee the implementation of the Accord.
Sept.1993–Mar.1994	President Habyarimana stalls implementation of power sharing agreed in the Accord. Militia training intensifies. Radio Mille Collines broadcasts promote the killing of Tutsis.
6 April 1994	President Habyarimana killed when his plane is shot down while landing at Kigali airport. Killings begin.
7 April 1994	Systematic murders of thousands of Tutsis and moderate Hutus by FAR. UN forces forbidden to intervene.
8 April 1994	RPF starts major offensive to end the genocide.
9 April 1994	Belgian and French troops arrive in Kigali to rescue expatriates.

21 April 1994	UNIMAR troops cut from 2500 to 250 by the Security Council of the UN following the death of the Belgian soldiers guarding Prime Minister Agathe Uwiliyingimana who is also killed.
30 April 1994	UN Security Council discusses Rwanda without using the word "genocide". Hundreds of thousands of refugees, both Tutsi fleeing from murder and Hutu fleeing from the RPF cross into Tanzania, Burundi, and Zaire.
17 May 1994	UN agrees to send troops (UNIMAR II) to Rwanda to defend citizens, but little happens because of concerns about cost sharing.
22 June 1994	UN troops still not in Rwanda. Murder of Tutsis continues. 10 700 bodies removed from Lake Victoria for burial.
30 June 1994	Massacres described as "genocide" by UN Human Rights Commission Special Rapporteur.
4 July–18 July 1994	Rwandan army is defeated. The government and a mass of refugees flee to Zaire. RPF sets up an interim government with a Hutu president and a Hutu Prime Minister.
Aug. 1994	UNHCR (United Nations High Commission on Refugees) estimated 200 000 Hutu refugees had fled into Zaire, Burundi and Tanzania to escape the RPF. Killing of Tutsis continues in refugee camps under the control of the Interahamwe *génocidaires*.
Aug.–Nov.1994	An International Tribunal established to oversee the prosecution of *génocidaires* in Arusha.
June 1995	UN forces reduced over 50% at Rwanda's request.
Dec.1995	The United Nations Tribunal for Rwanda charges eight people with genocide and crimes against humanity.
Nov.–Dec.1996	Refugee camps forcibly closed, Rwandans repatriated.

| Jan.1997 | Trials for genocide begin. The murders of potential witnesses and Human Rights observers begin. |
| Dec. 1999 | The International Tribunal in Arusha, Tanzania finds the sixth person guilty of genocide and crimes against humanity. |

Prepared from information in:
African Rights. (1995) *Rwanda: Death, Despair and Defiance* London.
African Rights. (1998) *Rwanda: The Insurgency in the Northwest* London.
Des Forges, Alison. (1995) *Chronology*. Human Rights Watch: Africa
Keane, Fergal. (1995) *Season of Blood: A Rwandan Journey* New York: Viking.
Murphy, Dervla. (1998). *Visiting Rwanda*. Dublin: Lilliput Press.

OBJECTIVES OF OUR MOVEMENT

People in Action for the Liberation of Rwanda "PALIR"

The objectives of "PALIR"

1. To stop the genocide of the HUTUS; to promote its recognition by the International Community and to pursue its perpetrators be they Rwandan or strangers.
2. To regain and defend the National Sovereignty against the predatory Imperialism of some Regional and International powers.
3. To set up an Administration, an Army and a Police Force that comes from all levels of the population.
4. To re-establish and maintain Public Order and Individual Safety.
5. To clean up the festering situation in Rwanda based upon Right and the Requirements of genuine and durable National Reconciliation.
6. To set up a legitimate State by re-establishing all physical and moral legal entities in their rights and freedom.
7. To prosecute the perpetrators of Crimes against Humanity, of Crimes of War, of Economic Crimes and other massive violations of Right committed since 1 October 1996.
8. To organize the peaceful and dignified return of all Rwanda refugees.
9. To install Democracy based upon workable multi-parties and pluralist elections.
10. To restore and guarantee Unity and National Peace.
11. To rekindle the Country and its habitants on the path of integral Development self-managed and shared.
12. To develop viable and fair External Relations.

Translation of the French copy of PALIR demands. Martin Kear provided this by fax 20 April 1999.

OBJECTIFS DE NOTRE MOUVEMENT

Peuple en action pour la liberation du Rwanda "PALIR"

Le PALIR a pour Objectifs de:

1. Arrêter le génocide des HUTU; Promouveir sa reconnaissance par la communauté Internationale et en poursuivre les auteurs aussi bien Rwandais qu'étrangers;
2. Reconquérir et défendre la souveraineté nationale contre l'impérialisme prédateur de certaines puissances régionales et Internationales;
3. Mettre en place une administration, une armée et des forces de l'ordre émanant de toutes les couches de la papulation;
4. Rétablir et maintenir l'ordre public et la sécurité Individuelle;
5. Assainir la situation caroérale du Rwanda sur base du droit et des exigences d'une réconciliation nationale vraie et durable;
6. Instaurer un Etat de Droit en rétablissant toutes les Personnes Physiques et morales dans leurs droits et libertés;
7. Poursuivre en justice les autres de crimes contre l'humanité, de crimes de Guerre, de crimes économiques et autres violations massive du Droit commises de puis le 01 Octobre 1996;
8. Organiser le retour pacique et digne de tous les réfugiés Rwandais;
9. Instaurer la Democratie Impliquant un multipartisme Opérationnel et des élection pluralistes;
10. Restaurer et garantir l'Unité et la paix Nationale;
11. Relancer le Pays et tout un chacun sur la voie du Développement intégral, autoporté et partagé;
12. Développer des Relations Extérieures viables et équitables.

COMMUNIQUE DE PRESSE
No. o 16/98 du 20/07/98

CONSEIL de securite ou caisse de resonnances pour la diplomatie USA?

Pouvait-on imaginer quinze diplomates, dont trois représentants de grandes puissances mondiales qui se réclament championnes du respect des Droites de l'homme, accoucher d'un texte ridicule.

C'est malheureusement, ce qui s'est passé avec la résolution adoptée àl'unsmimité par le Conseil de sécurité des Nations Unies en date du 14 Juillet 1998 aux les massacres des réfugiés Rwandais au Zaire.

Demander à deux Gouvernements de criminals, qui sont renié ces crimes à maintes reprises, qui ont tout fait pour faire échouer l'enquête des Nations Unies, demander a ces Gouvernements de mener des investgations sur leur propres crimes, de se juger eux-memes et de faire rapport au Conseil de Sécurité. Ce n'est PAS seulement ridicule, c'est injuste et s'est révoltant.

Pourquoi les Alliés n'ont-ils pas demané aux nazis de rechercher et de juger les criminels hitlériens? Pendant que KABILA et KAGAME arrêtent, emprsonnent et exécutent à liosir leurs adversaires Politiques, ils n'ont pas de soucis à se faire pour les crimes perpétrés par leurs armées. KIBERO* a été jeté aux oubliettes, 150,000 à 200,000 réfugiés sur le sol *airois deviennent un détail et le jen peurs toujours continuer sur tout le territoire Rwandais sous l'oeil et l'oreille complaisants de la Communauté Internationale.

Cette résolution met a nu le d'éréglement Complet do la machine onusienne*. En effet, le rapport des enquêteurs envoyés par le secrétaire General est clair: plus de 150,000 réfugies ont bel et bien été exécutés par les troupes de KABIRA appuyées par l'APR. Dès lors, on se demande pourquoi avoir inutilement exposé ses enquêteurs aux tracasseries du régime KABILA et parfois même à la mort comme lora des mandfestations organisées par le régime a MBANDAKA. Qu'espère le Conseil de Sécurité? Se souie-t-il réellement des Droites de l'homme? Ou alors on se tromp: Pour mos quines diplomates, les réfugiés Rwandais exterminés au ZAIRE no sont pas consideérés comme des hommes, et même si c'étaient des hommes, leur génocide est l'oeuvre de martiens et autres extraterrestres.

Si l'on peut écater d'un revers de main diplomatique l'émination de plus de 150,000 personnes sans aucun remord, à quoi set-il de créer des

* illegible print

commissa*ts aux Droits de l'homme? a quio riment les tribunaux de la HAYE et d'ARUSHA?

Les jurietes internationaux retiendront qu'un génocide peut être toléré ou condamné selon que les auteurs sont ou non protégés par les Americains. La morale et le Droit International en sortirent bafoués.

Les Américains mènent le jeu au sein des Nations Unies, les autres pays dont les français, les anglais, les russes et les chinois suivent aveuglement tant que leurs propres intérrêts ne sont pas remis en cause. Le Conseil de sécurité est devenu une simple chambre d'enregistrement, une caisse de résonnance au service de la diplomate USA

Le PALIR (Peuple en Action pour la libération du Rwanda) proteste énergiquement contre ce maquillage qui veut disculper les Américains et leurs protégés du génocide entrepris de puis 1990 contre le peuple HUTU. Ils en appelle aux Organisation de défense des Droits de l'homme de continuer à user leurs moyens afin que triomphe la vérité.

                    Pour le Comité Exécutif National du PALIR
                             Le Président.
                    (Sé)

Chers Expatriés

Vous entendres souvent le Gouvernement sanguinaire de KABILA dire à la Communayté Internationale que l'Objectif de notre Organisation (PALIR) est uniquement celui de verser du sang. C'est de pur men*onge et vous l'aures constaté vous mêmes pendant votre séjour dans notre Pays.

Nous avons nobles objectifs tels qu'ils vous sont présentés dans la note ci-jointe. Sans trop discourir, nous vous demandons très simplement et très humblement de dire la vérité et rien que la vérité.

                    Pour le PALIR.
                    (Sé)

                         * illegible print

TRAVEL INFORMATION REPORT

Department of Foreign Affairs
and International Trade

Ministere des Affaires etrangeres
et du Commerce intenational

CANADA

UGANDA   20-August-1998

The Consular Affairs Bureau of the Department of Foreign Affairs and
International Trade provides two types of up-to-date travel reports: a)
Travel Information Reports (TIRS) provide general information on
countries; and b) Travel Advisory Reports (TARS) indicate where
conditions may be unsafe to travel. Cancelling a pre-arranged trip based
on information contained in a Travel Report could entail a personal
financial obligation. You should contact your travel agent and/or your
travel insurer prior to cancellation to discuss the matter. The decision to
travel to a specific country is the sole responsibility of the traveller.
Contact 1-800-267-6788 or 613-944-6788/Internet address:
http://www.dfait-maeci.gc.ca / FaxCall: 1-800-575-2500 or 613-944-2500
or the nearest Canadian mission prior to departure for information on
current conditions.

GENERAL CONDITIONS

Uganda (Capital: Kampala) is located in East Africa west of Kenya
bordering Rwanda, Sudan, Tanzania, and the Democratic Republic of
Congo. Tourism facilities are adequate in Kampala but limited in other
areas. Due to the continuing incidents of rebel activity, all non-essential
travel to, or through, the north and north-west areas of Uganda and the
adjacent Sudanese border areas should be avoided. These areas include,
but are not limited to, Aura, where attacks have been carried out on
establishments frequented by foreigners, and Gulu-Kitgum-Patongo,
where rebels have begun to use land mines on the main roads (i.e.
Adjumani-Guluto, Kitgum-Gulu and Gulu-Patongo-Lira) and kidnap
foreigners. Essential travel should be by air only. Travellers in the country

should contact the Canadian Consulate in Kampala for the latest security information.

The contiguous areas of the Democratic Republic of Congo and Rwanda in western and southwestern Uganda are unsafe. Canadians are advised not to cross into either the Democratic Republic of Congo or Rwanda from Uganda. Tourist groups visiting southwest Uganda to view gorillas should not cross into the Democratic Republic of Congo or Rwanda no matter the assurances received from tour companies or local authorities. A tourist group, including a Canadian, was kidnapped in the Congo in August.

Travel by road in other parts of Uganda is discouraged due to occasional armed robberies and car-jackings. In general, travelling by road throughout Uganda is extremely dangerous. Drive defensively at all times; Ugandan drivers do not follow Canadian rules of the road. Petty crime is prevalent in urban areas like Kampala, and tourists are subject to purse and jewellery snatching. Travel to game reserves and parks should be organized with a reputable tour company. Avoid solo travel and camping. Travel to Murchison Falls National Park is unsafe.

REFERENCES

African Rights. (1995). *Rwanda: Death, Despair and Defiance* rev. ed., London.

Astill, James. (2002, May 23). Rape is still an everyday horror as eastern Congo's war winds down. *The Guardian Weekly*: Montreal, p.3.

Carter, Rita. (1998). *Mapping The Mind*. California: University of California Press.

Damasio, Antonio. (1994). *Descartes Error: emotion, reason and the human brain*. New York: Avon Books.

Des Forges, Alison. (1995) *Chronology*. Human Rights Watch: Africa.

Eckberg, Maryanna. (2000) *VICTIMS OF CRUELTY Somatic Psychotherapy in the Treatment of Posttraumatic Stress Disorder*. Berkley: North Atlantic Books.

Flannery Jr., Raymond B. (1992). *Post Traumatic Stress Disorder: A Victim's Guide to Healing and Recovery*. New York: Crossroads.

Glasser, William. (1965). *Reality Therapy, a new approach to psychiatry*. New York: Harper & Row.

Goujon, Emmanuel (2000, May 4). Agence France - Presse. *The National Post*, Section A. p.15.

Goujon, Emmanuel (2000, April 6). It takes time to give a million people a proper burial. Agence France - Presse. *The National Post,* Section A.

Goujon, Emmanuel (2000, April 6). Army deserters, leaders fleeing smell of danger. Agence France - Presse. *The National Post,* Section A.

Gourevitch, Philip. (1998). *We wish to inform you that tomorrow we will be killed with our families: stories from Rwanda*. New York: Farrar, Straus & Giroux.

Grana, Sam (NFB) and Patry, Yvan (Alter-Cine). (1996). *The Rwanda Series: Vol.1 Sitting on a Volcano; Vol.2 Hand of God Hand of the Devil; Vol.3 Chronicle of a Genocide Foretold*. [Videotape]. Montreal: National Film Board & Alter-Cine.

Keane, Fergal. (1995). *Season of Blood: a Rwandan Journey*. New York: Penguin.

Kingsolver, Barbara. (1998). *The Poisonwood Bible*. New York: Harper Flamingo.

Ledoux, Joseph. (1998). *The Emotional Brain: the mysterious underpinnings of emotional life*. New York: Simon & Schuster.

Levine, Peter A. (1997). *Waking the Tiger: Healing trauma: The innate capacity to Transform Overwhelming Experiences*. Berkeley: North Atlantic Books.

Leyton, Elliott. (1998). *Touched By Fire: Doctors Without Borders in a Third World Crisis* Toronto: M&S.

Mugabo, Lama. (2000, April 8). Confronting the face of Genocide. *The Vancouver Sun*. Section A.

Murphy, Dervla. (1998). *Visiting Rwanda*. Dublin: Lilliput Press.

Myss, Carolyn. (1996). *Anatomy of the Spirit: The seven stages of power and healing.* New York: Three Rivers.

Myss, Carolyn. (1997). *Why People Don't Heal and How They Can.* New York: Three Rivers.

Niehoff, Debra. (1999). *The Biology of Violence: How understanding the brain, behaviour, and environment can break the vicious circle of aggression.* New York: The Free Press.

Norretranders, Tor. (1991) *The User Illusion.* (Sydenham, J. trans.) New York: Viking.

Northrup, Christiane. (1994). *Women's Bodies, Women's Wisdom.* (revised 1998). New York: Bantam.

Ogden, Ph.D., Pat and Minton, Ph.D., Kekuni. (2000 Oct.) *Sensorimotor Psychotherapy: One method for Processing Traumatic Memory.* Traumatology: Vol. VI Issue 3.

Papero, Daniel V. (1990). *Bowen Family Systems Theory.* Boston: Allyn and Bacon.

Parnell, Laurel. (1997). *Transforming Trauma - EMDR: the revolutionary new therapy for freeing the mind, clearing the body and opening the heart.* New York : W.W. Norton.

Peress, Gilles. (1995). *The Silence: a photoessay of the 1994 Rwandan genocide.* New York: Scalo Publishers.

Pert, Candace B. (1997). *Molecules of Emotion: Why you feel the way you feel.* New York: Scribner.

Peterson, Scott. (2000) *Me Against My Brother: At War in Somalia, Sudan and Rwanda A Journalist Reports From the Battlefields of Africa* New York: Routledge

Restak, Richard. (1995). *Brainscapes; an introduction to what neuroscience has learned about the structure, function and the abilities of the brain.* New York: Hyperion.

Schiraldi, Ph.D., Glenn R. (2000). *The Post-Traumatic Stress Disorder Sourcebook: A Guide to Healing, Recovery, and Growth.* Los Angeles: Lowell House.

Shapiro, Francine. (1997). *EMDR: the breakthrough therapy for overcoming anxiety, stress and trauma.* New York: BasicBooks.

Williamson, Marianne. (1992). *A Return to Love: Reflections on the Principles of A Course in Miracles.* New York: Harper Collins.

Internet sites:

http://www.afbis.com/analysis/rwanda.htm (A press release on African Rights book, *Rwanda: The Insurgency in the Northwest* (1998) that outlines the on-going violence in post-genocide Rwanda)

http://news.bbc.co.uk/2/hi/health/2237005.stm (Article on research on counselling for trauma victims)

http://www.bodynamic.ca/theory.htm (Information on the theory, history and training for Bodynamic Analysis)

http://www.cognitivetherapy.com/basics.html (Information on Cognitive Behavior Therapy)

http://www.comebackalive.com/df/dplaces/rwanda.htm

http://www.fas.org/irp/world/para/interahamwe.htm (A Dec. 1999 summary of information on Interahamwe and PALIR)

http://www.peacelink.it/africa/weekly/08 98 (Summary of terrorist action in Africa in July, 1998)

http://www.peacelink.it/africa/weekly/09 98 (Summary of terrorist action in Africa in Aug. 1998)

http://www.sas.upenn.edu/African_Studies/Hornet.irin428.html

http://www.sn.apc.org/wmail/issues/960705/NEWS53.htm (An article from the Weekly Mail & Guardian on PALIR threats to US citizens)

http://www.traumahealing.com (Peter Levine's Somatic Experiencing website)

http://www.trauma-pages.com (An encyclopedic site on all aspects of trauma)

http://vislab-www.nps.navy.mil/~library/tgp/chrono98.htm (Chronology of Significant Terrorist Incidents, 1998, Dudley Knox Library Naval Postgraduate School)

http://www,usip.org/oc/sr/rwanda1.html (Rwanda: Accountability for War Crimes and Genocide—a Report on a United States Institute of Peace Conference)

http://www.worldatlas.com/aatlas/africa/facts/rwanda/htm

http://www,usip.org/library/regions/rwanda.html (A list of websites around various topics and Rwanda)

http://web.nps.navy.mil/~library/tgp/alir.htm (Terrorist Group Profiles, Dudley Knox Library Naval Postgraduate School from *United States Department of State. Patterns of Global Terrorism, 2000.* April 2001)